The Unrefined Cane Sugar Specialists

HOW the British *fell in love* WITH FOOD

*25 years of food writing & recipes
from the Guild of Food Writers*

COMPILED BY
Lewis Esson

PHOTOGRAPHY BY PETER CASSIDY

First published in Great Britain by Simon & Schuster UK Ltd, 2010
A CBS Company

Copyright © Guild of Food Writers, 2010
and Contributors listed on page 208.

Simon & Schuster UK Ltd
1st Floor, 222 Gray's Inn Road
London WC1X 8HB

A CIP catalogue record of this book is available from the British Library.

Editorial Director: Francine Lawrence
Editor: Heather Bateman
Design: Lawrence Morton
Food Photography: Peter Cassidy
Home economist for photography: Jane Suthering
Stylist for photography: Roïsin Nield
Illustrations: Lizzie Gardiner (except pages 45 and 76)
Additional photography: Oskar Proctor

The articles and recipes published here have been transcribed directly from their
original publications.

Printed and bound in China
ISBN 978-1-84737-649-7

Contents

Forewords

On the 12th April 1984, a group of people in the British food world gathered for lunch at London's first Intercontinental hotel to enjoy a superb lunch devised by the hotel's celebrated chef Peter Kromberg. Among others, Arabella Boxer, Jane Grigson, Michael Smith and Elizabeth David were in attendance. The purpose of this grand event was to discuss the formation of an 'association of food writers'. How exactly had this come about?

As long as I can remember, I have believed that an understanding and appreciation of good food is essential to human happiness, a conviction reinforced in 1947 when I joined The Wine & Food Society, of which I eventually became Chairman, and later Executive Director. In that capacity, and through various employments, I had been fortunate enough to know many of the past century's finest writers about food. I also travelled the world, and became aware of how much work, by contrast, was variable in quality, often through no fault of the writer.

Wine commentators, travel journalists, science correspondents and other specialists all had their own professional associations and appeared to enjoy the status justified by their skills; not so Britain's culinary scribes. Accordingly, when I took a job specifically concerned with the appreciation of good cookery, and married a writer and chef, I felt I had the chance to do something constructive about the problem.

Publicist Hilary Laidlaw-Thomson warmed to my wish to found an association, and we agreed that some of Britain's best practitioners should be invited to discuss the subject over lunch. Richard Foulsham, MD of Badoit, kindly picked up the tab, and Peter Kromberg planned a menu worthy of what I assured him would be an historic occasion.

Some of those I approached were sceptical, others enthusiastic – but all wished the project success. A chance encounter with Nadine Heidsieck, spouse of the head of the Champagne *maison* and herself a cookery writer, resulted in the offer of the family product as apéritif. Arabella Boxer, Elizabeth David, Christopher Driver, Jane Grigson, Alice Wooledge Salmon, Michael Smith and Katie Stewart said they would be delighted to attend and we were on the move. The then-Chairman of The Wine & Food Society, Dr Louis Hughes, having within his ambit nearly 10,000 culinary readers, agreed to act as host.

Remembering her early struggle to interest publishers in her own groundbreaking work, I had privately suggested and all agreed, that we should invite Mrs David to be our first President; her comments when we spoke had been very constructive. But when I proposed, during the course of the meal, that she should chair a 'recruitment' meeting of prospective members, she said she did not after all wish to join. Hamlet without the Prince? Or, more appropriately, strawberries *sans* cream.

I talked to Derek Cooper, who agreed the plan was too good to abandon, and between us we circulated a list of likely writers. That hotelier-extraordinaire, Ron Jones, offered us Claridge's hospitality for The Guild's first formal meeting, and this time, I invited Derek to take the chair. I can't remember how many potential recruits appeared, but I believe nearly a hundred signed up on the spot.

Since 1984, much has been achieved. This collection of writings by some of my fellow members demonstrates that the initiative taken twenty-five years ago has been more than worthwhile.

HUGO DUNN-MEYNELL, FOUNDER MEMBER OF THE GUILD OF FOOD WRITERS

I don't think any of the original members of the Guild could possibly have imagined how their creation would grow. In 1985 when our constitution was formally approved, the forty or so members who met (including such well-known names as Michael Smith, Derek Cooper, Colin Spencer, Glynn Christian, Arabella Boxer, Mary Berry, Alice Wooledge Salmon, Katie Stewart, Prue Leith, and Claudia Roden) still represented almost every newspaper and magazine in Britain and every radio and television programme that concerned itself with food.

Over the years some members remained determined to keep it small, others welcomed the multitude of culinary disciplines that we now have within our membership. However, we are now a body of almost 400 members still covering the more obvious areas of food writing, as well as welcoming the newer disciplines of websites and blogs. Many of our members are well known, yet many more distinguish themselves admirably without being household names. As Marguerite Patten once said, 'diversity of background is a strength'.

Our accomplishments and events are numerous: the prestigious annual awards; tackling serious issues through debate and forums; the establishment of a professional code of conduct; drawing up guidelines on plagiarism and recipe acknowledgement; establishing standard imperial and metric conversions; running CookIt! and WriteIt! (competitions in cookery skills and writing respectively for those aged 10-18); supporting Fairbridge (a charity helping inner city youth); offering bursaries to members, campaigning for better food in hospitals and schools; contributing to a collection of food and cookery books at Guildhall. We do all this in addition to offering our members the day-to-day support and network to carry on their daily business.

We do go from strength to strength. We choose to educate and continue to be educated ourselves, and in so doing, spread the word that food and eating should be a pleasure.

JANE SUTHERING, PRESIDENT OF THE GUILD OF FOOD WRITERS

Preface

When I was asked by the committee of the Guild to compile this book to celebrate our 25th anniversary, I have to admit that I did at first feel rather daunted by the idea. What was to be the theme? How on earth was I going to select content from among the millions of words that our members have crafted over the last quarter century?

Two main thoughts eventually prevailed. It seemed like the perfect vehicle to demonstrate how important the work of our members – some household names and others not – had been in helping to develop people's attitudes to and appreciation of food and eating over that period. All too often the credit for this is attributed to TV and celebrity chefs (some of whom, of course, are fellow Guild members) but this is to ignore all those whose inspirational words alone fired readers to try some new dish or ingredient.

The other thing that I knew the book had to achieve, if at all possible, was to be a good seller, so we could use the royalties to further the Guild's work encouraging young people to cook well and to write well about food with our CookIt! and WriteIt! campaigns and competitions.

What the exercise also afforded me personally was a wonderful opportunity to revisit some of my favourite writing and also to discover new joys. Hence you will find extracts here from Katie Stewart's *Times Cookbook*, which was my first and from which I really taught myself how to cook more than mince and tatties, as well as Elisabeth Luard's *European Peasant Cookery*, which I still take with me whenever I go on self-catering holidays. It would be invidious for me to say here what my new discoveries had been, but some of the writing in them has brought tears to my eyes with its simple evocative beauty.

Sadly, I know already that, inevitably, my selection will have lost me some friends, as it simply could not be a publication where everyone 'could get a look-in' – as one member put it. However, I do hope that when they see the book they will understand and appreciate what I have done and had to do.

Finally, I would like to give my sincere thanks to all those who have contributed to the book and to the families, friends, agents or publishers of those members who are no longer with us and who facilitated the use of their work.

Also I do have to thank our old and loyal friends at Billington's for their extraordinary generosity in the considerable sponsorship they put into the costs of the book in order to make it possible, also Ian Jesnick at Richmond Towers Communications for his pivotal role, and the team at Simon & Schuster for really getting behind it and making it a book to be proud of.

LEWIS ESSON, VICE CHAIR AND PUBLICATIONS COORDINATOR OF THE GUILD OF FOOD WRITERS

The food scene *prior* to THE Guild's formation

Jane Grigson

Michael Bateman

Katie Stewart

Alan Davidson

Deh-Ta Hsiung

Nicola Humble

Glynn Christian

Anne Willan

Cecilia Norman

Susan Campbell

Jane Grigson

Jane Grigson became interested in food when she began to spend three months of each year in France. Her book *Charcuterie and French Pork Cookery* was the result. This has also been translated into French, a singular honour for an English food writer. In 1968 she began her long association with the *Observer Magazine* for whom she wrote right up until her untimely death in 1990. She received both the Glenfiddich Writer of the Year Award and the André Simon Memorial Fund Book Award for her *Vegetable Book* (1978) and for her *Fruit Book* (1982), and was voted Cookery Writer of the Year in 1977 for *English Food*. A compilation of her best recipes, *The Enjoyment of Food*, was published in 1992 with an introduction by her daughter, the food writer Sophie Grigson. In her obituary for the *Independent*, Alan Davidson wrote 'She won to herself this wide audience because she was above all a friendly writer...the most companionable presence in the kitchen; often catching the imagination with a deftly chosen fragment of history or poetry, but never failing to explain the 'why' as well as the 'how' of cookery'.

Avocado

Jane Grigson's Vegetable Book
Michael Joseph 1978

The avocado, or avocado pear, was originally a native of tropical America. The name comes, via Spanish, from the Aztec ahuacatl, and has nothing to do with lawyers, or with egg drinks from South Africa – or with pears for that matter. Nowadays many varieties grow in other regions of the world. In this country we import them from Israel in the winter and South Africa in the summer.

A Ghanaian friend told us that in Accra there is a tree in every garden, like apple trees in some parts of England; everyone gets bored with the fruit during the season, as we get bored with endless Bramley windfalls in the autumn. In Kenya it is much the same. Barrow-loads are put by the road, at the end of gardens, with notices saying Help Yourself. The stray dogs make up their dietary deficiencies, becoming sleek and glossy on the tumbled fruit that no one bothers to pick up. Certainly avocados are good for you, being so nutritionally endowed that many Israeli babies are weaned on them. The price would have to come down before any baby of my acquaintance got the chance, but I pass on the idea.

Here in this country we have known about avocados since the 17th century, when they were given delightful nicknames such as midshipman's or subaltern's butter, as if in those days the children of our harsh services kept healthy when they were in the West Indies on windfall avocados, like the stray dogs of Kenya today. We ate them in England from time to time before the Second World War if we were well off and lived near a grand greengrocer. In other words they had not progressed very far in three centuries. Yet it took the Israelis ten years only, perhaps less, to get them into most of our supermarkets. By the seventies, they had become as much a cliché start to a meal as grapefruit.

If you visit an avocado-growing kibbutz, you will see that the groves of trees are kept at a height around ten metres by pruning. As you stand admiring the dense, dark leaved growth, a head will suddenly pop out eight or nine metres up, like a Jack in the Green. Then another to the right, lower down. Then again, a minute later, both heads are at normal level as the pickers bring their mobile lifts to earth, to roll out the avocados into central bins. The Israelis invented these lifts, and now export them, even to California. Naturally the best avocados cluster at the tops of the trees. The small chariot-like platforms on an angled stem and four wheels can be propelled forward and back, up and down, left and right, by pulling and kicking levers, so that the picker can go swiftly to the highest desirable clutch, selecting the avocados that are just right for the harvest. Then they are graded and taken rapidly to refrigerated ships, where the even coolness prevents them ripening further, to arrive at our markets hard and firm, but not too far away from the soft, brown-splashed ripeness that makes them so delicious to eat.

As you will see from the following section I feel that there are few recipes to improve on avocado nature, with an olive oil vinaigrette. There are a few magnificent partnerships, avocados with pineapple, or with grapefruit, with spiced or salt beef, with wholemeal bread and butter, but I cannot bear to see a few cubes of avocado wasting their substance in a vast fruit salad. No doubt if avocados covered the orchard grass, I should be happy creaming them into meat stews and soups, as they do in Latin America, to avoid waste. Here, they demand more considerate treatment, as star items for special meals.

HOW TO CHOOSE AND PREPARE AVOCADOS

Judging by the hard unripe avocados one occasionally gets in restaurants, and in restaurants that pride themselves on their food, some people still do not know that they should be kept until the whole surface is slightly yielding, with an extra softness around the stalk. If you hold an avocado in your hand and gently feel round the skin with a slight pressure, you can soon tell if it is right.

This does not mean that you should never buy a hard avocado. It is often convenient to do so, if you can only shop once or twice a week. In a warm kitchen it will soon ripen; I allow two or three days, and if it gets to the proper state before it is needed, I put it into the vegetable drawer of the refrigerator. Green-skinned avocados often become patched with brown. This is a sign that they are ready. The warty, purple-brown-skinned avocados can only be tested by feeling them. Do not let the lumpy skin put you off; these dark, pebbled fruit of the Hass variety have the best flavour of all.

If you see really bruised looking avocados, you may be able to get them at a reduced price that makes them a bargain. Eaten the same day, they are really good and buttery. Mash them to a cream with seasoning and vinaigrette and serve the paste on buttered wholemeal bread or in sandwiches. Or use them to make avocado butter to serve on steaks.

If you are ever in an avocado-growing country in the season, keep an eye open for tiny, freak avocados. They look like small courgettes, about 5 cm (2 in) long or less. They have no stones, but thin quills instead that are easily pulled out. Peeled and sliced, these delectable miniature avocados make excellent salads.

The one problem with avocados, after settling the matter of ripeness, is that they discolour when cut. It does not matter from the flavour point of view, but the appearance loses its freshness. Always have ready a wedge of lemon to rub over the new surfaces. No lemon? Then use orange or citrus juice of another kind, or some vinaigrette, according to the recipe you are following.

To halve an avocado, cut down from the stalk, then go round the stone. The two parts can then be twisted free. For slices, remove the peel which comes away neatly with the aid of a sharp knife, and rest each half, cut-side down, on a board, so that it can be cut lengthways into pear-like slices.

To cut avocados into circles and – inevitably – rings, peel the whole thing then slice it across, working carefully when you get to the stone so that the rings are as even as possible. Should you need chunks of avocado, it is best to slice the fruit across in this way first, rather than lengthways, then you can divide circles and rings rather as if you were dealing with a pineapple.

Although it is waxier and less fibrous, an avocado has something in common with the base of a globe artichoke. Both, for instance, are deliciously partnered by shellfish and mayonnaise or mornay sauce. One French chef has invented recipes using avocado with meat, in something of an artichoke style. Apart from an avocado butter with steak, they are not altogether successful. But it is a hint worth knowing, especially if avocados ever become cheap enough for experimenting.

Avocado Fool

I used to think that the word fool as applied to mixtures of fruit and cream – or custard – derived from the French fouler, *to crush. It would have been appropriate. But it seems I was wrong, and the word means what it says more or less, being a synonym for something of small consequence. Two similar names, given to other light and quickly made puddings, are trifle and whim-wham. Affectionate names, denoting pleasure and fun and an easy simplicity. Lime juice is by far the best flavouring for avocados used in this way, but lemon juice can be used instead.*

3 avocados

2 limes or 1 large lemon

unrefined golden icing sugar

150 ml (5 fl oz) whipping or double cream

Peel the avocados and cut them up into the goblet of a blender, or sieve through a *mouli-légumes*.

Slice the limes or lemon in half, and cut one thin slice from the middle; divide each lime slice into three, or the one lemon slice into six wedges and set aside.

Squeeze the juice from the rest of the limes or lemon, and add it to the avocados, together with a tablespoon of icing sugar.

Blend the avocados to produce a smooth cream, or mix the sieved avocado well to an even mash. Whip the cream until stiff, fold in the purée and add more sugar to taste.

Divide between six glasses, and chill for two hours.

Decorate with the reserved lime or lemon wedges, sticking them into the top of each fool like a tiny fan. Serve with sponge or shortbread fingers.

Harold Wilshaw's Avocado Salad

1 ripe avocado

lemon juice

olive oil

salt, pepper

250 g (8 oz) shelled broad beans

soured cream

chopped parsley

Peel and dice the avocado, sprinkling it immediately with lemon juice, oil and seasoning. Cook the beans, then skin them – this is essential. Arrange beans and avocado on a plate, preferably a bright pink plate to show off the different greens. Pour over a little soured cream and sprinkle with parsley.

There is no need to restrict this salad to June. It works well with frozen broad beans.

Michael Bateman

Michael Bateman began writing about food in the 60s when food was not seen as a serious subject by the British press. At *The Sunday Times* he broke new ground by writing detailed exposés of food additives, prison food and school dinners. Hailed as the first modern investigative food journalist, he also edited the *Lifespan* section of the paper's magazine, where, in 1980, he launched the ground-breaking Campaign for Real Bread. The weekly debates and events eventually brought about a change to the bread sold in shops and supermarkets up and down the country. Michael went on to become Deputy Editor of the *Sunday Express Magazine* and then Food Editor of the *Independent on Sunday Magazine* from its launch in 1989 until his tragic death in 2006.

Campaign for Real Bread

Campaign for Real Bread
THE SUNDAY TIMES 1980

We believe the consumer has a right to bread which is tastier, healthier, and better value. Today *Lifespan* launches *The Sunday Times Campaign for Real Bread*. But isn't all bread 'real'? Of course. But like ale, some breads are more real than others. More real than the technological bread of the Sixties and Seventies.

Throughout the bad times, *The Sunday Times* has always championed the cause of better bread. Now, at long last, we detect a swing in the right direction. Today very many more housewives confidently bake their own bread. Small bakers, who had been disappearing are returning as high quality bread shops.

WE ARE CAMPAIGNING FOR HEALTH, QUALITY AND VALUE:

Health. Most health authorities recommend wholemeal bread as the staple. Wholemeal bread is made from flour which contains the wheatgerm and its essential oils, and the bran, which is vital roughage. Yet wholemeal bread is difficult to obtain, and shop assistants often don't know wholemeal from wheatmeal and brown.

Quality. What is lacking from the majority of loaves today is flavour. Most loaves cooked the technological way are underbaked, so they have no appreciable crust. If they had, they could no longer be squeezed to see if they are 'fresh'. Taste and flavour also come from the flour: the more wholemeal flour in the dough, the more wholesome the flavour.

Value. Healthy, good quality bread costs more. But it is good value. Mass-produced bread is cheaper because it is easier to make, and because it contains more water in proportion to flour.

THESE ARE OUR AIMS:

1. To improve the variety of breads sold in shops.
2. To encourage bakers to tell customers exactly what they are buying.
3. To make wholemeal bread available everywhere.
4. To collect and publish news of good bakers.
5. To find, test, and publish the best bread recipes.

In our Campaign for Real Bread we are criticising plant-baked bread, which is bought by 70 per cent of us. This week we have a reply from the people who invented it, the *Flour Milling and Baking Research Association*, Professor Brian Spencer:

'I think you should tell all your readers that all bread is good, but it comes into two categories. If you want a Rolls-Royce, and all the comforts, you have to pay for it. If you are not satisfied with plant bread, the answer is to go to the bread shop for hand-crafted bread. You pays your money and you takes your choice. There isn't a problem.

And there is no way, unless you can rapidly train 25,000 craftsmen and set them up in small shops, that you can change things. But things aren't going to change, the number of small bakers we have in this country is about what the country can sustain. The plant bread strikes helped them, but not all of their new customers stayed with them.

It is wrong of you to say some bread isn't good. A lot of people aren't desperately well-educated, and if they are told white bread isn't good for them, and they don't like brown bread, they may cut down on bread and eat less nutritious foods.

All bread is good, but it comes in two kinds, the better tasting loaf which I prefer, and the plant-baked bread.

Incidentally, plant-baked bread makes vast savings; it costs the country £80 million a year in subsidies to the EEC to import the hard North American wheats used in the traditional loaf. The Chorley Wood Bread Process uses more soft European wheats, and saves the government millions. You accuse us of making plant bread with more water. But you have to use enough water to make a handleable dough. Plant loaves need slightly more water because of the soft wheat used, but it's less than is used in brown, and much less than in wholemeal.

I think what you printed was your opinion given as stated fact.'

The Grant Loaf

This is the original of the famous loaf which home cooks make all around the world. It was created by food reformer Doris Grant as an alternative to the ubiquitous white loaf of the post-war years. There isn't an easier loaf you can make – you do not knead the dough. You could substitute 1 ½ oz (40 g) of medium cut oatmeal for 1 ½ oz (40 g) of the wholemeal flour for a different texture and flavour.

Makes 3 loaves

3 lb (1 ½ kg) stoneground wholemeal flour

1 oz (30 g) fresh yeast or 3 level teaspoons dried yeast *

2 teaspoons unrefined golden caster sugar

2 pt (1 ¼ litres) lukewarm water

2 scant teaspoons salt

* If using modern activated yeast, add one pack directly to the flour.

Cream the fresh yeast in a small bowl with the sugar. Add ¼ pint (150 ml) of the water at 95–100°F (35–38°C). The temperature is important: it is best to check with a cooking thermometer. Leave for 10 minutes to froth up. If using dried yeast, mix with 3 tablespoons of the water and then add 3 teaspoons sugar.

Put the flour into a large bowl and add the salt. In very cold weather, warm the flour slightly, just enough to take off the chill. Pour the yeast mixture into the flour and add the rest of the water. Mix well – by hand is best – working from the sides of the bowl to the middle till the dough feels elastic and leaves the sides of the bowl clean. Divide the dough, which should be slippery but not wet, between three 2 pt (1 ¼ litre) bread tins, warmed and greased.

Cover the tins with a cloth and put in a warm place for 20 minutes, or until the dough is within ½ in (15 mm) from the top of the tins.

Preheat the oven to 400°F (200°C, Gas 6) and bake for 35–40 minutes.

The Sunday Times Book of Real Bread
RODALE PRESS 1982

Katie Stewart

Katie Stewart's *The Times Cookery Book* taught more than one generation how to cook. It was the only book in many homes and the one that everyone turned to when looking for the right way to go about any dish. More than anything, it featured traditional recipes, well explained to just the right level of detail. Katie was involved in the founding of the Guild of Food Writers and has written many books. In 2000 she won the Guild's Award for Cookery Journalist of the Year and in 2008 she received the Guild's Lifetime Achievement Award.

Roasts

The Times Cookery Book
COLLINS 1972/PAN 1974

Roasting is one of the most traditional methods used for cooking meat, poultry and game. Originally, the term implied spit-roasting in front of an open fire, but this has been superseded by cooking in a tin in the oven.

Meat chosen for roasting should be of good quality and well hung. Less tender cuts, or very small joints, can be pot roasted. In this case the meat is cooked in a covered container, with liquid added, and simmered gently over direct heat or in the oven. The longer, more moist, cooking keeps the meat juicy and makes it tender.

The presence of a certain amount of fat in the meat gives flavour and keeps it moist during roasting. Joints should be lightly greased with a little dripping, lard or vegetable fat before going into the oven. The traditional method is to 'sear' or cook the meat, at a higher temperature (450°F, 230°C, Gas 8) for a short time – usually about 15 minutes – then reduce the heat to moderately hot (375°F, 190°C, Gas 5) for the remainder of the cooking time. A hot oven seals the surface, browning it and closing in the natural juices. Basting is the accepted procedure for protecting the outside of the meat while it cooks through. The melted fat from the tin, spooned over the joint from time to time, forms a screen, filtering the heat so that the joint cooks under the best conditions. Where possible the joint should be placed on a stand in the roasting tin or on a bed of vegetables so that it cooks above the level of any juices or gravy which might drain from the meat. A few scraped carrots and a peeled onion, cut in thick slices and placed in the roasting tin, allow the heat to reach all surfaces of the joint evenly. Low temperature roasting at 325°F (170°C, Gas 3) is excellent for small and stuffed joints and for cheaper cuts of meat, and is very good for turkey or any joint over 5 lb (2 kg 250 g) in weight, where the long cooking time required makes a 'seared' outside thick and hard. Low temperature roasting is not suitable for pork since the meat requires to be thoroughly cooked, nor for small chickens. Both of these produce better results when roasted at a higher temperature.

After taking the roast out of the oven (with the exception of venison) allow it to stand for 10–15 minutes. The flesh carves more easily and retains more juices this way, and, so long as the skin is not broken (this applies to chicken or turkey, in particular) or the meat carved, the joint will not lose its heat.

Beef is nicest slightly underdone; lamb is also nice underdone but is more often well done – never overcook or it becomes dry. Veal, pork and venison should all be well done. Chicken and turkey should be well cooked but not overcooked; juices coming from the birds still tinged with pink indicate that more cooking is needed.

HOW TO MAKE
GOOD GRAVY

Gravy is an important accompaniment for any roast meat, poultry or game. Stock is required for all gravies and should be made from poultry giblets or a stock cube or vegetable cooking water.

For a thin gravy to serve with roast meat or game, strain off all the fat from the roasting tin, but tip back into the tin any flavouring vegetables or crispy brown bits. Add a pint (600ml) of stock or vegetable water. Stir and bring to the boil, and boil briskly until reduced by half. Taste and correct the seasoning. Strain into a hot sauce-boat; skim away any fat that rises to the surface. Makes ½ pint (300 ml).

For a thick gravy to serve with roast meat or poultry, strain off all but 1 tablespoon of the fat from the roasting tin and stir in 1 tablespoon flour – sufficient to absorb all the fat in the pan. Stir over the heat until the flour has absorbed all the fat, and browned. Stir in 1 pint (600 ml) stock or vegetable cooking water. Bring up to the boil stirring well all the time to get a smooth gravy. Cook for 2–3 minutes after boiling. Taste and correct seasoning, and strain into a hot gravy boat. Makes 1 pint (600 ml).

There is an interesting variation on the method of making gravy for a roast. Before the meat is put to roast, place 1 tablespoon of flour in the centre of the roasting pan. Place the joint of meat (or chicken) on top and put the dripping in the tin. Roast in the usual manner basting the joint. During the cooking the flour absorbs juices from the meat and combines with the dripping in the pan to become a dark brown colour. When the meat is done, lift out of the tin. Pour off excess fat and, stirring or whisking well, add 1 pint (600 ml) of stock or vegetable cooking water to the pan. Bring to the boil, stirring well, simmer for 2–3 minutes. Strain into a hot gravy boat and serve. Makes 1 pint (600 ml).

Roast Beef with Yorkshire pudding

Sirloin and wing rib on the bone, or boned and rolled, can be used for this recipe. Top rump and topside are the choice pieces of beef for roasting.

Serves 4–6

Time Taken: 2–2½ hours

1 (2–3 lb) (1–1½ kg) piece of top rump or topside

dripping or lard

bed of roasting vegetables

For the Yorkshire Pudding

4 oz (100 g) plain flour

pinch salt

1–2 eggs

½ pint (300 ml) mixed milk and water

1 oz (25 g) dripping or lard

Wipe the meat and spread lightly with a little dripping or lard. Place extra fat in the roasting tin. Set the joint on a bed of roasting vegetables, place in the centre of a very hot oven (425°F, 220°C, Gas 7) and roast for 15 minutes. Lower the heat to moderately hot (375°F, 190°C, Gas 5) and roast for the remaining cooking time, allowing 15 minutes per lb (450 g) plus 15 minutes for a rare roast, and 20 minutes per lb (450 g) plus 15 minutes for a well-done joint. Baste frequently. Any roast vegetables, such as potatoes or parsnips, should be blanched in boiling water for 5 minutes, then well-drained and placed around the joint. Give them at least 1 hour of cooking time in the oven and baste frequently.

While the roast is cooking, prepare the batter for the Yorkshire pudding. Sieve together the flour and salt into a basin. Make a well in the centre, add the egg and about half the liquid. (Use liquid in the proportion of two-thirds milk and one-third water.) Using a wooden spoon, mix from the centre, gradually drawing in the flour from the edges of the basin. Mix to a smooth batter, then gradually stir in the remaining milk. Pour into a jug and leave until ready to cook.

About 40 minutes before the end of the cooking time, raise the oven heat to very hot (425°F, 220°C, Gas 7). Place the joint lower down in the oven. Put the lard or dripping in an ovenproof dish or small roasting tin and heat on the top shelf in the oven until smoking hot. Quickly pour in the batter all at once. Replace in the oven and cook for about 40 minutes, or until risen and crisp.

Alan Davidson

Alan Davidson was a giant of the food world. A former diplomat, who served in Washington, The Hague, Caro, Tunis and Brussels, he was eventually appointed Ambassador to Laos in 1973. While living in Tunis, his wife asked him to find a fish cookbook as she was unfamiliar with any of the local types. There being no such book, he wrote one himself, with the help of Giorgio Bini, the world's greatest living authority on Mediterranean sea fish. A copy of the book found its way to Penguin via Elizabeth David and was published in 1972 as *Mediterranean Seafood*. Alan left his post in Laos to take up a career as a food writer. For *North Atlantic Seafood*, he travelled throughout the region, gathering thousands of recipes from Portugal to Iceland. In 1999 he produced the seminal *Oxford Companion to Food*, which won several awards.

A Note On Soft-shell Crabs

North Atlantic Seafood
Macmillan 1979

Since some people really do think that soft-shell crabs are a separate species, and since there is much of interest to be said about them, I provide this note. It is, however, essentially a footnote to the preceding entry, on the blue crab, since that is the species which is eaten in the soft state in the United States; and eaten on a scale which cannot be matched on the Atlantic coast of Europe, although in principle other crabs can be so treated.

Like other arthropods, crabs can only grow if they are able to cast off periodically their rigid exo-skeleton or shell, and grow a new and larger one in its stead. This is an uncomfortable process, and the creatures are for a short time bereft of their natural defences, after they have wriggled out of the old shells. The degree of softness varies from species to species. The blue crab is very soft indeed when it emerges, and will normally take refuge in some relatively safe nook for a day or so until the new shell is reasonably hard.

A crab which is just about ready to shed is called a 'comer' or 'peeler'. The condition can be recognized, at an advanced stage, by the appearance of a red line along the edge of the 'paddlers' at the rear of the crab. During the actual process of shedding, the crab is a 'buster', 'peeler' or 'shedder'. At the moment of emergence from the old shell it is a 'soft crab' in the full sense of the term. Soon afterwards, as a slight hardening becomes apparent. it is termed a 'paper shell'. Further hardening turns it into a 'buckram' or 'buckler'. At this stage the new shell is still flexible, but the crab is no longer soft enough to be treated as a soft-shell crab, and its muscles are thin and watery. Within twenty-four hours or so of the shedding the new shell will be hard and the crab can resume a normal life.

There is a further complication in all this. The female must mate with the male immediately after her own shedding. When she is almost ready, the male will pick her up, clasping her beneath him, and carry her to a suitable spot. She then sheds and mating takes place. Crabbers are of course very pleased if they catch a couple on this amorous journey, since they gain simultaneously a hard male and a female shedder. Such a pair are called 'hard doublers'. If, however, mating is successfully achieved, the female will become a 'sponge crab', carrying a large mass of eggs, of an orange-lemon colour, on her abdomen. It is illegal to have in your possession either a sponge crab or a buckram.

Catching and marketing the soft crabs is no easy business. They cannot in fact be caught while they are soft. They have to be caught in advance and kept in special 'floats' until they moult. These floats must be patrolled regularly so that damaged crabs can be removed and crabs which have just moulted be culled, i.e. gathered for market. The culling must be done swiftly, since the period of softness is so short, and conveyance to market must be rapid, too. The peak season for Chesapeake Bay crabbers comes in May.

Soft crabs may be bought frozen. It is then only necessary to thaw them before they are fried or grilled.

CUISINE If soft crabs are bought alive, they must first be dressed, thus: 'With a sharp knife, cut off the apron or flap that folds under the rear of the body. Turn the crab and cut off the face at a joint just back of the eyes. Lift each point at the sides with the fingers, clean out the gills, and wash the crabs in cold water. Pat dry with a paper towel.' (Seafood Marketing Authority, Annapolis.)

It is usual to fry the prepared soft-shell crabs in butter, after patting them dry and flouring them. It is best to use clarified butter, as advised by Anna Wetherill Reed (The Philadelphia Cook Book of Town and Country, 1940). She also recommends that when the fried crabs have been removed to a serving platter the cook should add some lemon juice to the butter remaining in the pan, and strain the combination over the crabs.

I find that the unusual texture of the soft-shell crab is enhanced by serving it on half of a soft roll, and eating it as a sort of open sandwich. I ate some prepared in this way at Tilghman, with tartare sauce, and found them excellent thus. (A tartare sauce can be made very easily by adding to mayonnaise some finely chopped gherkin and parsley, and perhaps a little minced onion. But a better procedure is to start by rubbing two hard-boiled egg-yolks into a paste, with seasoning. Turn this into a liquid by adding olive oil and tarragon vinegar. Then add also some very finely chopped chives, gherkin and capers, a little French mustard and a touch of cayenne pepper. Blend this mixture with a suitable quantity of home-made mayonnaise.)

Deh-Ta Hsiung

Deh-Ta Hsiung was born in Peking and grew up in a family of scholars and gourmets. He came to England to finish his studies at Oxford and London, then worked in films for over twenty years. In the late 1970s he started to teach and write on Chinese culture and food; in 1980 he wrote Marks & Spencer's first book on *Chinese Cooking*. When Deh-Ta wrote the following piece, most people in the West were still convinced that wines simply didn't work with Chinese food – a myth that he soundly dispelled.

Wine and Chinese Food

DECANTER MAGAZINE
1982

Choosing wine or wines to go with Chinese food always seems to present problems for most people, partly because the order of different courses served at a Chinese meal bears no resemblance to the Western convention of soup-fish-poultry-meat-cheese-pudding sequence.

But on a closer examination, one soon realizes that a Chinese meal is served according to a carefully worked out programme based on the yin-yang principle in Chinese culture. This ancient Chinese philosophy believes that harmony arises from the proper blending of opposites, not of irreconcilable opposites, but of complementary pairs.

The main distinctive feature in Chinese cooking is the harmonious balance of colours, aromas, flavours and textures both in a single dish and in a course of different dishes. For instance, chicken breast meat which is white in colour and tender in texture goes well with green pepper which is bright green and crisp; and to pair this dish one would choose beef with celery or carrots. In seasonings, yin and yang, reveals itself in classic partnerships like sweet and sour, soy sauce and rice wine, ginger and spring onions and so on.

The yin-yang principle extends still further to Chinese menu planning. The order in which different courses or dishes are served depends more on the method of cooking, and the way the ingredients are prepared before cooking rather than on the actual food itself. Let us take a typical dinner menu for 8–10 people:

FIRST COURSE: 4 cold starters or an assorted hors d'oeuvre dish.

SECOND COURSE: 2 or 3 quick stir-fried dishes or deep-fried or even braised dishes.

MAIN COURSE: 2 or 3 long-cooked dishes, which can be steamed, braised or roasted, but usually consist of a whole duck, chicken, fish and joint of meat.

PUDDING: only served at formal banquets in China; soup is often served for lesser grand occasions.

RICE COURSE: noodles and dumplings are often served instead of or as well as rice at the end of a big meal.

FRESH FRUIT: is often served right at the end of the meal.

Choosing wines for a menu like this should present no problems at all; since there are 8–10 people, you will need at least five if not six bottles of wine. Now if you follow the yin-yang principle, you would not dream of serving white wine only throughout the meal. To start with, choose a medium or dry sherry as an aperitif to go with the cold first course; alternatively select a champagne or a sparkling wine, or any light wine, such as muscadet, chablis, graves; or a less dry white such as hock, moselle or any white wine made from the Riesling grape.

For the next course, when hot stir-fried dishes are served, you need a stronger wine with more fruitiness and flavour such as an Alsace, a white burgundy or Pouilly Blanc Fumé from the Loire; an Orvieto secco or Frascati from Italy, or a Pinot Chardonnay from California. For those who prefer red wine, choose a good Beaujolais, Mâcon, Chinon, Bourgueil or a lightish claret from Bordeaux; or any light red wine from Italy (Valpolicella, Bardolino or Barolo).

The main course calls for a more robust and full-bodied red wine. For the claret lovers, there is plenty of suitable good red wine such as an aromatic Pomerol (my personal favourite) or St. Emilion. Médoc or red Graves may be a shade too delicate for those really rich dishes, but the firmer and tastier burgundy should suit well. So would a powerful and fragrant Rhône or a Chianti Classico, or a matured Rioja from Spain, Cabernet or Shiraz from Australia or Cabernet Sauvignon or Pinot Noir from California.

At a recent Chinese food and western wines luncheon held at the Golden Duck Restaurant in London, we sampled no less than 35 different wines during a 16 course meal. We started off with Crab Spring Rolls served on a bed of cabbage relish, Deep-Fried Prawn Snowballs and Curried Wantons. The Chablis and Sauvignon were both excellent accompaniments, but the Italian white seemed to be lacking in fruit when tasted side by side with a Californian Chardonnay.

The next course began with a perfect example of the yin-yang principle: Fish Slices in Rice Wine Sauce with Black Fungus (Wooden Ears). This is a classic Peking dish that requires the highest skill on the part of the cook, and in this instance it was one of the best I have ever sampled. Full marks to Chef But, a younger brother of the chef from the restaurant Memories of China, London SW1. Steamed Dumplings with soy and ginger dips were served next; they were delicious and everybody liked them, but strictly speaking they should be eaten much later.

So was the next dish of Scallops in Black Bean Sauce, Cantonese Style, a touch too fiery for this early stage, especially compared with the last dish of the course, "Sea Spice" Chicken Shreds – chicken breast meat cooked in what is know as "fish sauce". This style of cooking from Sichuan has often been misunderstood in the West; in reality, no fish is used – the sauce usually consists of garlic, ginger, spring onions, soy sauce, chilli sauce, wine, vinegar and sugar, and is normally used for cooking a fish dish, hence the name fish sauce. Here because of the addition of sugar to the chilli and other seasonings, the result was a fragrant and full flavour, while the Cantonese-style scallops almost numbed one's palate.

The main course was Crisp and Aromatic Duck served with plum sauce, cucumber and spring onions, wrapped in pancakes. This Sichuan dish is claimed to be the forerunner of the world-renowned Peking Duck. Whatever is the truth, it is on the menu in most Peking-style restaurants. A fresh duckling is first marinated for several hours with star anise, Sichuan peppercorns, ginger, spring onions and rice wine, then it is steamed vigorously for 2½–3 hours to drain off its excess fat, then finally it is deep-fried in hot oil until golden brown and crispy. Another triumph for young Chef But, and the Gewürztraminer from Alsace was a perfect partner.

Crispy Beef with Carrots came next, I think it was then that we had our first red, a five-year-old Rioja with a pronounced oaky flavour. Sweet and Sour Fillet of Pork followed, our host said it was a challenge to see what wine could be matched to this very popular Chinese dish. But I thought that this dish was out of place here and, besides, the sauce seemed to have so much tomato ketchup, that no wine would be solid enough not to be overwhelmed by its piquancy.

The last dish in this course was Sizzling Lamb on Griddle, a Chinese version of Teppanyaki which originated from Japan. Tender lamb marinated in soy and wine, rapidly stir-fried in hot oil over high heat with spring onions for a very short time, was brought to the table sizzling on a heated iron plate. "A dramatic dish," remarked David Wolfe, and it was most delicious too; we had a ten year old Rubesco from Torgiano, and it made a dignified and very compatible partner. Yangchow Fried Rice made its welcome appearance, so did a plate of stir-fried mixed vegetables. Believe it or not, we still had room for Singapore Rice Vermicelli with shrimps and vegetables.

The meal ended with sesame sprinkled Toffee Apples and Bananas. We all agreed that what we needed here was a Sauternes or Barsac. I observed with interest that although coffee was offered on the menu, everyone opted for jasmin tea. After eating and drinking for nearly four hours, a pot of hot green tea was most refreshing and invigorating.

The lunch was a most successful experiment and for me a highly rewarding experience, and I must thank Shura Shihwary, Serena Sutcliffe and David Peppercorn for inviting me to their event.

Nicola Humble

Nicola Humble is a Senior Lecturer in English Literature at Roehampton University. She has a particular interest in the history of food and food writing, and has co-edited a volume of *Mrs Beeton's Book of Household Management*. Her *Culinary Pleasures: Cookbooks and the Transformation of British Food* is the first serious study of the British culinary reawakening since the Victorian era. Winner of the Guild's Food Book of the Year Award in 2006, it also won a Special Award at the 2006 Gourmand World Cookbook Awards. Nicola's ability to 'float adjacent to the historical moment' invests her study of nouvelle cuisine with a unique clarity. She is currently working on a book about the cultural history of cake.

Nouvelle Cuisine

Culinary Pleasures
<small>FABER 2005</small>

Nouvelle cuisine hit Britain in the late 1970s, and by the beginning of the 1980s it was everywhere. The movement had originated in France a decade earlier, when two food critics, Henri Gault and Christian Millau, wrote an article describing a new sort of cooking being practised by a group of young chefs who challenged the time-honoured conventions of the professional French kitchen. These chefs, who included Paul Bocuse, Roger Vergé, Michel Guérard and the two Troisgros brothers (Jean and Pierre), rejected flour-based sauces, long cooking of meat and what they saw as the overcomplicated, indigestible classics of French haute cuisine. Instead they shortened menus and cooking times, used more fish and less meat, and constructed sauces based on reductions of juices and stocks, essences and spices. This was food redesigned for a health-conscious generation, aware of the dangers of a diet high in fat and cholesterol, body-conscious but physically indolent.

Gault and Millau outlined the principles behind the new cooking in the form of a manifesto, converting the practice of individual chefs into a movement that immediately attracted the attention of the French and then the international press. According to their account, *la nouvelle cuisine* was governed by a set of key principles: avoid unnecessary complication (so use simple cooking methods), shorten cooking times (which necessitated younger, fresher ingredients), shop regularly at the market, reduce choice on the menu (so as not to have a huge stock of ingredients all requiring refrigeration), ban obsolete or boring principles (such as the notion that game must be marinated), banish heavy flour-based sauces, make use of advanced technology (in practice this tended to mean an eager embracing of the food processor and a consequent parade of terrines, mousses and purées), apply knowledge of dietetics (reduced sugar and salt, no frying) and – possibly most crucially – invent constantly. Reflecting in 1996 on the movement he had helped to kick-start, Gault noted that:

this nouvelle cuisine, wishing to be without roots and open to every influence, was the band wagon on to which jumped, along with the authentic cooks, a crowd of mountebanks, antiquarians, society women, fantasists and tricksters who did not give the developing movement a good name. Furthermore fashions, mannerisms and trickery attached themselves to this new culinary philosophy: miniscule portions; systematic undercooking; abuses of techniques in themselves interesting (mousses, turned vegetables, coulis); inopportune marriages of sugar, salt and exotic spices; excessive homage paid to the decoration of dishes and 'painting on the plate'; and ridiculous or dishonest names of dishes.

That just about sums it up. The new method of "plating-up" in the kitchen rather than allowing the customer to serve himself from dishes brought to the table was seized on by restaurants large and small, good and bad, as the perfect way to institute portion control. Every chef who fancied himself an artist now had licence to swirl his plates with multi-coloured sauces (the food always sat on top, obedient to the principle that nothing must be disguised in the new cooking), serve meat and fish in tiny medallions rather than hefty slabs, and let his imagination run free in the invention of startling combinations of ingredients (duck and pawpaw, lobster and mango). But the vast majority of chefs who embraced the movement with such enthusiasm in fact exhibited a paralysing conformity: every pudding had its flood of fruit coulis (another product of the food processor, invariably oversweetened, with the chemical kick of icing sugar), all vegetables were infants, handturned into identical little barrels, and kiwi fruit was the new parsley.

The ubiquity of the kiwi fruit slice perched on British restaurant food of the early 1980s indicates the extent to which most of the adopters of nouvelle cuisine had simply got it wrong: the point was to continue to invent, not to enshrine the inventions of others in a sort of cultural aspic. Pink peppercorns and raspberry vinegar met a similar fate: desperately trendy and overexposed (and actually not very nice), the bottles gathered dust in homes all over the country. Because it was not just restaurateurs who bought nouvelle cuisine: magazines seized on the new culinary style because it made such pretty pictures. And that, of course, was the point about most of the new ingredients – their colours and shapes were much more important than their taste, hence the fondness in these years for the flavourless but graphic star fruit. So delicatessens and even supermarkets began to stock the new ingredients, manufacturers to make the requisite oversized black or white octagonal plates (the shape apparently helped chefs perfect the pattern of the food), and the readers of the magazines to attempt to reproduce the dishes for their dinner parties.

It is hard to imagine that many of those dinner parties were very successful. Nouvelle cuisine was essentially restaurant food, a theatrical performance requiring bustling waiters, gleaming napery, silver cutlery and a succession of surprises issuing forth from the kitchen to "oohs" and "aahs" and fanfares. It also helped the effect if the meal cost a lot. It is no accident that this food reached its high point in the Thatcherite 1980s, when a new class of entrepreneurs and city boys was desperate to display its wealth. Spending was good in the 1980s, the more conspicuous the better. In this rampantly consumerist decade, food became one of the key ways of demonstrating wealth and status. And what was more conspicuous than paying a fortune for a beautifully produced meal that left you hungry? This was food as art object rather than as a source of sustenance. It was the era of the specialist food magazine – publications like *A la Carte* and *Taste* presented exotic foods in gorgeous double-page spreads, tweaked by stylists and airbrushed like models. The aesthetic of the new food formed an interesting contrast with the browns and beiges and earthenware platters of the 1970s wholefood movement and with the vibrant hues of Mediterranean dishes. This food was colourful, but with a delicate, almost pastel palette: creamy sauces tinged with pink, green and yellow, the pink of salmon, the fresh greens of pistachios and mange-tout, the soft reds of radicchio and oak-leaf lettuce (almost entirely without flavour or texture, but a very pretty colour). The food looks artistic and tasteful (in the non-culinary sense) – like the perfect lady in her camels and soft pinks, it looks expensive.

Nouvelle cuisine produced a response in the British press unheard of for a mere matter of food: analyzed, fêted and fulminated against, it was the wonder of the age. Elizabeth David gave a characteristically measured but ascerbic response to the new cooking in the preface to the 1983 reprint of *French Provincial Cooking*, noting that it was not really so new at all:

> In 1960, when this book was first published, it seemed to me that so called cuisine classique with its rigid traditions and immutable rules had already been unrealistic and hopelessly out of date at least since 1939, let alone by fifteen years after the end of the Second World War. Belatedly, then, in the early 70s a group of younger professional chefs began to make rebellious announcements about lighter food and less of it, about vegetables being undercooked in the Chinese style instead of stewed to pulp, about fish being poached or grilled until the flesh just came away from the bone rather than tumbling from it in a shower of flakes. Very laudable aims all these were too, if not perhaps as startling to the ordinary public as they seemed to the young men themselves.

Mocking, as do most other commentators, the finicky presentation of the new chefs ("the five green beans sitting lonely on one side of a huge white plate, three tepid chicken livers *avec ses quelques feuilles de salade* nine inches distant on the opposite edge"), she nonetheless acknowledges the necessity and inevitability of continual culinary evolution. The main problem with nouvelle cuisine, in her opinion, is not its innovations but the attitude its presentational pretensions imply towards the customer:

> The enticement of the wonderful smells of fine cooking, now diffused and muddled by the obligatory plate service, the intense visual stimulus once inseparable from a meal in a good French country restaurant but now destroyed by misguided imitation of Japanese-style presentation, could quite easily be restored to us. In other words, it is not so much the cooking that is wrong, except in the most blatantly arrogant establishments, as a certain coldness and ungenerosity of spirit, an indifference to the customer, now manifest in establishments operated on nouvelle cuisine principles.

Glynn Christian

Glynn Christian is best known in the UK as one of the earliest TV cooks. In 1974 he co-founded Mr Christian's, the iconic delicatessen off London's Portobello Road. Using his unrivalled experience of gourmet and specialty foods, he packed the shop with everything he thought a good cook would want. When BBC Breakfast Time began in 1983, Glynn broadcast live from a sliced-bread factory three times weekly, sometimes cooking and regularly updating availability and costs of fresh ingredients. Glynn has written many books and *Real Flavours: the Handbook of Gourmet and Deli Ingredients* was shortlisted for the Guild's 2006 Food Book of the Year.

Truffles

Glynn Christian's Delicatessen Food Handbook
MACDONALD 1982

When an author as august as Colette describes a fungus as the 'most capricious and most revered of black princesses' you can be certain it is rather more than a mushroom. The truffle, black diamond of cookery, is one of the rarest of all the world's exotic treats; in Périgord in France, regarded as the epicentre of truffledom, they cost 1600 francs per kilo in 1982 when still uncleaned and straight out of the soil. That's about £5 an ounce and on top of that we have to pay for processing, transport and for the profits of those who sell such delights.

Truffles have been popular and acknowledged as special for thousands of years and like all rare things have been credited with aphrodisiac powers, particularly by Francis I of France, but I suspect this was rather a matter of expecting more for your money than passing gastronomic gratification.

The flavour of black truffles is found in nothing else – indeed it isn't found in truffles most of the time. The delicacy is fugitive, easily overpowered and expected to perform tasks of which it is incapable. It is more a perfumer or catalyst than a flavouring and the true flavour is only passed on to other foods by standing together or cooking together very gently for a longish time. Truffle is best with other fragile flavours, such as exalted foie gras or creamy scrambled eggs. Although a standby of buffets, banquets and ballrooms, the practice of decorating with slithers of cold truffle is nonsensical and wasteful in the extreme – the truffle has not been brought to full flavour and the food will not be perfumed by it. Far better to use slices of black olive, which have been blanched to desalt them. An extraordinary number of people will believe it is truffle if you tell them so; everyone will if you don't.

The 19th century was blessed by a boom in the truffle harvest, as is manifest in cookery books of the time which use truffles like we use tomatoes. It was nothing to be served a whole one as a starter, baked with a little madeira and seasoning, and served on a crisp, linen napkin. Now the harvest is around 100 tonnes a year when conditions are right. You need warm rainy summers to follow a spring in which the right types of breeze have encouraged the spores to travel, settle and germinate. Dry summers can reduce the harvest by at least 25 per cent.

Truffles are gathered between the end of November and mid-March or so. They're probably at their best in January. Usually they are found under oak trees in 'burnt' areas, so-called because no other vegetation can or will grow there. They can only be found by being sniffed out by trained dogs or pigs, all of which contributes to the high cost. But if they grow under oak trees, why are there no English truffles? Well, there is an English truffle, the Bath or Red truffle, but it has largely been lost to us by the creeping of our towns and cities into our fields and by a dearth of those who have the knowledge to train animals to find them. However, I once had a Lithuanian working for me who said regularly, 'Oh I know where to find truffles all over England'. Initial excitement gave way to inertia on my part, a dampening of disbelief. Imagine my face when he returned months later with a small paper bag full! There were black ones and white ones – and one extraordinary fragrant one the like of which I've never come across before or since. I knew rather less about truffles than I do now and probably ruined some of them in my experiments – but . . . truffles to experiment with. My friend told me he knew where to go because he had actually sown the spores all over England, having brought them from Europe after the war. I've not seen him for years now, but somewhere in England there are treasures as valuable as any Graeco-Roman silver hoards.

There are two major types of truffle, the black and the white. The black truffle – *tuber malanosporum* or *tuber brumale* – is best known as the Perigord truffle. Its dark flesh becomes jet black when fully ripened. Found only in France in Perigord-Quercy, Provence, the Comtat Venaissin and the southern slopes of the Cévennes.

Tuber Magnatum is the white Piedmontese truffle which has a white flesh and smooth yellow skin. Less expensive than the black, it is slightly more pronounced in flavour and usually eaten raw, grated finely over pasta or on a hot brioche, a specialty of sidewalk cafés in Florence. Neither type has yielded to being cultivated with any success.

Although supplies are hard to come by, some of the Arabic countries are growing and harvesting a type of white truffle commercially. They grow in sand, especially in North Africa. In few, very few shops in London you can buy a tin holding well over 1 lb (½ kg) in weight for something in the region of £8–£10 (Christmas 1981).

Their flavour is very light but the excitement they give is enormous. With a huge hot cheese and cucumber soufflé I served a great bowl of sliced white Egyptian truffles, gently poached for a few seconds in a reduction of dry madeira. The astonishment was so extraordinary I'll never do it again. The soufflé got cold as the table stared at the truffles

– and everyone thought I was so rich they stopped bringing bottles of wine when they came to dinner. If you do find these, buy them and use them extravagantly, to layer patés, smother scrambled eggs, stuff rolls of smoked salmon, float in consommé, flavour seafood sauces for pasta. Brush them well first to remove the sand and soak in some reduced sherry or madeira with a touch of salt and pepper first.

Black truffles are sold fresh, tinned or bottled. After the laborious brushing and peeling and sorting, which can only be done by hand, truffles stay fresh for just three to four days and will be sold in the chilly winter markets of French villages whole or in pieces. Otherwise the truffles are preserved in one of two ways; they are either cooked before canning or bottling which gives some control over weight loss, or they are slightly salted and sterilized after packing which keeps all the flavour and bulk but converts 25 per cent of the weight into liquid. If you have a fresh truffle and wish to keep it, poach it in Madeira and leave it in this liquid, itself a wondrous addition to sauces.

Frankly, though, I am disillusioned. I've never been knocked out by the flavour of a black truffle, even when it has been left for days to perfume a sirloin of beef. In fact the flavour that seems best is that of the madeira in which a truffle has been poached. Even the whole, baked truffle I enjoyed at the Ménage à Trois restaurant in London's Beauchamp Place wasn't such a thrill as, say a slice of foie gras or a few spoonsful of caviare. I'll walk a long way to eat freshly grated white truffle, but the black ones? I don't understand the fuss.

Anne Willan

Born in Newcastle, Anne Willan studied and taught cooking in London and Paris before moving to the United States. She was associate editor of *Gourmet* and founder of *L'Ecole de Cuisine La Varenne in Paris*. Among her many accomplishments, she edited the 20-volume *Grand Diplôme Cookery Course*, which earned an André Simon Award, wrote *The Observer French Cookery School*, which won a Glenfiddich Award, and *Cooked to Perfection*, which won a Guild Award. She was made a Grande Dame of Les Dames d'Escoffier International in 1999 and in the same year the International Association of Culinary Professionals honoured her with their prestigious Lifetime Achievement Award.

Confit

French Regional Cooking
HUTCHINSON 1981

"Confit" is an almost exclusively French method of salting meats and poultry, then preserving them in fat. It is hard to understand why it is not universal, since making confit is simplicity itself, requiring only three or four ingredients and little time or skill. Although usually associated with duck and goose, in fact any meat with a fairly high fat content can be preserved this way; all over southwestern France and throughout the length of the Pyrenees to Languedoc, the charcuteries are full of confit of pork, tongue, sausages, even pig's feet, as well as of poultry. In the mountains, where storing food for the winter is still an important activity, the autumn, when the pigs are killed, is the high season for confit. Confit is perfectly good made with the fatty breed of duck found in the USA.

Whatever the meat or bird, it is normally preserved in large pieces. These are thickly coated in coarse salt, with thyme and bay leaf added, and left to pickle for between 6 and 36 hours. Pickling time depends on the flavour wanted and the thickness of the meat; the longer it is left, the stronger the flavour will be, although eventually the confit can become inedibly salty. The confit is then cooked in large quantities of fat; goose is normally cooked in goose fat, which can be bought in tins, duck in duck fat and pork in lard. However, lard can be used for everything, or fat left from previous confits can be reused after straining, although after three or four cycles it becomes too salty. The fat must be sufficient to cover the meat, which is cooked extremely slowly on top of the stove or in the oven, until it is almost falling apart – so soft, say country cooks, that a straw can be inserted right through the meat.

When cool enough to handle, the meat is packed in a crock and completely covered with melted fat to seal it. A tight seal is vital, for all air must be excluded from the meat and the crock should be banged on the table to extract air bubbles. When the fat has set, any air pockets must be filled with more melted fat. Then a cloth is laid on the fat, topped with a thick layer of coarse salt right to the edges of the crock,

and the whole pot is covered with stout paper tied with string. In a cool place, the paper lid is sufficient covering for a month; in a refrigerator, the confit will keep much longer. If left in a warm place, confit goes rancid and acquires a musty taste.

In any case, confit should be left at least a week to mature before being eaten. It has a flavour all its own, though it can be compared to ham. Drained of the preserving fat, it is used to enrich soups and stews, particularly those based on vegetables, but most often confit is served alone, cooked gently in a little of its fat until it is hot and brown; the crisp brown skin on confit of goose and duck is a particular treat.

As accompaniment, potatoes fried in fat from the confit are a must – the best are wafer-thin, and crisp with a hint of garlic. Vegetable accompaniments may be added to balance the richness of confit. Lentils or dried beans are popular, or a stew of green peas and onions, or a purée of sorrel, spinach or chestnuts, while confit of goose deserves the luxury of a few wild mushrooms. Confit is also good cold, particularly in a salad dressed with tarragon vinegar and walnut oil, another south-western speciality.

Confit de Canard Confit of Duck

Often only the legs and thighs of the duck are used for confit, and the breast, called a "magret", is cooked like a steak. If you intend to serve the duck alone instead of using it to flavour other dishes such as cassoulet, reduce the amount of salt in this recipe by one-third.

Serves 3–4

1.8 kg (4 lb) large duck

45 g (1 ½ oz) coarse salt

1 tsp ground black pepper

2–3 sprigs of thyme

2–3 bay leaves, crumbled

1.5 kg (3 lb) lard or goose fat, more if needed

Cut the duck in 8 pieces, trimming the neck and wings and removing the backbone; these bones can be used for soup.

Rub each piece of duck with some of the coarse salt and put it in a crock or terrine. Sprinkle with pepper and the remaining salt, and add the thyme and bay leaves.

Cover and leave in a cool place for 6–12 hours, depending on how strong a flavour you want, turning the pieces occasionally.

When ready to cook, wipe the excess salt from the duck pieces. Set the oven at low (150°C, 300°F).

Lay the duck pieces skin side down in a flameproof casserole and cook over a low fire for 15–20 minutes or until the fat runs and the duck browns lightly.

Add enough lard or goose fat to cover the browned duck, cover and cook in the oven for 2 hours or until the duck is very tender and has rendered all its fat.

To preserve the duck: pour a layer of rendered duck fat in the base of a small terrine and leave until set. Pack the pieces of duck on top and pour over enough fat to cover them completely, adding melted lard if necessary.

Cover the crock and keep in a cool place at least a week for the flavour to mellow. If sealed with a cloth sprinkled with salt and then covered with paper, confit will keep for several months in a cool place.

To serve the confit by itself: leave it in a warm place until the fat runs. Drain it, then fry it in a little fat until it is very hot and the skin is crisp and brown. Transfer to a platter and serve very hot. Keep the left-over fat for frying.

Confit d'Oie
Confit of goose

To substitute goose for the duck in the above recipe, double the quantities of all the seasonings, including the salt.

Cecilia Norman

Cecilia Norman trained as a home economist and teacher. When she was given a cookery book which had printer's errors in the ingredients, she contacted Pitman Publishing and was invited to lunch by the editor. On perusing her recipes, the editor asked Cecilia to write a book on microwave cooking. Having no experience as an author and none of the microwave, Cecilia was reluctant, but when told, 'Well my dear, it is up to you', she made up her mind to meet the challenge. *Microwave Cookery for the Housewife*, the first British book on the subject, became a best seller. Many books followed and in 1980 Cecilia opened the first Microwave Cooking School in the UK. She is now on the Board of the University of the New Age and offers advice to the elderly on how to continue eating a well-balanced diet.

Microwave Cookery at Home

Microwave Cookery for the Housewife
Pitman 1974

During the 1960s the microwave oven quickly proved itself a valuable asset to all types of catering establishments, because of the extreme speed and facility with which pre-cooked meals can be re-heated ready for serving and frozen foods thawed. For example, a frozen pre-packed meal which might take 45 minutes to reach a serving temperature in a conventional oven from the frozen state or about 20 minutes from a refrigerated state can be ready for serving after 1½ to 4 minutes from the frozen state or 45 seconds to 1½ minutes from a refrigerated state in a microwave oven, the times varying according to the power of the oven.

During World War II it was found that microwaves pass easily through rain, smoke and fog, all of which block light-waves. Their special properties made it possible for images of distant objects such as enemy shipping and aircraft to become visible on a radar screen. It was in the course of this radar research that the heating properties of microwaves were discovered.

Now microwave cookery is proving itself equally valuable in the home, not only for quick re-heating or for the thawing of frozen food but also for basic cooking. As these recipes will show, the microwave oven will save hours of time in cooking almost any item of food and in hastening the processes involved in the preparation and completion of a dish.

Microwaves have many of the same characteristics as light-waves. Electric light is generated in an electric light bulb but microwaves are generated from electrical energy in a vacuum tube operating as an oscillator called a magnetron.

Microwaves will pass through such substances as glass, porcelain, china, earthenware and paper. As they pass through without effect those substances will remain cool. When microwaves meet metal they are reflected from it and the metal also remains cool. But when micro-waves encounter the moisture contained in food they are absorbed by it. The millions of molecules which comprise the food begin to jump about, rubbing against one another and causing friction. This results in massive heat, which forms the cooking process. It could be compared with the proverbial boy scout rubbing two sticks together to start his fire.

This is the reason that foods cooked by microwaves become hot much more quickly than those cooked in a conventional oven. With the advent of the microwave oven, a change in the technique of cooking has arrived. Microwave cooking is not an improved method of cooking by conventional means. It is an entirely new approach to the exercise, for it is a new method of introducing heat to food. The food is exposed to electro-magnetic waves and the heat is generated inside the food itself.

This calls for a certain amount of re-thinking on the part of the cook, just as the first gas and electric cookers did in the case of cooks who had spent most of their lives grappling with temperamental kitchen ranges.

The microwave oven is not designed to replace conventional cookers but should complement them. Few appliances are more than 70 per cent efficient. Although some microwave primary cooking may seem slow, at least there is no 10-minute wait for the oven to reach the correct temperature. The ideal way of cooking is to use your conventional oven in conjunction with your microwave oven and your freezer. For example, when cooking Yorkshire puddings, which will not cook in a microwave oven, make a batch of them in your conventional oven, freeze them and reheat when necessary in the microwave.

Although at the moment the microwave oven is mainly used for re-heating foods previously cooked by conventional means, this recipe book will show that it is not only possible but easier to prepare a great variety of dishes from basic ingredients. Do not think in terms of buying a tinned ready-made sponge pudding to reheat, either by steaming on your conventional cooker or by re-heating in the microwave. It is cheaper to prepare the mixture yourself; you will then be sure that there are no added chemicals and preservatives. Beef burgers are so easy to prepare from minced beef, onion powder, salt and pepper. Just shape on a floured board and cook in the oven for 1 minute. The cost of the basic ingredients is at least halved. Crème caramel, which is obtainable in ready-mix form which needs no baking, can be left on the grocer's shelf. It is not the mixing of the eggs and milk that is difficult, it is the pre-heating of the oven and the long water-bath cooking that is tedious. Tedium is not a word applicable to microwave cooking.

Naturally you will need to practise. Once you have used an electric mixer and blender it is difficult to imagine how food preparation could have been done without them, but their use had to be learnt, and so it is with the microwave cooker.

Microwave ovens are not radioactive. They have no connection with X-rays or radioactive fall-out. They simply convert electrical energy into radio waves, and they 'are equipped with safety devices which ensure that there is no risk of microwaves escaping into the room. The principle in every model is the same. The door cannot be opened while the oven is in operation. Once the door is opened the unit shuts off. There are also other in-built safety factors, such as various devices to check any leakage of microwaves through the door when it is locked and cooking is in progress. The primary door seals the microwave energy back into the oven, and secondly there is a gasket made of materials which will absorb any possible leaking microwaves. If your oven has a drop-door, therefore, never rest anything on it or you may damage the door's perfect alignment and fit.

This safety factor is especially important in a home where there are small children. There is no electric hot-plate to burn their hands and no switches that can be accidentally turned on to produce fumes. There is a main switch now standard with all microwave installations; if this is switched off after use, no harm will come if the button on the oven itself is pressed accidentally. However, remember to keep half a glass of water in the oven when it is not being used so that there is something to cook for a short time if a child activates the oven, since the magnetron can be damaged if the machine is operated when empty. The oven can be damaged but not the child. A microwave oven is heavy and so it is virtually impossible to pull over. The doors are fairly stiff and require some strength to open. It is safer also for the half-awake husband cooking his own bacon: no burning himself with hot fat, nor will it matter that in searching for a bandage he forgets to switch off the oven, for the microwave oven having been pre-set to cook for a certain length of time will automatically switch itself off, so avoiding the acrid smells of burning pervading the whole house, to say nothing of the problems of cleaning a blackened frying-pan.

As the sides of the oven remain cool, food particles do not burn against them and the oven stays clean, needing only a quick wipe over with a damp cloth.

Cooking odours, which often cling, will not be noticeable to visitors since the "smelly" part of cooking can be carried out earlier in the day.

Microwave cookery virtually dispenses with the need for saucepans. In most cases it is possible to cook in the serving dishes. Vegetables may be strained after cooking and then returned to the cooking dish, which will remain hot by conduction, although dinner plates will have to be warmed by other means. Meat dishes which include sauces can nearly always be prepared, cooked and served in the same casserole. At the most one other dish will be required for preparing the food. Since many dishes can be cooked in the serving bowl which comes to the table, and some on the plate on which it is to be eaten, the washing-up chore is most satisfyingly reduced. Indeed food can be cooked in disposable paper containers if liked.

Should your family be quite incapable of cooking they will at least be able to push a button, so prepare the breakfast the previous night and leave it in the refrigerator on individual plates. Write the heating time on a piece of paper and then cover the whole plate with plastic film. When the food is hot the family can discard the plastic film and paper and enjoy a hot and fresh breakfast.

The microwave oven has numerous advantages for the housewife and is a true release from a great deal of time-consuming labour. As the following recipes will show, it is invaluable for preparing meals quickly and for re-heating a meal for a latecomer.

It is a boon for entertaining, as sauces and gravies and all the details involved in the last minute serving can be made well beforehand and then reheated.

It has been mentioned previously that foods re-heat very quickly and this enables any member of the family to cook, and also enables the hostess to devote her individual attention to her dinner guests. Even when a pressure-cooker is used for last minute vegetables it cannot be left unattended, since the timing is even more precise than in microwave cooking. Now vegetables can be pre-cooked (either conventionally or by microwave) and they will only require a moment's re-heating while the plates are brought to the table. Dishes of different foods may be re-heated in the oven at the same time and there will be no transference of flavour. After dinner coffee may be pre-percolated and the jug (not metal, of course) left in the oven, with the switch just ready to press.

Among the many advantages of the microwave oven speed comes high in the list. As cooking periods are so short, food often shows a great improvement in flavour and colour and retains a higher proportion of nutriment.

Several hours can be saved in the thawing process of meat and poultry. A joint is ready for cooking 30 minutes after leaving the freezer. Frozen fruits should only be half-thawed, taking 2 minutes approximately.

For speedy last-minute cooking a jacket potato will be ready in 4 minutes and baked apples, stuffed as you wish, will take 1 minute for each apple. And when you have forgotten to buy bread, a large loaf from the freezer will be thawed for eating in 5 minutes. Microwave cookery means freedom, cleanness and speed.

Upside-down Pudding

This attractive and economical sweet can be varied by using other fruits such as apricots, peaches or mandarin oranges. Soft red fruits such as strawberries or raspberries are not suitable as the colour runs and the fruit goes mushy.

1 oz (30 g) unrefined light muscovado sugar

1 oz (30 g) margarine

small can of pineapple, drained

a few glacé cherries, halved

Cake Mixture:

2 oz (60 g) margarine

2 oz (60 g) unrefined golden caster sugar

2 oz (60 g) self-raising flour

1 egg

Line or grease a 7-in (18-cm) round glass cake-dish.

Cream brown sugar and 1 oz (30 g) margarine. Spread over base and around sides of dish.

Arrange fruit on base. Glacé cherries should have the smooth side facing the dish. Prepare cake mixture by the creaming method: i.e. cream margarine and sugar together until light and creamy. Add 1 tsp of flour, followed by the beaten egg and then the remainder of the flour. Place creamed mixture on top of fruit.

Cook 6 minutes turning dish a ¼ turn every 1½ minutes.

Turn out on to a hot dish. Serve immediately or re-heat when needed for ½ minute.

Rum Truffles

This is a useful way to use up left-over cake. Truffles can be quickly prepared for unexpected guests.

6 oz (170 g) stale cake crumbs (fruit cake is ideal)

1 oz (30 g) butter

2 heaped tbsp apricot jam

1 oz (30 g) cocoa

1 oz (30 g) ground almonds

½ tsp vanilla essence

2 tsp rum

chocolate vermicelli

Place butter in the dish to melt ½ minute.

Add jam and cocoa. Put in oven to melt ½ minute.

Mix in vanilla essence, rum, ground almonds and cake crumbs.

Form into balls and roll in chocolate vermicelli.

Leave to cool in refrigerator.

Susan Campbell

Writer and illustrator Susan Campbell's first food books included the iconic *Poor Cook* (1972), which she co-wrote with Caroline Conran, and *A Guide to Good Food Shops*. *The Cook's Companion* was among the earliest food books created and designed by the infant publisher Dorling Kindersley. Susan has put great energy into the Guild's Fairbridge Campaign, helping teach disadvantaged young people how to cook.

Hands

The Cook's Companion
MACMILLAN 1980

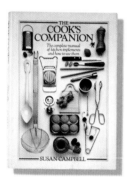

Somewhat perversely, the first chapter of this book is not devoted to any tools at all but to hands. Hands may be regarded as an integral part of any tool, since a tool is usually held in the hand to make it work. This chapter, however, deals with the many tasks in the kitchen that can be performed by hand, without the help – or in some cases hindrance – of any tools. By reading this chapter first you may save yourself the expense of buying some of the special equipment described further on, as well as the time and bother of washing up things that you can perfectly well manage without.

No really satisfactory domestic tool has yet been invented for fiddly jobs like peeling shrimps or shelling peas, but there are dozens for simple tasks like mixing. Bare hands are as good if not better than many of these, especially when making cakes, pastry and bread. When mixing sponges, for example, use the whole of your hand with the fingers spread out to fold the flour into a foamy egg and sugar batter. Feel with your fingertips for any pockets of unmixed flour. When mixing pasta and brioche dough, make a little well of flour on a pastry board and gently incorporate eggs into it with your fingers. Do the same for pâte brisée and add the butter by pressing it in with the heel of your hand.

Rub fat into flour with your fingertips when making pastry, and mix in water with them as well, but only if you are blessed with cool hands. But if your hands are warm they will be all the better when kneading bread dough. By doing this with your hands, you will know the right moment to stop for you feel the smooth elasticity of dough that is ready to 'prove'. Warm hands are also useful for creaming together butter and sugar, as the warmth will help the butter to soften. This also applies when kneading together flour and butter for beurre manié to thicken a sauce. Use your whole hand to knead a slab of butter to soften it before incorporating it into puff pastry or brioche dough – this knocks some of the water out of it as well. (You can also use your fingertips to mark the number of turns you have given your puff pastry.) Smear butter round baking dishes and cake tins with the tips of your fingers; the warmth helps to soften it and you can get right into the corners.

It goes without saying that your hands should be scrupulously clean

Opening a cooked crab

Stand the crab on its edge. Press down hard where the top shell joins the tail: you should hear a slight crack. Prize the top shell away from the rest of the body, pressing hardest where the tail joins it.

(1)

(2)

(3)

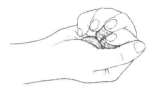

Cracking walnuts

Squeeze two walnuts together in your hand – one of them will crack against the other.

Skinning almonds

Pour boiling water over unskinned almonds to loosen the skin. When it cools, press each nut between your fingers so that the skin slips off. The almond will slide backwards into your hand.

Shelling prawns

Uncurl the prawn to loosen shell. Pull the shell from tail end, then gently pull the head and legs from the end.

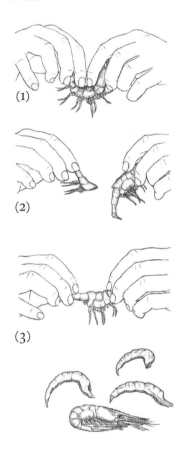

(1)

(2)

(3)

for all these jobs. It helps if you remove any chunky rings and bracelets which may get in the way and be difficult to clean. Flour your hands for dough and pastry making, so that they are nice and dry. Do the same when using your hands for shaping things like dumplings, quenelles, plaited loaves and knotted rolls, chapattis, pizzas, capelletti, wun tun noodles, Chinese dumplings and marzipan animals.

Wet your hands when mixing and shaping raw minced meat with herbs and eggs for beefburgers or meat balls. This will prevent the mixture from sticking to them. Do the same when mixing tabbouleh, a Middle Eastern salad of burghul – cracked wheat – soaked in water and then mixed with oil, lemon juice and minced onion.

Another Middle Eastern speciality, Syrian kibbeh, depends for its shape on a cook with long, slender fingers. A hollow, torpedo-shaped shell of cracked wheat, raw minced meat and onions is first shaped round the finger. It is then stuffed with another mixture – this time of raw meat, onions and nuts – sealed up and deep fried. Couscous, from North Africa, is broken up and worked over by hand, both before and after cooking. This is to separate the grains and is one of the occasions when an ability to tolerate heat proves useful.

In fact, many of the tricks of the cook's trade depend on being able to tolerate considerable heat with the hands. If you are unable to do this and you do burn yourself, hold the finger or hand under cold running water for several minutes. Some people say that clutching your ear lobes with the afflicted fingers will also relieve the pain. An experienced chef thinks nothing of removing a blanched onion from a pan of boiling water with his fingers or testing a bubbling sauce for flavour by dipping a clean finger into it. You can test rice for tenderness by squeezing a cooked grain between thumb and forefinger. Similarly, you can see if a piece of roasting meat is done by gently pressing it with the fingers – raw meat is soft and mushy, medium done is soft but springy, and overdone meat is hard and unyielding. With this method you can dispense with meat thermometers and timers.

There are many other jobs that you can do by hand and so dispense with pieces of equipment that will merely clutter your kitchen. You can, for example, do without egg separators, olive stoners and nutcrackers. Separate eggs by cracking the shell in half and, using each half as a cup, tip the yolk from one to the other, letting the white fall into a bowl underneath. A chef will tip the raw egg into the palm and, cupping the yolk, let the white run away between the fingers. If he has hairy hands, he may finish by rolling the yolk on the back of his hand, where the hairs will catch any remaining white. Stone an olive by pressing it between thumb and forefinger – the stone squirts out and the olive skin stays behind.

There are dozens of other tasks in the kitchen which you may find are done best by hand. The decorative presentation of food can only be done by hand, for example: arrange fruit prettily on open tarts and fan out apple slices like a pack of cards on the base of crème pâtissière. Run the side of your thumb round the edge of a soufflé mixture before putting it in the oven – this makes a little trough which helps to prevent the rising mixture from toppling over. Take the gut from a trout by hooking your finger into its gill and pulling gently. Skin fish fillets by hand, getting a grip on a slippery tail by sprinkling it with salt. Finally, always sprinkle salt into a dish by hand if you want to know exactly how much you are putting in – a pinch of salt means just that.

1984 TO 1989

The 'foodie' Years & the Rise of THE Celebrity Chef

Elisabeth Luard

Rick Stein OBE

Jeremy Round

Maurice Hanssen
WITH
Jill Marsden

Anna Del Conte

Richard Cawley

Yan-Kit So

Caroline Conran

Nichola Fletcher

Marguerite Patten OBE

Raymond Blanc

Elisabeth Luard

Elisabeth Luard is an award-winning food writer, journalist, novelist and broadcaster. Among her many cookbooks, *The Flavours of Andalucía* won a Glenfiddich Award in 1992 and *Sacred Food* received a Gourmand World Cookbook Award in 2001. She has also written an autobiography about her forty-year marriage to writer and co-founder of *Private Eye*, Nicholas Luard, *My Life as a Wife*, and her autobiography with recipes, *Family Life*, won a Guild of Food Writers Award in 1996. The *London Review of Books* called her *European Peasant Cookery*, 'a monumental work of scholarship... a book that no serious cook should be without'.

Potatoes

European Peasant Cookery
Transworld 1986

The potato, a relative newcomer to the European peasant larder, has none the less had a prodigious influence on European life. The first potato plants arrived in Spain in the baggage of the Conquistadores returning from Peru in 1540. The Incas had cultivated the potato for centuries to supply their mountain fortresses high in the Andes mountains, where their usual crop of maize could not survive. Just as Amsterdam was built on herring bones, so were Machu Pichu and Quito built on the potato. The Spanish court failed to see the tuber's culinary potential, but they found the pale mauve blooms very pretty and bedded the plants in flowerpots. The English received their first plants when Francis Drake brought some back from North America. Elizabeth I was not at all sure what to make of them, and she too planted them in her ornamental flower beds.

For the next two centuries the potato as a food source was treated with suspicion. A few brave souls took a chance and planted potatoes on the stony hillsides of Galicia, in the vegetable gardens of Lyons (even then the good burgers of Lyons were in the gastronomic vanguard), and in the flat fields of the Low Countries. Over in England some progress was being made. A dish of potatoes is recorded as appearing on King James's dinner table in 1619. Even with royal patronage the poisonous looking roots were widely considered untrustworthy, and in 1630 the Parliament of Besançon, in south-west France, outlawed the tuber, declaring it responsible for a particularly virulent outbreak of leprosy.

Nevertheless, the potato patch spread slowly across the fertile fields of Europe throughout the next century. From the sunlit valleys of Spain to the frozen mountains of Scandinavia the miraculously adaptable food-plant flourished.

Nowhere was it more successful than in the soft climate of Ireland. It was Elizabeth I's favourite sailor, Sir Walter Raleigh, who took the first potato plants to the green hills of the Emerald Isle. A mere century and a half later, virtually all other crops had been abandoned in its favour. A single damp Irish acre put down to potatoes by one Irish peasant, equipped with a spade and a hoe, yielded enough food to fill his family's black iron cooking pot all year – with some left over for the family pig. The population of Ireland tripled – from three million in 1750 to nearly nine million a century later. In 1841 the blight struck the potato. By 1846 a million and a half Irish men, women, and children had died of starvation. Of those who survived thousands emigrated to the New World.

Between 1750 and 1850 not only the Irish but the whole population of Europe exploded – victualled increasingly by the ever-adaptable jack-of-all-foods. An English traveller in Westphalia in 1780 reports the change in diet:

> Peasants tire of oatbread eaten dry with salt and water. I can heartily recommend the potato boiled and then moistened with a little milk, roasted in the ashes and eaten with a little butter, or eaten cold as a salad. Grated and mixed with eggs, oats and sugar it makes an excellent rissole. On this diet the peasants of Sauerland endure hard heavy work, and yet live as healthily as fish in the sea.

Whether boiled or baked, eaten as potato bread or in soup, used for animal fodder or fermented and distilled into alcohol, there was virtually no culinary need the potato could not supply. Just as the potato had been essential to the supremacy of the Incas in Peru, so it now dominated the politics of Europe. Revolution, war, the growth of empires – all were fuelled by the pressures of an expanding population. That curious basket of sprouting tubers in Francisco Pizzaro's luggage has proved as powerful as any of Alfred Nobel's explosive mixtures.

The best potatoes are those freshly dug from your own garden – the finest I have ever tasted grew in the stone-strewn, sheep-manured 'tattie patch' beside a shepherd's farmhouse on the rocky Atlantic coast of a Hebridean island. They were always freshly dug and scented the kitchen with smells of peat and bracken. The soft mists seem to make Scottish potatoes particularly delicious – feathery pillows, plump and sweet. Their skins are pale gold and translucent, and stretched so tightly over the snowy flesh that they pop when you bite into them. Hebridean potatoes are scrubbed, never peeled, and cooked in boiling water with salt. They are eaten scalding hot, straight from the pot, with cold unsalted butter and salt, washed down with the Scots' favourite strong tea. Better than the finest caviar to an appetite sharpened by a long day walking the heather in search of a lost new-born lamb.

Janssons Frestelse Anchovies and Potatoes

This dish was re-christened 'Jansson's Temptation' in the eighteenth century after a deeply religious Swede, Erik Janson (whose name was apparently misspelt during the long Atlantic crossing). Janson, the tempted one, was forbidden any enjoyment by his devout church. This simple but delicious dish from his native land was his one transgression. The Swedish tinned anchovies are usually billed as Marinated Sprats.

Serves 4

20 salted anchovy fillets
(2 small tins)
2 lb (1 kg) potatoes
½ Ib (250 g) onions
pepper
1 pint (600 ml) single
cream

Peel and slice the potatoes finely. Peel and slice the onions finely. Open the tins of anchovies. Save the oil – if you buy the anchovies from a barrel, you will need to soak them for 10 minutes in milk to de-salt them a little, and you will need 1 oz (25 g) butter.

Pre-heat the oven to 400°F (200°C, Gas 6).

Layer the potatoes with the onions and the anchovies into a deep gratin dish. Sprinkle with freshly ground pepper as you go. There should be enough salt in the anchovies. Finish with a layer of potatoes.

Pour in half the cream. Trickle the anchovy oil over the surface, or dot with butter. Cover with foil.

Put in the hot oven to bake for 15 minutes. Then pour in the rest of the cream and turn the heat down to 300°F (150°C, Gas 2). Leave to cook gently. The potatoes will take another hour to soften. Ready when they yield to a knife.

Remove the lid for the last 20 minutes to allow the top to gild.

That's all. Simple perfection. No wonder Erik was tempted. A blueberry pie to finish in celebration of the American connection.

Rick Stein OBE

Rick Stein, with his ex-wife Jill, owns four restaurants, a delicatessen, patisserie, seafood cookery school and forty hotel bedrooms in the small fishing port of Padstow on Cornwall's north coast. Rick attributes their success to a simple observation: 'Nothing is more exhilarating than fresh fish simply cooked'. This enthusiasm led him to write his first book *English Seafood Cookery*, which won Glenfiddich Cookbook of the Year in 1989. He then made the first of his award-winning TV series Taste of the Sea, and has since made nine more. In 2003, Rick was awarded an OBE for services to West Country tourism.

What Fish Can You Buy?

English Seafood Cookery
PENGUIN 1988

The choice of fish in all but the very best of fish shops in Great Britain is poorer than on the Continent, but things are improving. You shouldn't have too much difficulty in getting hold of red mullet, black bream, John Dory and squid nowadays. If you can't find what you want, you will further the cause of better fresh fish supplies by ordering it. Any fishmonger will tell you that it's lack of demand that leads to a poor selection, not lack of supply.

Don't be too dogmatic about what you mean to buy at a fishmonger. If another fish looks fresher and shinier than the one you came in for, buy that. There are few recipes which can't be made with a different fish, so long as it is similar to the one named. In the Padstow fish shop the other day, I was standing behind a couple who asked if there was any monkfish. There wasn't. On the slab were some extremely fresh and cheap John Dory, which were pointed out to them. 'No,' they said. 'We really wanted monkfish.' They left with nothing. A man reading our menu another day said to me, 'Do they ever have John Dory up at the fish shop?' I said they did and added that they had some excellent small monk tails at the moment. But it was John Dory he wanted. Fish is wild food; you have to take what you can get, not necessarily what you want, and if you can't get what you want you just might find you get what you need!

I shan't bother you with a chart of when is the best time to buy each fish, since I've never seen such a list which was correct. As a general rule, fish are in poor condition after spawning but fine to eat at any other time of year when you can get them.

A Rather Special Fish Pie

The more familiar fish pie is made with mashed potato, flaked fish, eggs, parsley, and cheese, but this haddock pie is based on a medieval recipe and is topped with pastry. The original recipe contained a great deal of sugar and has too long a cooking time for modern tastes. I have left a pinch of sugar in – to good effect – and I have used puff pastry instead of shortcrust for a lighter result. The vegetables are sautéed in butter first, so the fish doesn't overcook.

1 lb (450 g) haddock fillet

10 oz (300 g) potatoes, peeled

2 oz (60 g) butter

3 oz (90 g) carrots, peeled and cut into thin rounds

3 oz (90 g) onion, peeled and chopped

4 oz (120 g) white of leek, sliced into thin rounds

pinch of unrefined golden caster sugar

4 oz (120 g) button mushrooms, thinly sliced

salt and freshly ground black pepper

a little lemon juice

1 oz (30 g) fresh chopped parsley

4 tablespoons (60 ml) double cream

8 oz (240 g) puff pastry

1 egg

Cut the fish into ½-in (1.25-cm) strips. Cut the potatoes into ¼-in (6-mm) slices, place them in salted water, bring to the boil and boil for 3 minutes; drain.

Melt the butter in a heavy-based saucepan and cook the carrots, onion and leek gently for 5 minutes, stirring three or four times. Add the pinch of sugar and the mushrooms and cook for a further 3 minutes. Season with the salt and black pepper.

Put into a pie dish. Add the drained potatoes, fish, lemon juice, parsley and cream; season again.

Set your oven at 425°F (220°C, Gas 7).

Roll out the pastry on a lightly floured surface until it is 1 in (2.5 cm) larger than the pie dish.

Beat the egg and brush the rim of the dish. Cut strips from the outside of the puff pastry and use it to line the rim. Brush with beaten egg.

Cover with the main sheet of pastry, trim off the edges and crimp the pastry. Cut a small hole in the centre of the pie to allow steam to escape. Brush with beaten egg and bake in the top of the oven for 20 minutes.

A simple green salad goes excellently with this pie.

Jeremy Round

Jeremy Round was the first – and highly-acclaimed – cookery writer for The *Independent*, from its launch in 1986 until his tragically early death in 1989. This, his only book, is a collection of his best recipes. Round's emphasis on good produce, eaten at its seasonal best, shines through the book and gave significant impetus to the movement towards a return to the use of seasonal food throughout the UK. His recipes were both innovative and practical: everything always worked and everything was delicious. In his memory, the Guild set up their annual Jeremy Round Award for Best First Book of the year.

Seasonal Strategies

Shopping Seasonally

The Independent Cook
BARRIE & JENKINS 1988

This book grew out of a series of articles, originally called 'The Month in the Kitchen', which I wrote in an attempt to discover when and why fresh foods were at their best – by which I mean most delicious.

Many people would argue that such a seasonal approach to food has become outdated. Developments in the retail scene have had an extraordinary effect on food shopping over the last couple of decades: half the market is now controlled by the five biggest supermarket chains, whose massive buying power has altered patterns of British production and food imports out of all recognition. Their professed aim is to offer ever wider choice and better quality.

Likewise, ask top chefs about seasonal foods and, putting aside a few obvious examples of some soft fruits, shellfish and game, most will tell you that fast, international supply lines and modern storage techniques mean that they can obtain almost anything throughout the year. Nowadays, fresh raspberries adorn hot soufflés in January as well as ice-creams in July; scallops and asparagus pop up together in late summer mille-feuilles as often as they do separately in their different official seasons.

To a certain extent, the chefs have a point because they often have access to specialist suppliers who make sure they are getting the best of what's coming into the country or being grown in special conditions here. Their white currants in December may be better than the ones the rest of us can buy in the height of the season from our local green-grocer, if we can buy them at all. And to a certain extent, yearning for the 'good old days' of the six-week pea season is more a comment on the whimsy of eighties' nostalgia than a realistic alternative to modern market forces.

But the fact remains that fresh produce, as sold to the domestic consumer, changes seasonally – even from week to week – to a remark-able degree, despite the stated intentions of the largest retailers to regularise supplies and destroy seasonality. This was brought home to me again and again during the year in which I wrote the articles.

Take fruit as an example. Strawberries are now offered for ten months of the year from more than half a dozen different countries. But, for flavour, nothing comes close to the English outdoor-grown strawberries that can only be found for perhaps ten weeks. And seasonality applies equally to new exotica. Flagship branches of supermarkets are often keen to offer tamarillos, loquats and the like, but apply little real care in selecting them. So the adventurous customer can end up buying a nasty, sour, unripe specimen, hating it, thinking this is what the fruit is like – and never buying another.

This is the crunch. Most food exporters, producers and retailers care very little about an item's eating quality as against it's 'eye-appeal' and ability to keep. Many characterful and tasty varieties never see the neon light of supermarket-shelf day because they aren't particularly glamorous to look at and start to go off in a day or two, or cannot be produced in large or consistent enough quantities. So, for example, you have little chance of coming across sorrel or medlars unless you grow or gather them yourselves.

Underlying this attitude is an assumption that taste is subjective and that there is no point in assessing products for their eating quality. Astonishingly, this affects the whole food business – from gigantic national concerns, such as the citrus trade in Israel or the tomato trade in the Netherlands, to the buyers for individual supermarket chains. This is why it is so important that we learn to make judgements about eating quality ourselves.

Damson Sauce

For a particular breed of home cook who might be called the broodies, the end of the damson season means preserves, wine and a freezer full of purée. The rest of us find that we have an energy problem. You know the picture: you get home with a couple of pounds of the sour little black plums. But you feel tired and the idea of jelly-making defeats you. So you leave the brown paper bags in the salad box of the fridge. For the next three days, they nag at your conscience, but then you forget about them until you next go to stow a lettuce. The bags have dissolved in black sludge and everything is sprouting grey-green fur.

Tut tut! Next time, buy only half a pound and rescue them for this tastebud-jolting relish, excellent with fatty lamb or pork chops.

Serves 3–4

8 oz damsons, stoned

4 tbsp dry sherry

1 oz unrefined golden caster sugar or light muscovado sugar

½ level tsp salt

2 tbsp groundnut oil

1 tsp peeled and minced garlic

1 tsp peeled and grated fresh root ginger

finely chopped fresh hot green chilli pepper (as much as you might enjoy)

Bring fruit to the boil with the sherry. Cover pan and cook for 5 minutes or so until soft.

Liquidise, or sieve, and pour back into the pan with the sugar and salt. Reduce to a jammy consistency.

Heat the oil in another pan until almost smoking. Add the garlic, ginger and chilli. Push this around for a second or two until it has given up its surface moisture but not quite begun to colour.

Add the fruit purée and stir briskly until hot and glossy.

Maurice Hanssen (with Jill Marsden)

Maurice Hanssen began his professional life in pharmaceutical development but then quickly moved into the development of health foods, playing a pivotal role in the creation of the UK Health Food Manufacturers Association in 1965. At the time of writing this book, he was Chairman of the academic and parliamentary consumer group The National Association for Health, which monitored all food and medicines legislation, and a member of the European Food Law Association. The book made him a household name in the UK and abroad, alerting millions of consumers to the increasing chemicalization of food, and forcing food companies and governments to reassess the future of food manufacturing.

Meat Products

E for Additives
THORSONS PUBLISHERS
1984

Regulations governing meat products and spreadable fish products were laid before Parliament in October 1984. Like the E numbering provisions, these will come into full operation by July 1986.

Polyphosphates (E450) allow manufacturers to add water to meat products without it becoming obvious. If the meat is cooked or raw and contains added water, then they will have to declare: 'with not more than x per cent added water.' X is the maximum added water content of the food. On the other hand, if the meat is uncooked and cured, such as bacon, of which more than 10 per tent is added water, then the declaration has to say 'with not more than y per cent added water'; but that doesn't mean this represents the amount of added water – y represents a multiple of 5 by which the percentage of water in the product exceeds 10 per cent! Finally, to make matters clear to our (presumably computer owning!) consumer – if it is cooked pure meat then the declaration has to say 'with not more than z per cent added water', z being an indication in multiples of 5 of the percentage of water added.

There is a list of parts of the carcass which may not be used in uncooked meat products – and may therefore be used in cooked meat products. You will be glad to know what use manufacturers of cooked meat products can make of the slaughtered animal because they can use the brains, foot, large intestine, small intestine, lungs, oesophagus, rectum, spinal cord, spleen, stomach, testicles and udder. There has to be an argument for manufacturers to tell us just what parts of the animal are used and how much, not just the blanket description 'offal'.

A meat pie weighing 100 g to 200 g must have a meat content of not less than 21 per cent. If the pie weighs less than 100 g the meat content can shrink to 19 per cent of the food, otherwise the meat content can soar to the dizzy heights of 25 per cent as a minimum but, of these percentages, the lean meat content need only be half so, at the worst, a ¼ pound pork pie may contain just over ⅓ of an ounce of lean meat – and it may include unexpected parts of the beast.

The true nature of the contents are then disguised in taste and appearance by the use of flavour enhancers, such as monosodium glutamate (number 621). It can then be coloured, flavoured and, after the addition of the appropriate amount of water, you can have, at the worst, a very fatty pie but one which looks and tastes good. Though of course there are many pie manufacturers who certainly do use the finest ingredients, it would be worth their while making clear claims. The fat content of burgers and sausages is also controlled, in general so that fat content of the meat part of the product does not exceed 35 per cent.

Many German meat products are labelled with their fat content. In order to be able to eat sensibly we should demand that such information be available throughout the E.E.C.

AZO DYES   An azo dye has a particular chemical structure of the atoms in its molecule. It could be this 'azo' construction within the molecule to which a proportion of the population is sensitive, or it might be because of impurities. About a fifth of people who are sensitive to aspirin (usually middle-aged adults and more commonly women than men) are also sensitive to azo dyes. Other groups which may be affected are asthmatics and people who suffer from eczema.

The kinds of reactions that occur in sensitive people are contractions of the bronchi – the tubes allowing air into the lungs – (and asthmatic attacks), nettle rash, watering eyes and nose, blurred vision, swelling of the skin with fluid and in extreme cases shock and reduction in blood platelets with the production in the blood of anti-platelet antibodies. (The blood platelets are involved in blood clotting to seal wounds.)

It has been suggested by the late Dr Ben Feingold that azo dyes are among those substances which could trigger off the hyperactivity syndrome in children. The following are azo dyes:

E102 .... Tartrazine	'Coal tar dye' is an old name – it means nowadays that the dye is synthetically made and doesn't occur in nature. It would include all the above plus:
E107................................. Yellow 2G	
E110................... Sunset yellow FCF	
E122............................. Carmoisine	E104 .... Quinoline yellow
E123............................... Amaranth	E127............................. Erythrosine
E124........................... Ponceau 4R	E131 .... Patent blue V
E128................................. Red 2G	E132......................... Indigo carmine
154 .... Brown FK	E133 .... Brilliant blue FCF
155 .... Chocolate brown HT	
E151 .... Black PN	
E180 .... Pigment rubine	

Anna Del Conte

Anna Del Conte read History and Philosophy at Milan University but left Italy in 1949 to learn English in London, where she also met her husband. In 1975 when her first book, *Portrait of Pasta*, was published, she became the first cookery writer in England to specialize in Italian food. Her books have won many prizes, including awards from the Guild of Food Writers and the Accademia Italiana della Cucina. In 1994 Anna was awarded the Verdicchio d'Oro Prize for 'having contributed to the diffusion of the right and documented knowledge of Italian food and cooking'; in 1999 one of her many articles in *Sainsbury's Magazine* was awarded the prestigious Glenfiddich Award.

Limone
Lemon

Gastronomy of Italy
BANTAM PRESS 1987

For me the lemon tree is the most beautiful tree there is, magical in the way that it can produce both flowers and fruit at any time of the year. The flowers, known as zagara, have a pungent yet delicate fragrance; they contain essential oils used in the production of eau-de-Cologne.

The fruit was used for its aromatic properties in Roman times and the Middle Ages as well as during the Renaissance. Lemons have also been used in medicine since ancient times. The Egyptians prescribed the juice of lemons to fight fever, the Arabs to cure cardiac diseases, and during the Renaissance it was used to prepare syrups to ward off the plague. Lemon juice still has a place in medicine, being used,

please turn to page 62 ●◆

Tagliatelle al Limone

Serves 4

tagliatelle made with 200 g (7 oz) Italian oo flour and 2 free-range eggs, or 500 g (1lb 2oz) fresh tagliatelle, or 250 g (8 oz) dried egg tagliatelle

40 g (1 ½ oz) unsalted butter

grated rind and juice of 1 organic lemon

3 tbsp chopped fresh herbs, such as parsley, sage, rosemary and chive

150 ml (¼ pt) double cream

salt and freshly ground black pepper

40 g (1 ½ oz) freshly grated Parmesan cheese

Melt the butter in a small heavy saucepan. Add the grated lemon rind, the chopped herbs, cream, salt and pepper. Bring slowly to the boil and simmer, stirring constantly, for a couple of minutes.

Add the lemon juice to the pan and bring back to the boil, then take the pan off the heat and keep warm.

Cook the tagliatelle in plenty of salted boiling water until al dente. Drain but do not over-drain, and then transfer to a warmed bowl.

Dress immediately the pasta with the sauce and a sprinkling of Parmesan. Toss very well and serve at once with the remaining cheese separately.

Gastronomy of Italy
BANTAM PRESS 1987

among other things, as an antacid, an anti-emetic, an anti-arthritic and against scurvy.

It is, of course, in the culinary world that the lemon plays its most important role, being an essential ingredient in many dishes. Among these are pollo al limone – chicken with a lemon stuck inside, vitello tonnato, ossobuchi and frittura piccata. Fish dishes cry out for lemon juice. Can you imagine fresh raw anchovies that are not first marinated in lemon juice, or a fish baked with herbs without those few drops squeezed from a lemon? And, even though purists object, fritto misto di pesce is always served with lemon.

Riso al limone is a modern recipe created by Giovanni Goria, a member of the Accademia Italiana della Cucina. The rice, cooked with the usual soffritto, is flavoured halfway through with chopped sage and rosemary. It is finished with grated lemon rind, egg yolk and the juice of half a lemon. Parmesan, and the extra butter that is *de rigueur* for a real risotto, are added before serving to make it creamy. A favourite dish of mine is tagliatelle al limone: the pasta is dressed with melted butter flavoured with lemon juice, cream and Parmesan. The recipe is given on the previous page.

Sweets, cakes and pastries all benefit from a hint of grated lemon rind. On a hot summer's day, a gelato di limone is the best gelato there is, and a spremuta di limone – lemon squash – the most thirst-quenching drink. A granita di limone combines gelato and spremuta in a most satisfying way.

When you buy lemons, choose thin-skinned ones which are not too hard and have a nice smooth skin. Before using, press down on a hard surface and roll back and forth with your hands: this way you will get more juice out of the lemon.

Richard Cawley

Richard Cawley studied fashion design in Paris and London and then worked at the fashion house of Belville Sassoon. When, in 1984, he won the Mouton Cadet cookery competition in the *Observer*, he overnight exchanged a career in fashion for one in food. During his time in Paris, Richard had also studied life drawing at the École des Beaux Arts and this, his third book, he illustrated with his own drawings and paintings. He went on to write and present two TV series 'That's Entertaining' and 'Guess Who's Coming to Dinner'. It is, however, probably for his later appearances on the now iconic Ready Steady Cook – usually paired with fellow Guild Member Patrick Anthony – that he is probably best known.

Simple Pleasures

The Artful Cook, Secrets of a Shoestring Gourmet
MACDONALD ORBIS 1988

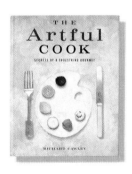

Inside Freddy Ashley's home all was peace and quiet and spotless purity. The walls were freshly whitewashed, the table and board floor were scrubbed to a pale straw colour, the beautifully polished grate glowed crimson, for the oven was being heated, and placed half way over the table was a snowy cloth with a paste-board and rolling-pin upon it. Freddy was helping his mother make biscuits, cutting the pastry she had rolled into shapes with a little tin cutter. Their two faces, both so plain and yet so pleasant, were close together over the paste-board and their two voices as they bade Laura come in and sit by the fire sounded like angels' voices after the tumult outside.

FROM *Lark Rise to Candleford* BY FLORA THOMPSON, OXFORD UNIVERSITY PRESS 1945

Flora Thompson's description of the beautiful quiet calm of the Ashleys' kitchen in *Lark Rise to Candleford* seems like a haven of peace into which I should love to escape from the hurly-burly world we live in almost a century later. How pleasant it would be to be invited, like Laura, to 'come in and sit by the fire'. The Ashleys, like everyone else in the village of Lark Rise, were very poor and although no-one would now care to return to an age of such poverty and hardship, in some ways they were much better off than we are now. In our computer-dominated age, unfortunately, we seem almost to have lost the capacity to enjoy the truly simple but essential pleasures of life. The ancient ritual of sharing a meal with close family or friends is surely one of the most pleasant ways to relax, and with this in mind the menus in this chapter are intended to give pleasure rather than to impress. Some of the meals are composed of a very small selection of basic ingredients simply combined and prepared. Others are based on old-fashioned, much-loved and comforting classics, like Boiled Salt-Beef and Pease Pudding or nursery favourites like Queen of Puddings.

Now that so much of the food we eat comes to us so carefully manicured and glossily packaged it is easy to lose track of where it comes from. It is for this reason that I have begun this chapter with a quick and easy recipe for delicious home-made bread. Simple and nourishing, bread has been one of the world's essential staple foods in one form or another since ancient times. Although it would be rather impracticable for most of us to adopt a total 'back-to-nature' life style, the comfortable pleasure of making bread never grows less, and with the help of modern technology in the shape of 'fast-action' yeast, it is easy to fit this task into our busy lives.

There is a tendency today to be over-fussy when preparing food but the simplest things are always best – provided you have shopped for the freshest and best ingredients. One of the nicest meals of all for me is a perfectly plain omelette with a simple green salad in a good dressing and some fresh crusty bread. With a glass of cold white wine it becomes a feast.

Miss Bailey's Pudding with Gravy

This is a genuine old Yorkshire recipe. Miss Bailey died in the 1960s, and was already quite old when I first knew her. This recipe was given to her by her mother who probably got it from hers, so it is certainly over a hundred years old to my knowledge, and is probably very much older.

2 large onions, peeled and chopped

30 g (1 oz) beef dripping (Miss Hilda Bailey would have insisted on dripping, but use lard if you have none)

1 heaped tbsp cooked white rice

85 g (3 oz) fresh white breadcrumbs

1 heaped tbsp grated suet

1 level tbsp porridge oats

½ tsp dried sage (1 tsp if using fresh)

½ tsp dried thyme (1 tsp if using fresh)

salt and freshly ground black pepper

2 eggs

115 g (4 oz) plain white flour

300 ml (10 fl oz) milk

Put the onions in a small saucepan and add enough cold water to not quite cover them.

Cook uncovered, over a moderate heat for about 15 minutes or until the onions are soft and the water has all evaporated. Watch carefully when they are almost cooked and be careful that they do not burn.

Heat the oven to 220°C (425°F, Gas 7) and put the dripping (or lard) into a medium-sized metal roasting tin, ovenproof dish or large round metal flan tin (obviously not the loose-bottomed kind).

In a large bowl, mix together the cooked onions, the rice, the breadcrumbs, suet, oats, sage and thyme, and season well with salt and pepper.

Beat the eggs with the flour and milk to make a smooth batter and mix this with the onion mixture. (It doesn't seem to make much difference if you make the batter in advance and leave it to rest.)

Pour the mixture into the hot fat in the pan and bake for 15 minutes in the centre of the oven, then turn down the heat to 180°C (350°F, Gas 4) and cook for another 45 minutes.

Serve cut into squares or wedges on warmed plates, with some of the gravy from the following recipe.

Notes Many such savoury puddings were popular in Victorian times, in both town and country, as they took the edge off the appetite before the expensive meat course was served. These puddings were always served like this as a first course, never with the meat, and many hungry children were tricked into almost losing their appetite completely before the meat was on the table by the old saying "im as eats most puddin' gets most meat" (to be read with a Yorkshire accent).

Yan-Kit So

Born in her ancestral village of Zhongshan, in Guangdong province, Yan-Kit was brought up in Hong Kong, where her university degree was a starred first in history. The D.Phil she later gained at London University focused on 19th-century Sino–Burmese border issues. Her first book, *Yan-Kit's Classic Chinese Cookbook* (1984), was greeted with much critical acclaim, and she has been credited with introducing Chinese cuisine as haute cuisine. Reviewing her second book, *Classic Food of China*, Jane Davidson wrote: 'There are cooks, and there are historians, and there are writers, and there are linguists. To be all four must be an unusual combination. Dr So wields her pen and her chopsticks with deftness, displaying her academic powers and her practical skills with charm and modesty.'

What Makes Food Chinese

Yan-Kit's Classic Chinese Cookbook
Dorling Kindersley
1984

Whatever the arguments about the greatness of Chinese cuisine, it is undeniable that certain features make the food look Chinese, smell Chinese and taste Chinese.

One feature, unique to Chinese cooking, is the technique of stir-frying. Here, a small amount of oil is poured into a heated wok and a few condiments are added to 'arouse the wok' and lend fragrance to the main ingredients which are rapidly stirred and cooked in a short time. This very rapid cooking technique requires specially prepared ingredients. In Chinese cooking the ingredients are cut up into uniformly small pieces so that they will both absorb the taste of the seasonings that they are marinated in, and retain their freshness, juiciness and, in many cases, crispness.

Another speciality of Chinese cuisine is its use of dried products. Before the invention of canning and deep-freezing, drying was the Chinese way of preserving food. But even though canning has become a Chinese industry and frozen food products are now exported abroad, dried products are still widely used and are very often more expensive than corresponding fresh ones. This is because the dried products, when reconstituted, add an extra dimension to the taste and richness of the finished dish. For instance, the flavour and fragrance that dried Chinese mushrooms so miraculously lend to other ingredients are beyond the capabilities of fresh mushrooms. The same can also be said of dried scallops, dried oysters, dried shrimps and dried abalone, one of the most exotic ingredients in Chinese cuisine.

Nowhere in other cuisines is there such a pronounced emphasis on texture. Exotic ingredients like shark's fin, bird's nest, edible jellyfish or duck's feet, and everyday ones such as cloud ears, bamboo shoots or cellophane noodles, often have little taste, yet the Chinese go to any amount of trouble preparing them, combining them with other ingredients to lend them taste. Why? Nutrition apart, it is the texture,

Eight-Treasure Vegetarian Assembling

Eight is a significant number for the Chinese, for in Buddhism, which for many centuries exerted great influence in China, there are eight treasures in life: the pearl, lozenge, stone chime, rhinoceros horn, coin, mirror, books and leaf. The symbolism of these eight treasures is not lost in Chinese food: any dish comprising eight or more main ingredients can term itself 'eight-treasure'.

Serves 6 – with 3 other dishes

35 ml (2 heaped tbsp) cloud ear mushrooms, reconstituted*

15 g (½ oz) golden needles (dried tiger lily buds), reconstituted*

50 g (2 oz) cellophane noodles

5 ml (1 tsp) salt

67.5 ml (4½ tbsp) groundnut or corn oil

100 g (4 oz) mange tout, trimmed

6 thin slices fresh ginger root, peeled

6 spring onions, sliced diagonally

15 ml (1 tbsp) fermented red bean curd cheese, mashed with 5 ml (1 tsp) own juice or water

8 bean curd puffs, halved * *

8 canned baby corn on the cobs, halved lengthwise

100 g (4 oz) canned straw mushrooms

75–100 g (3–4 oz) canned ginkgo nuts

175 ml (6 fl oz) vegetable or clear stock, mixed with 2.5 ml (½ tsp) potato flour

2.5 ml (½ tsp) unrefined golden caster sugar

30–37.5 ml (2–2½ tbsp) thin soy sauce

sesame oil to taste

Drain the cloud ears and golden needles but leave damp. Break up the large pieces of cloud ears.

Soak the cellophane noodles in plenty of boiling water for 30 minutes. They will expand and become pliable. Drain. Cut with scissors to shorten.

Bring a saucepan of water to the boil and add 2.5 ml (½ tsp) of the salt and 7.5 ml (½ tbsp) of the oil. Add the mange tout and, as soon as the water returns to the boil, drain in a colander. Refresh under cold running water and drain again.

Heat a wok over a high heat until smoke rises. Add the remaining oil and swirl it around. Add the ginger, then the spring onion and stir for a few seconds, then add the red bean curd cheese and stir to blend. Add the cloud ears, toss and stir, then adjust the heat to moderate.

Add the cellophane noodles, golden needles, bean curd puffs, baby corn, straw mushrooms and ginkgo nuts, and mix together. Season with the remaining salt, sugar and soy sauce.

Pour in the stock and cook, covered or uncovered, until much of the stock has been absorbed. Add the mange tout, mix well and heat through.

Sprinkle with sesame oil to taste. Remove to a warm serving dish. Serve hot.

❧ *see photo on previous page*

* To reconstitute mushrooms, rinse then place in a bowl with enough warm water to cover by about 4 cm (1 ½ in). Leave for about 20 minutes or until they have become swollen and soft.

* * To make the puffs, cut 2 cakes of bean curd into quarters. Place the 8 cubes on changes of kitchen paper to drain excess water. Half fill a wok or deep-fryer with groundnut or corn oil. Heat to 200°C (400°F) or until a cube of stale bread browns in 40 seconds. Deep fry the bean curd for about 15 minutes until golden and crisp. Remove with a strainer and drain on kitchen paper. The puffs can be made in advance and kept in the refrigerator for up to 2 weeks.

whether crisp, elastic or slippery, that they provide that makes them invaluable. Emphasis on texture is also apparent at a more basic level: leaf vegetables, whether boiled or stir-fried, must retain their crispness; noodles must be served al dente.

Monosodium glutamate (MSG) is a white crystalline substance which adds a meaty sweetness to food. It is used widely in Chinese restaurants, but as some people react badly to it I do not use it in home cooking, nor have I used it in this book.

WHAT IS A TYPICAL CHINESE MEAL?

To the Chinese, a meal constitutes rice or another grain, with a few dishes. The number of dishes accompanying the rice depends on the number of people sharing the meal, but a family of six may have three or four dishes at dinner, and perhaps one less at lunch. Obviously the more the dishes, the more festive and special the occasion. Whatever the number of dishes, they should be well balanced so that in one meal a variety of ingredients, including meat, seafood and vegetables, are eaten, and different cooking methods appreciated.

LAYING THE TABLE

As a Chinese meal is a communal affair, a round table is usually used, being more conducive to sharing of the dishes. For each place setting you need one rice bowl, a matching saucer and a pair of chopsticks. As the name so aptly suggests, the rice bowl is for the rice, the saucer underneath is for food taken from the communal dishes before you eat them, or for the bones you gently spit out. The chopsticks are placed vertically to the right side of the bowl and saucer – the Chinese do not seem to have made concession to left-handers!

HOW TO SERVE A MEAL

On a day-to-day basis, all the dishes are served together in the centre of the table (with extra rice kept warm for second or third helpings). There is no specific order for eating the dishes, so one may have a mouthful of chicken followed by another of bean curd, followed by yet another of fish. However, for more formal occasions, the dishes are served individually. The sequence of order varies from place to place, but generally one or two seasonal 'delicacies' are served at the beginning, followed by substantial dishes of meat and poultry, with special soups in the middle and a fish to end the dishes. ('To have fish' is pronounced exactly the same as 'surplus', in Mandarin and Cantonese, so the Chinese frequently use this pun and choose fish to symbolically end the main dishes.) Then, one fried rice and often one noodle dish will be served. This is the host saying, with traditional polite modesty, 'Excuse my humble fare which may not have been sufficient, so please fill up with some grain food!'

HOW TO EAT RICE   The proper way is to raise the bowl with one hand and perch it on your lower lip and then, holding the chopsticks with the other hand, to shuffle the rice into your mouth without dropping the grains on to the table or floor. Rice symbolizes blessings in life for the Chinese and it is therefore vital for you to grab your blessings rather than pick away at them.

EATING OTHER DISHES   When you pick up a piece of food from one of the central dishes, it is quite all right to do so at the same time as another person so long as your chopsticks do not end up fighting in the dish. Having picked up the pieces, remember to make a gesture of touching the rice in the bowl, however momentarily, before putting the food into your mouth.

When a piece is large in size, whether with or without bone, it is polite to eat it in bites, rather than in one gulp. The bones can be sucked, quietly, before being gently spat out on to the side plate.

The main aim should be to enter into the spirit of the meal and to enjoy yourself. Don't forget, however, if you are host, to always put some choice pieces on to the bowl or saucer of your guests.

USING CHOPSTICKS   Perch the chopsticks on the first knuckles of the third and middle fingers so that they lie parallel to each other, resting in the crook of the thumb. Lay the thumb on top of the chopsticks to secure them – the lower chopstick should remain more or less stationary while the upper one is manoeuvred by the first and middle fingers in a pincer movement.

Caroline Conran

Caroline Conran was Cookery Editor of *The Sunday Times Magazine* for thirteen years and is author and co-author of many cookery books, including *Poor Cook* (with Susan Campbell). She translated and edited English versions of books for the chefs of the nouvelle cuisine, Michel Guérard, Roger Vergé and the Troisgros Frères. Always inspired by the food of Southern France, where she has had a house for many years, Caroline's most recent book is *Under the Sun*. Her *Good Home Cooking* was in the vanguard of a movement in favour of home cooking and the rediscovery of British food.

Meat, Poultry and Game

Good Home Cooking
CONRAN OCTOPUS 1985

Until the Industrial Revolution, meat, together with bread, cheese and ale, was the preferred diet of everyone in Britain; and many cottagers kept a pig who was respectfully called 'the gentleman that pays the rent'. Beef was mostly for gentry and pork, ham and boiled bacon were for the cottagers: this was supplanted in sheep-rearing areas by mutton. Veal was a little-known delicacy, but poultry was everybody's favourite: the art of rearing poultry was highly skilled and complicated and the results were, as we now realise, much better flavoured than today's factory-farmed, pellet-fed poultry.

Game, after the Middle Ages, was not for the poor, who could face imprisonment or even worse for poaching. Rabbits they were allowed to take, but game belonged to the land owner himself and in England and Scotland it usually still does (although deer poaching in the Scottish Highlands is secretly a rather skilled and respected trade, the poachers often using crossbows, which have the advantage of being silent). In England, of course, we take a frightfully poor view of this sort of thing, whereas the Irish are often portrayed as born poachers who love every minute of it, as anyone who has read *The Experiences of an Irish R.M.* (by Somerville and Ross) will know. However it finds its way to you, British game is second to none and is something to cheer your table in autumn and winter.

Home-made Pork Pie

> There is nothing to equal a good English farmhouse pork pie, if the crust is not, as it all too often is, thick heavy and stodgy. Flaky crust should merge imperceptibly into doughy, the doughy into jelly that is not extraneous to the meat employed and the jelly into the meat, like mingling geological strata.
> *A Book of Food*, P. MORTON SHAND 1927

The pork pie is a real institution, the favourite lunch, along with a ploughman's lunch, of most English pub-goers. Many pies are bought to eat at home too, especially at weekends; and as for picnics, who would want to go without one? To make a pork pie, on the other hand, is almost unheard of, although it can be extremely enjoyable. The instructions here are for a hand-raised pie, but some people find it easier to use a mould.

Serves 6–8

1 lb (450 g) belly of pork

4 oz (100 g) streaky bacon

1 lb (450 g) pork bones and trimmings

2 bay leaves

2 leaves of red sage

10 black peppercorns

1 lb (450 g) boneless pork shoulder or loin

2 scant tsp salt

pepper and nutmeg

1 egg, for glazing

Hot Water Crust Pastry

1 lb (450 g) plain flour

5 oz (150 g) lard, diced

2 pinches salt

Remove the rinds from the belly of pork and streaky bacon. Put them with the bones and any other trimmings into a pan with the bayleaves, sage leaves and peppercorns; cover with water and make stock by simmering gently until clear, reduced by half and deliciously flavoured.

Strain this stock and return it to the pan to reduce again, ending up with about ½ pint (300 ml). Allow to cool, when it will set to a jelly, and remove the fat from the top.

Chop the bacon and two kinds of pork by hand or in a food processor. Chop one third finely, leaving two thirds rather coarsely chopped.

Mix with the salt, a lot of coarse black pepper (at least 20 turns of the peppermill) and a good deal of grated nutmeg.

TO MAKE THE PASTRY

Bring the lard and ¼ pint (150 ml) water to the boil in a saucepan. If you are using a hinged pie mould you can increase the quantity of fat up to half the weight of flour, but use the amounts suggested in the ingredients above for a hand-raised pie, as it makes the pastry easier to handle.

Put the flour and salt into a bowl and as soon as the lard and water mixture boils, pour it into the middle and mix it together with a spoon. As soon as it is cool enough to handle, knead it well and cover it with a cloth. Leave it in a warm place to rest for 20 minutes.

Now cut off one quarter of the dough and leave it in a warm place, wrapped up.

SHAPING THE PIE

Put the rest of the dough on a greased baking sheet, spread it out a little and put a jar about 4½ in across by 6 in high (11 x 15 cm) in the middle.

With your hands, work the dough up the sides of the jar until it is within an inch (2.5 cm) of the top.

Tie double greaseproof paper round the pie and put it in the refrigerator to chill for a while.

Preheat the oven to 350°F (180°C, Gas 4). Now put a teatowel in the jar and pour on boiling water, enough to soak the cloth.

The next step is easier with two people – one holds the pie whilst the other twists the jar and lifts it out, the heat will have released it. Pack in the pork mixture; make sure it is even or the pie may tip over.

Roll out the remaining pastry, and cut a round lid about ¼ in (6 mm) wider in diameter than the base of the jar.

Make a hole in the centre. Paint the edges with beaten egg glaze, place the lid on top of the pie and pinch the edges together to make a scalloped rim.

BAKING AND FINISHING

Bake the pie for 1 hour, remove the greaseproof paper and brush all over with egg glaze. Cook for a further 15–20 minutes. Allow to cool, then chill for 1 hour.

Alternative
You can put one hard-boiled egg right in the middle of this pie; it looks very pretty when cut.

Have your jellied stock at warm room temperature, when it is syrupy but not quite set. Pour it through a funnel into the cold pie through the hole in the pastry. Allow to set in a cool larder or the bottom of the refrigerator overnight, but take the pie out at least an hour before you want to eat it. It should be a triumph of pie-making.

TO SERVE

Serve with a superlative green salad, some fresh tomatoes, and beer.

Nichola Fletcher

Nichola Fletcher is an award-winning goldsmith, the manager of a venison business and a food writer. For her thirty-five years' work with venison (she started Britain's first deer farm), she was nominated for a Slow Food Award and Best Food Producer in the 2007 BBC Food and Farming Awards. Nichola writes mainly (but not exclusively) about game meats and the history of food. Her first book, *Venison, The Monarch of the Table* (1983) remained in print for twenty years, as did *Game for All* (1987). *Charlemagne's Tablecloth: a piquant history of feasting* (2004) won a Gourmet Voice Silver Award in Cannes and was also shortlisted for Food book of the Year in the Guild of Food Writers Awards. *Nichola Fletcher's Ultimate Venison Cookery* (2007) won a Best in the World Gourmand World Cookbook Award.

Venison: The Meat

Game For All: With a Flavour of Scotland
GOLLANCZ 1987

Alexis Soyer rated venison as 'the second greast pedestal ... of English cookery'. Since turtle soup (his first great pedestal) has met its demise, that elevates venison to first place, exactly where I should have put it myself.

Venison is a highly desirable meat for today because of its marvellous flavour which exists without the help of fat. I don't wish to pursue too vigorous an anti-fat campaign, for many meats lose their flavour without it, but in today's climate of cholesterol conscious consumers it is worth taking a closer look.

Young venison (most farmed venison is sold at around eighteen months) may have only 5 per cent fat, though admittedly a fully mature stag of five or six years may have 20 per cent by the end of a good summer. Beef has around 20 per cent and lamb 25 per cent. Furthermore, half of venison's fat consists of polyunsaturates (that's the less harmful sort) as opposed to beef and lamb's mere 5 per cent. Another advantage is that all venison's fat is distributed on the exterior of the carcase – there is no marbling – and is easily trimmed off if so desired.

But in case you think me hopelessly biased, I'll mention a sdisadvantage. Like mutton fat, it has a high melting point, so where venison fat is around, serve it piping hot and skim the gravy diligently or your enthusiasm may congeal. An almost total lack of cholesterol may be an enormous advantage for diabetics and dieticians, but it does mean that sympathetic cooking is required in order that it should remain moist. This is particularly so with roasting, and I do urge you to read that most important section.

Enough of fat – what of taste? Red deer are naturally forest animals, grazing mainly on grass in the clearings, with small amounts of leaves, apples, acorns etc. In the Highland glen he does his best with heather and grass, and a few raided trees or potatoes if he can find them. Frequently there is nothing at all and then he dies. On farms, deer grown for venison graze on grass, supplemented by hay, potatoes, apples etc when necessary: in other words, a fairly natural diet. They are, by and large, healthy creatures and grow well enough without growth stimulants and antibiotics. So the meat is good.

In the section on hanging game, I have pointed out that the conditions under which a deer lives, be it wild, park or farmed, have far less bearing on the final flavour of its meat than the conditions imposed on the carcase after dispatch. Age has a far greater effect, for old venison needs much longer hanging to make it tender, and this affects the flavour. Young venison can be hung to acquire a good venison flavour or else hung until gamy, but it will always be tender. It is up to you to ask for what you want.

Since deer farming is a new industry and its venison is thus relatively scarce, considerable amounts of wild venison are also consumed. When you know its origin and likely age, you can deal with it accordingly, but once the head is removed it is almost impossible to age a carcase. That is why so many people have had unfortunate experiences with wild venison. However well-meaning, the vendor simply doesn't know what he is selling and can therefore offer the consumer little helpful advice.

Very briefly, there are exceptions, I know – here are the wild species most commonly sold in this country: roe deer generally produce the most reliable wild venison. Roe are tiny, have a relatively short life, and fine-textured meat. Fallow deer may be wild or from a park (they are also farmed in small numbers). The meat is a little darker and at some times of the year has considerably more fat. It can be excellent, but beware the old buck! Sad to say, wild red deer, the majority of which comes from the Highlands, are the least reliable, due mainly to the difficult terrain over which they are stalked. When well shot and carefully handled, though, the young Prince of the Glen has a great deal to offer.

GRILLING AND SAUTÉING

Generally speaking, venison steaks and chops are perfectly straightforward, but bear in mind: because it is lean, venison does not take kindly to being fiercely cooked past the medium rare stage. But all trace of pinkness can be eliminated by cooking quickly to medium rare so that both sides are well browned, then resting the meat in a plate-warming oven. This process also relaxes the steaks and keeps them juicy. The length of time depends on thickness.

Unless you like very rare or 'blue' steaks, thick steaks also need to be rested after initial fierce cooking, rather like small roasting joints. Otherwise the outside will have dried up long before the centre has cooked.

If you need to cut down on fat, brush the meat with a thin coating of oil and quickly brown in a pan or under the grill. Thin pieces cook quickest and therefore need less oil, but do undercook, then rest as before or the meat will be very dull. The unhealthily delicious taste of grilled butter can be replaced by pressing a few spices or fresh herbs on the surface. But without any additions, venison is healthier and tastier when not overcooked.

The Fallow Deere

Crazy Paving Venison Galantine

This galantine comes from an excellent charcutier in Provence, and is rather unusual in that it uses other meats with the normal pork. It is good for a buffet lunch as a little goes a long way. Don't be put off by the sheets of pork fat. You will need to order them, but if I can get it in Auchtermuchty then I'm sure your butcher will also oblige. Ask him to cut it extremely thin: as near to ⅛ inch as possible. This gives a beautifully professional finish as well as being necessary to hold everything together.

You will need a rectangular terrine or bread tin, and a former for it so that the galantine can be pressed; so try and find something suitable before you start. A small piece of thick plywood is ideal. If you resort to foil and tin cans, take extra caution in slicing.

Serves 8–10

8 oz (225 g) venison steak

8 oz (225 g) venison liver

6 oz (170 g) belly of pork

12 oz (340 g) sheets of pork back fat

1 wine glass brandy or red wine

5 juniper berries

black pepper

butter

sea salt

Marinate the steak, liver and belly of pork (but not the sheets of pork fat) overnight in the brandy or wine, juniper berries (crushed) and ground black pepper.

Next day, take them out and pat them dry. Cut into long strips ⅓ in (1 cm) square in cross-section. Heat some butter in a pan and quickly brown the meat all over. Do this in batches so the butter remains really hot.

Line the bread tin or terrine with the sheets of pork fat making sure there are no holes. Lay the sautéed strips of meat lengthways down the tin, alternating the three kinds and filling in the gaps so that it is packed tightly. Season well with the sea salt in between each layer.

Sprinkle a tablespoon or two of the marinade over the meat. Most of this will ooze out during the pressing but it flavours and moistens the meat as it cooks.

Fold the remaining pork sheets over the top to make a lid and press on some folded foil to keep it in place. Then encase the whole tin in foil and stand it in a tray of warm water.

Bake in a very moderate oven 325°F (170°C, Gas 3) for 1½–2 hours. Remove all the foil and stand the terrine in a dish in case of spillage, and fit the former. Weight heavily till cold.

To turn out the galantine, stand the dish in hot water for a few moments to melt the fat slightly. Use a very sharp knife to cut slices, and you will see the neat white rim with a crazy paving of the different meats inside.

Insalata di Piccione Pigeon Salad

This is one of the best ways I know to eat cold pigeons as the meat stays so beautifully succulent. It is ideal for people who don't like rare meat, which is how a pigeon salad is normally presented. You could use any game bird – in Italy they cook partridges like this too. Mallard is particularly good using orange zest and juice instead of lemon. The recipe will stretch to do eight people as an hors d'oeuvre.

Serves 4

4 pigeons

4 plump cloves garlic

1 ½ pt (900 ml) clear stock

Dressing

4 tsp Dijon mustard

8 pinches salt

black pepper

4 tsp unrefined golden caster sugar

4 tbsp lemon juice

4 tbsp white wine vinegar

12 tbsp good olive oil

4 tbsp chopped herbs

lettuce hearts or salad leaves

Pop a clove of garlic into each pigeon and lay them in a pan, breast downwards.

Pour in enough stock to cover them and season if necessary. If you don't have stock, pack some browned vegetables in beside the pigeons and cover with water. Bring to the boil and simmer very gently for 2 hours until the birds are really tender. The stock will reduce, but as long as the breasts are kept covered there is no need to dilute with water.

Make the dressing: Stir the mustard into the salt and a generous amount of pepper. Beat in the sugar, lemon juice, wine vinegar, olive oil and herbs till well amalgamated.

Lift the pigeons out of their stock and prick them deeply all over with a fork. While they are still hot, immerse them completely in the vinaigrette. They should be turned around in this till cool. I find the easiest way to keep them covered is to put each one into a double polythene bag with vinaigrette and tie them tightly.

The pigeons can be eaten while still warm but they keep quite well in their bags for a day or two in the fridge. Serve at room temperature.

To serve, arrange the salad leaves on a plate, sprinkle them with the pigeon's vinaigrette, and lay the pigeons on top. They may be served whole or cut in half, or else just the breasts can be taken off.

The left-over broth is now a sumptuous consommé so don't throw it away.

Marguerite Patten OBE

Marguerite Patten OBE, the original TV 'celebrity chef', has a career that spans more than sixty years. It began before World War II, when only a quarter of British households owned a fridge. During the war she was a senior Food Adviser in the Ministry of Food, advising people on how to keep families healthy on the rations available. In 1947 she became the cookery expert of the very first BBC television magazine programme, Designed for Women, and in 1956 the BBC appointed her President of their Cookery Club. Each month for five years viewers sent in recipes, which Marguerite tested and then demonstrated on TV. Marguerite's tally of cookery books is approaching 170, with worldwide sales of more than 17 million, and she has been honoured with four Lifetime Achievement Awards: in 1995 by The Guild of Food Writers; in 1996 by the Trustees of the André Simon Memorial Fund; in 1998 by BBC Good Food; and in 1999 by Waterford Wedgwood. In 2007 she was awarded Woman Of the Year and in 1991 the OBE for 'services to the art of cookery'.

We'll Eat Again

We'll Eat Again
HAMLYN 1985

These words were issued by the Ministry of Food at the start of food rationing.

'You want to get through your work and difficulties with the same spirits you expect of the Forces in action ...
Well, thanks to government planning, the foods that will feed you and your family to the point of fighting fitness are right at your hand. They have been deliberately chosen to that purpose. To release ships and seamen on the fighting fronts, you on the 'Kitchen Front' have the job of using these foods to the greatest advantage.'

'Your rations and allowances. Spread these so that you get part every day, making sure that each member of your family gets his proper share.'

'Vegetables. These provide many of the vitamins so essential for good health and buoyant vitality.'
NOTE: in summer we had a good selection of vegetables and fruits, many home-grown. In winter our choice was limited to seasonal apples and pears; fresh tomatoes and other salad ingredients were unavailable, so we depended on grated root vegetables and cabbage greens.

'Unrefined or whole-grain foods - flour, oats, etc. These also supply valuable health factors, and, of course, add bulk to build up satisfying meals.'

The Ministry of Food

The Ministry of Food controlled the distribution of food during the war and afterwards, and was responsible for giving information on food rationing, and the wise use of all foods. The recipes and Food Facts leaflets they published enabled people to make the best use of the rations available plus unrationed foods.

Praise must be given to the Ministry of Food for the way they initiated and carried out their food policies and also to the farmers of Britain, plus the land girls, who worked such long hours. The people in Britain must be extolled for their long endurance of the many shortages; most of us kept healthy during those traumatic years.

The rations per person per week

Bacon or ham .... 4 oz (115 g)

Meat to the value of .... 1 s 2 d (6p today)
Sausages and offal were not rationed, corned beef often formed part of the meat ration.

Butter ....2 oz (50 g)

Cheese ....2 oz (50 g)
sometimes 4 oz (115 g)

Margarine .... 4 oz (115 g)

Cooking fat .... 4 oz (115 g)
often dropping to 2 oz (50 g)

Milk ....3 pints (1,800 ml)
sometimes dropping to 2 pints (1,200 ml).

Household (skimmed, dried) milk was available, i.e. 1 packet each 4 weeks.

Sugar ....8 oz (225 g)

Preserves ....1 lb (450 g) every 2 months

Tea ....2 oz (50 g)

Eggs .... 1 shell egg a week
at times 1 every 2 weeks.

1 packet of dried eggs each 4 weeks.

Sweets ....12 oz (350 g) each 4 weeks

Cream — it was illegal for farmers to produce cream

The points system

In addition, there was a monthly points system. The 16 points allowed you to buy one can of fish or meat or 2 lb (900 g) of dried fruit or 8 lb (3.6 kg) of split peas.

Extra benefits

People doing extra-heavy work and munitions workers were allowed extra meat. Agricultural workers, who had no canteen facilities, were allowed extra cheese. Cod liver oil and later concentrated orange juice were issued free to young children and expectant mothers. Vegetarians gave up their meat coupons in exchange for extra cheese.

After the war

In 1945 we celebrated both VE and VJ days – victory in Europe and Japan. I wrote a special *Victory Cook Book* to recall the wonderful sense of victory. I was one of the fortunate people who celebrated in front of Buckingham Palace and cheered the King, Queen and Winston Churchill. The happy victory days did not mean the end of food rationing, food became scarcer in 1946, due to a shortage of money to buy wheat from Canada and, in 1947, very severe weather meant potatoes were limited.

The *Post-War Kitchen* continues the information to the eventual end of rationing in 1954. Britain was rationed for 14 years – longer than any other country in the world.

Raymond Blanc

Raymond Blanc, although totally self-taught, is one of the country's most respected chefs. Born in France, Raymond started his career in England as a waiter, taking over one day when the chef was ill. In 1977, he and his wife Jenny opened their first restaurant, Les Quat' Saisons in Oxford, which won the Egon Ronay Restaurant of the Year Award and prestigious Michelin stars. In 1984 he created the hotel and restaurant Le Manoir aux Quat' Saisons in Great Milton, Oxford – the only country house hotel in the UK to have achieved two Michelin stars for a total of nineteen years. Since then, Raymond has set up a cookery school and a chain of brasseries. In January 2009 he was awarded a Lifetime Achievement Award at the Tatler Restaurant Awards.

Recipes from Le Manoir aux Quat' Saisons
MACDONALD ORBIS
1988

Serves 4

Total recipe time: 10 minutes

2 egg yolks
1 tsp Dijon mustard
250 ml (9 fl oz) best quality non-scented oil
1 tsp white wine vinegar
2 tsp lemon juice
salt and freshly ground white pepper

Variations

Mayonnaise is a mother sauce from which others can be made – by adding tomato coulis, paprika or saffron etc. To make a light rouille, replace the non-scented oil with olive oil and add 1 pinch each of saffron and cayenne pepper, and 2 garlic doves, crushed and puréed.

Sauce Mayonnaise

Mayonnaise is an emulsified sauce which illustrates the magical power of egg yolks. Smooth and delicious, this classic sauce is very simple to make.

In a large mixing bowl whisk together the egg yolks, mustard, 2 pinches of salt and 3 turns of pepper.

Start adding the oil in a steady trickle, whisking energetically until the oil is absorbed and the mixture turns pale yellow and thickens – usually after adding 150 ml (5 fl oz) oil.

Loosen the consistency with 1 teaspoon wine vinegar and 2 teaspoons lemon juice, then whisk in the remaining oil. Taste and correct the seasoning if necessary.

STORING

In a covered container, mayonnaise will keep for 2 to 3 days in the lower part of the fridge. If you are not going to use the mayonnaise immediately, make it with grapeseed oil, which prevents it from separating in the fridge.

CHEF'S NOTES

All ingredients used must be at room temperature – especially the oil. If too cold, it will be difficult to incorporate.

Incorporating the oil: At first this must be done gradually, and with constant, vigorous whisking. The emulsion is created at this stage and the emulsifying agents within the egg yolk cannot cope with too much oil at a time. This is the most important stage of mayonnaise making. Once the sauce is emulsified it will be stable. The rest of the oil can be added in greater quantities and with less vigorous whisking.

If the mayonnaise separates, put 1 teaspoon of Dijon mustard (which contains an emulsifier) in another bowl and gradually incorporate the separated mayonnaise, whisking vigorously.

*Recipes from
Le Manoir aux
Quat' Saisons*
MACDONALD ORBIS
1988

We ought to look forward to giving dinner parties – but do we? Often, they become a dreaded test upon which lives, career promotions, smarriages, divorces – perhaps even wars – depend. I often wonder to what extent the quality of a meal affects the decisions of world leaders. Might a terrible dinner lead to war and a wonderful meal bring world peace, no less?

Short of saving the world, let us merely aspire to saving face. Start by deciding not to panic at any cost! All you need is proper planning. Take your choice of courses; if your main course is a complicated dish requiring a lot of work and attention, make a cold starter and a simpler dessert, so that you avoid panic and a loss of confidence.

Plan ahead and order the ingredients in advance. Many of my recipes give you ample opportunity to prepare parts of the dishes well ahead.

Never test new dishes on your guests; they are not there as guinea pigs. Let your family or long-suffering and well-trusted friends help you with some honest criticism first. Your social life will then not suffer (family and friends soon forget, but a disastrous dinner party lingers long in the memory of disappointed guests). More importantly, you will be familiar with the recipe and find you can prepare it better and faster, knowing the pitfalls and difficulties.

Start by making some of the easier recipes (those marked with one chef's toque). Read the recipes carefully before plunging in; you should be able to visualise the dish and yourself preparing it. Understand all the stages and get a feel for how they should turn out. You need not slavishly adhere to all the recipes. Consider them as a guide and feel free to leave out or substitute ingredients, especially if these are difficult to obtain.

Read the introductory chapters; they will help you to succeed and to select the right ingredients. Freshness is of prime importance; learn where to buy the freshest ingredients. I have included a list of reliable wine merchants and specialist food suppliers who will be only too pleased to advise you on the wine best suited to your menu. One more piece of advice – nag! – demand, blackmail if you must, but insist on quality service. Only constant nagging will promote the necessary changes in the food supply industry, so never be reticent – you deserve the best!

And so, to work. The whole process should be easy and fun, from planning to shopping and cooking. Your efforts will be well rewarded by the smiles of delight and admiration on the faces of your guests. Congratulations!

1990 TO 1994

Home & away.
In *search* OF exotic *flavours*

Jill Norman

Margaret Shaida

Marie-Pierre Moine

Jenny Linford

Arabella Boxer

Henrietta Green

Sri Owen

Jill Norman

Jill Norman's *The Complete Book of Spices* won both a Glenfiddich and an André Simon Award and has enjoyed many years of success in several countries. Jill's expertise in herbs and spices has reached such a wide audience that she is frequently asked to identify spices, sent in small amounts to her by people all over the world. Recently, *Encyclopaedia Britannica* asked Jill to be their expert to update all of their entries on herbs and spices. Jill also created the Penguin Cookery Library in the 1960s and 1970s, bringing many first-class authors, such as Elizabeth David, to the list.

Chillies

The Complete Book of Spices
DORLING KINDERSLEY
1990

Members of the capsicum family, chillies and sweet peppers come in all shapes, sizes and colours, ranging from tiny, pointed, explosively hot birds-eye chillies, to large, fleshy peppers with a mild flavour. Indigenous to Central and South America and the West Indies, they had been cultivated there for thousands of years before the Spanish conquest, which eventually introduced them to the rest of the world. Columbus wrote that in the Caribbean island of Hispaniola axi (an Indian name for capsicum) was stronger than pepper and that people would not eat without it. On Columbus's second voyage in 1495, de Cuneo wrote: "In those islands there are also bushes like rose bushes, which make a fruit as long as cinnamon, full of small grains as biting as pepper; those Caribs and the Indians eat that fruit like we eat apples."

In 1569 the celebrated doctor Nicolas Monardes wrote at length about chillies and their successful adoption in Spain in his book on plants of the New World. Echoing him, the 17th-century herbalist John Parkinson noted that in Spain and Italy chillies were: "set in pots about the windowes of their houses". He also listed 20 types of capsicum, describing them as olive-shaped, heartshaped, spear-like, cherry-shaped, and "broad and crumpled".

Today there are probably 200 different types of chillies grown in all parts of the tropics. They are used ripe, when they may be red, orange, yellow or purple, and unripe, when they are green. When buying fresh chillies, make sure they are crisp and unwrinkled. Ripe chillies are available dried, crushed, flaked and ground, and form the basis of many products. With pepper, ginger and turmeric, capsicums are the most widely cultivated spice crops today.

CULTIVATION

Distribution India has long been the largest producer of chillies and is a major exporter, along with Mexico, China, Japan, Indonesia and Thailand. All these countries are also great consumers of chillies. Sri Lanka, Malaysia and the United States are the main importers.

Appearance & growth Chillies are grown in the tropics from sea level to altitudes of 2,000 m (6,600 ft). Sweet peppers and chillies will grow in warm temperate zones too, but are susceptible to frost, and so are cultivated from seed in nurseries and transplanted later. *C. annuum* and *C. frutescens* are believed to come from one original species, so the two types are frequently confused. The *C. annuum* plant usually grows to 30 cm–1 m (1–3 ft) high. Most sweet peppers, as well as some of the hot varieties, come into this group. *C. frutescens* is a perennial plant, which grows up to 2 m (6 ft); this species includes most of the small, pungent forms of chilli.

Harvesting Green chillies are picked three months after planting; other varieties, such as cayenne, are left longer to ripen. The harvest usually lasts three months. After picking, the chillies are either dried in the sun or artificially. Most chillies are grown annually as they become smaller and less pungent after the first year.

Aroma & taste Chillies have little aroma, but they vary in taste, from mild to fiery hot. Generally, the large, round, fleshy varieties are milder than the small, thin-skinned, pointed types. Capsaicin, the pungent principle that gives chillies their kick, is present in the seeds, veins and skin in varying amounts. depending on the species and the state of ripeness. Try removing the seeds and the veins to reduce fire.

USES

Culinary In the tropics, chillies enhance the bland flavour of the staple foods: rice in India and Southeast Asia, beans and corn in Mexico, and cassava in South America. They provide the heat in curry powders, are used in pickling spice, in pepper sauces, chilli oils and essences. Chilli extracts are even used in ginger beer and other drinks. Caution: When handling chillies, wash your hands well and avoid touching your eyes, and any sensitive areas or cuts.

Medicinal Fresh capsicums are rich in vitamin C: they help in the digestion of starchy foods and may be taken as a tonic. Caution: in large doses, chillies may cause stomach and intestinal burns. Even when taken in small quantities, chillies can burn: soothe a sore mouth with plain rice, bread or beans. Do not drink: it will make the burning worse.

Ceviche

In this Mexican hors d'oeuvre, the fish is tenderized by marinating in lemon juice for several hours.

Serves 4

175 g (6 oz) salmon

175 g (6 oz) brill or turbot

175 g (6 oz) cod fillet

juice of 2–3 lemons

1–2 fresh green chillies, seeded and finely chopped

1 small mild onion, chopped

½ avocado, peeled, stoned and cubed

2 tomatoes, skinned, seeded and chopped

125 ml (4 fl oz) olive oil

handful of coriander leaves, chopped

salt and pepper

Remove any skin or bones from the fish and cut the flesh into small cubes. Put the cubes into a dish with the lemon juice, turn to coat all the fish and leave to marinate in the refrigerator for a minimum of 5 hours.

Drain the lemon juice from the fish and combine with the chopped vegetables, olive oil and coriander.

Season with salt and pepper to taste and pour over the fish in a serving dish. Leave in the refrigerator until ready to serve.

Shami Kebab

Serves 4

500 g (1 lb) minced lamb

50 g (2 oz) yellow split peas

1 small onion, chopped

4 cloves garlic, chopped

1 tsp ground cinnamon

1 tsp chilli powder

1 tsp garam masala

small bunch of coriander leaves, chopped

handful of cashew nuts, chopped

a little salt

2 eggs

30 ml (2 tbsp) lemon juice

oil for deep frying

Combine the minced lamb, split peas, onion, garlic, spices, chopped coriander, cashew nuts and a little salt.

Mince or process briefly to blend thoroughly. Stir in the eggs and lemon juice.

Divide the mixture into eight. Wet your hands and form each piece into a small flattened ball.

Heat the oil in a deep fryer and fry the kebabs in two batches. Turn once and cook until brown on both sides, about 3–4 minutes. Serve hot or at room temperature, garnished with more chopped coriander leaves.

Margaret Shaida

Margaret Shaida was born in the United Kingdom but married an Iranian and lived in Iran for twenty-five years. There she learned Persian cooking techniques from her mother-in-law, her friends and her extended family in their own kitchens. As a result, she wrote one of the best surveys of this important cuisine. In *The Legendary Cuisine of Persia*, she includes much information on the cultural history of Persia as well as the techniques required for reproducing the recipes in the home kitchen. The book won the Glenfiddich Food Book of the Year Award in 1993.

Bread
First Things First

The Legendary Cuisine of Persia
LIEUSE PUBLICATIONS
1992 /GRUB STREET 2000

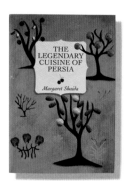

Such is the importance of bread (*nân*) in the cuisine of Persia that the first chapter of a seventeenth-century book written by the chef of the royal kitchens of the Safavid Court was given over to bread alone. As the author pointed out, 'bread precedes all other food'. There seems little reason to break with tradition here. Bread is the staple food of the Iranians in all regions, except for the narrow Caspian littoral in the north where rice supplants it. It makes an appearance at every meal, be it the most splendid banquet or the humblest repast.

Persian poetry has many references to the staff of life, and it is always treated with the greatest respect. Even today it is a sin to allow bread to fall to the ground or to drop 'beneath the feet'. Bread is never thrown away. A sufficient quantity is bought fresh every day and consumed immediately, or if not, then certainly it will be eaten up at the next meal. Dried bread is broken into pieces and added to soups and stews, dunked in tea, or ground into breadcrumbs.

> Here, with a loaf of Bread beneath the Bough,
> A flask of Wine, a Book of Verse – and Thou
> Beside me singing in the Wilderness –
> And Wilderness is Paradise enow.

In many regions, bread is used in place of cutlery and is thus vital in the eating process. Most modem Iranians cannot contemplate a meal without bread and there are dozens of different types to satisfy all tastes: soft thin breads to accompany kebabs, wholemeal breads to eat with savoury dishes, thicker breads to eat with cheese and herbs, soft sweet breads or crispy breads to eat with tea. They are unlike the loaves of the West in that they are 'flat' breads, but they are all, without exception, well leavened and light. At least four of them are nationally popular.

Bread is rarely made in urban homes in Iran today. Every city block has two or three specialist bakers who prepare one type of bread three times a day: in the morning for breakfast, at noon for lunch and in the evening for dinner. Each bread serves a specific purpose and will be bought to suit the meal that is being prepared in the home.

Marie-Pierre Moine

Marie-Pierre Moine was born in Paris and has been a gourmande since childhood days at her grandparents' house in the Touraine. Educated in Paris and at Oxford, she was part of the team behind *Taste* magazine in the 80s and subsequently spent over two years as its Editor. She has written many cookery books. Her 1990 book *Cuisine Grand-Mère* was widely held to herald a return in interest in French home cooking after the attenuated years of nouvelle cuisine. Marie-Pierre has received much acclaim for her regular column in *House & Garden*.

Cuisine Grand-Mère
Barrie & Jenkins 1990

Pain de Poisson de Tous les Jours
Family Fish Loaf

In de Gaulle's brave new France circa 1960, modern women like my mother, ex-career girls not full-time wives and mothers, were busy swopping colourful recipes that were at the time a little daring – in their relaxed use of canned food, spices and foreign, exotic ingredients. Plats uniques *became the 'in thing' for dinner parties, with paella playing a starring role.*

The following fish loaves are typical of the period. There was a sharp difference between family food – thrifty, filling but experimental – and dishes for entertaining – elaborately garnished and evidently more expensive. The basic fish loaf recipe was purely for family use. Note that it lists ketchup among its ingredients, the first recorded use of the stuff in my home-grown cards. Fish loaf and assorted jokes about yet another biblical miracle on the shores of the Loire became a family institution. The second recipe was pour les invites *– for guests. I still prefer it to the basic dish, but, then, wouldn't I just?*

Serves 6

450 g whitefish, skinned and boned

1 bay leaf

1 bouquet garni

sea salt

freshly ground black pepper

60 g tomato purée

2 tablespoons tomato ketchup

5 eggs

paprika

cayenne pepper

oil for greasing

60 g butter

Put the fish with the bay leaf and bouquet garni in a sauté pan. Cover with cold water, season with salt and freshly ground black pepper and bring to the boil, then simmer until the flesh is tender enough to flake easily. Drain well, remove any bones and put through a *mouli* or food processor. Stir in the tomato purée and ketchup.

Beat the eggs as for an omelette. Stir them into the fish mixture until well blended. Season with a good pinch of paprika and cayenne.

Heat the oven to 180°C (Gas 4). Grease a large loaf tin, abour 2.5 litres. Pour the mixture into the tin. Line a large baking tin with a folded newspaper. Put the loaf tin in the centre of the baking tin. Pour boiling water to come halfway up the sides of the loaf tin and cook the fish loaf in this *bain-marie* for 40 minutes, or until firm.

Unmould the fish loaf on to a dish. Melt the butter in a small saucepan and pour over the fish loaf just before serving. Delicious with *anchoïade* – a sweet, salty pounded anchovy paste.

Gigot Leg of Lamb

One word of caution: you may be disappointed, but I am not going to offer a proper recipe for the greatest of all French festive meat dishes. *Gigot* has to be boldly cooked; there can be few adjustments and no camouflage. And the list of variables to be taken into consideration is more daunting than usual. First there is the lamb itself and the way it is butchered and prepared. Then comes the roasting tin and the oven with its own little quirks. Last but not least, we have the cook, the carver and the guests, with their different hands and palates. And when *gigot* is at stake people always have strong views and great expectations. Quite rightly so. After all, *gigot* is the food of high days and holidays.

I have eaten other people's *gigot* and made a quiet note of it. I have on occasion achieved my idea of *gigot* bliss, only to be met by barely polite noises. So rather than a recipe, let me tell you what works for me.

In an ideal world, I will use young Welsh or English lamb, butchered and trimmed French-style, studded with lots of garlic, well seasoned and rubbed with rosemary and thyme. I would have discussed the meat with my butcher, then decided whether or not to sit the *gigot* on a few good knobs of butter. Before I put my *gigot* in the hot oven, I would dribble a little olive oil over it, then cook it very fast, basting a few times with the juices and a trickle of white wine.

Meanwhile, I would plead with the rest of the family, who like their lamb ultra-pink, for the *gigot* to be granted an extra few minutes in the oven and, hopefully, for injury time afterwards to relax. In the end I would serve it with *haricots* verts, young flageolets and this garlic sauce.

Sauce à l'Ail Garlic Sauce

Don't be put off by the 225 g garlic. It is not a printing error and this easy sauce is more aromatic than pungent, because the garlic will be boiled three times. You'll also find that peeling the cooked cloves is a real cinch: simply squeeze them between your thumb and forefinger and they'll just pop out.

Serves 6

225 g cloves of garlic
300 ml single cream
sea salt
freshly ground black pepper

In a medium-sized saucepan filled with plenty of cold water, bring the garlic cloves to the boil. As soon as the water starts bubbling, drain the cloves. Then return them to the pan, cover with fresh cold water and bring to the boil again. Drain, then repeat the process one more time.

Now squeeze the cloves (see above). Combine the cream and peeled cloves in the pan and heat through gently until piping-hot but not boiling, stirring occasionally. Purée the mixture, season with a little salt and more generously with pepper and serve with *gigot*.

Jenny Linford

Jenny Linford is a freelance food writer, journalist and author of fifteen books, ranging from cookery books to ingredient guides. Since starting as a food writer in 1991, she has campaigned for high-quality, independently-produced food. She is author and researcher of *The London Cookbook* and *Food Lovers' London*, a multicultural guide to the city's food shops and restaurants, now in its fifth edition. An inveterate food shopper, Jenny founded Gastro-Soho Tours in 1994, offering guided tours of London's best cuisine. She has also researched and written for the British Library's Food Stories website.

Introduction

Food Lovers' London
MACMILLAN 1991/
METRO PUBLICATIONS
1995

When I was a child my family moved to Florence and English food took on an especial importance. Visitors were entreated to bring packets of 'ordinary' tea, cheese and onion crisps and Walls' sausages. One small shop near the Duomo, Ye Olde English Store, sold a quaint mixture of English food: tinned asparagus, lemon puffs and Gentleman's Relish. Small jars of Marmite cost a few thousand lire more than they should have but were savoured nevertheless. Now that I am back in London, I buy fresh pasta, basil and Parmesan and try to recreate the sunny tastes of Tuscany.

This book started out of personal nostalgia but turned into an enjoyable and fascinating journey of discovery. London, where I have lived for so many years, suddenly revealed glimpses into new and varied worlds: the aesthetic delight of a Japanese fish counter, dainty, pistachio-dusted, baklava from a Turkish patisserie, the hustle and bustle of Brixton Market, freshly baked bagels in a busy Jewish bakery in Golders Green, being offered a free soft drink in Southall to commemorate a Sikh martyr who had preached tolerance to all.

Since I first wrote *Food Lovers' London* in 1991, food shopping in Britain has changed enormously. In those days, if I wanted mascarpone cheese or lemon grass, I had to visit an Italian delicatessen or a shop in Chinatown. Today, my nearest supermarket stocks these and many other foodstuffs alongside them. Supermarkets, however, cannot offer everything or keep it in the best conditions, especially 'exotic' fruits and vegetables. Tired-looking rambutans or rock-hard mangoes in a supermarket compare badly with the excellent quality and good value fruit on offer in Gerrard Street, Asian greengrocers or West Indian markets.

London has so many gastronomic riches to offer, but they are under threat on many fronts. If you've bought this book, I'm guessing that you too love food and I do urge you to support your local food shops and markets and enjoy the pleasure of shopping in this way.

ASIAN FOOD SHOPS
Ambala

ADDRESS 112 Drummond Street, NW1
TELEPHONE 020 7387 7886/3521
TRANSPORT Euston LU/Rail
OPEN Daily 9 am–9 pm

Ambala have been selling Asian sweets since 1965, when their first small shop opened on this site. Ambala is now a thriving chain and the original shop has been revamped in bright colours with marble counters. Customers return again and again for excellent fudge-like barfis, sticky jalebi and takeaway packets of rasmalai. Savoury snacks include crisp vegetable samosas and packets of Bombay mix.

JEWISH FOOD SHOPS
Platters

ADDRESS 10 Halleswelle Parade,
Finchley Road, NW11
TELEPHONE 020 8455 7345
TRANSPORT Golders Green LU, then bus 82, 102, 260
OPEN Mon–Sat 8.30 am-4.30 pm, Sun 8.30 am-2 pm

This friendly, well-established business, run by the eponymous Platters family, offers a range of fresh, own-made, classic Jewish deli fare, from moreish fried gefilte fish to chopped liver. A particular highlight is the hand-carved smoked salmon, skillfully sliced by Len (now in his eighties), which attracts regular customers from as far away as Birmingham.

MIDDLE EASTERN
Green Valley

ADDRESS 36 Upper Berkeley Street, W1
TELEPHONE 020 7402 7385
TRANSPORT Marble Arch LU
OPEN Daily 8 am–10 pm

Warmly recommended by cookery writer Claudia Roden, this spacious Lebanese shop just off the Edgware Road has an eye-catching array of pastries, arranged temptingly in the window. Stock is impressively comprehensive: fresh produce, groceries, a halal meat counter and an in-house bakery. Customers with a sweet tooth are well-catered for with an ice-cream counter, pastry counter and a huge assortment of prettily packaged nougats, candied nuts and Turkish delight.

SPANISH & PORTUGUESE
Garcia R. & Sons

ADDRESS 248 Portobello Road, W11
TELEPHONE 020 7221 6119
TRANSPORT Ladbroke Road LU, Notting Hill Gate LU
OPEN Tue–Sat 8.30 am–6 pm

The Garcia family have had a Spanish food-shop on Portobello Road for over 40 years. Their present spacious shop retains a pleasantly old-fashioned feel. The deli counter does a roaring trade in Jamon Serrano and costly Jamon Iberico (from acorn-fed black-footed pigs), which are deftly sliced to order. In addition, there are groceries such as chorizo sausages, pimenton, paella rice, tinned seafood, bacalao and olive oil. Turrons are kept throughout the year, with the range expanding at Christmas time.

Lisboa Delicatessen

ADDRESS 54 Golborne Road, W10
TELEPHONE 020 8969 1052
TRANSPORT Westbourne Park LU
OPEN Mon–Sat 9.30 am–7.30 pm, Sun 10 am–1 pm

When Carlos Gomes opened this shop over 20 years ago, it was the first Portuguese delicatessen in London and he and his partners 'imported' their own stock in suitcases from Portugal. All the essential ingredients for Portuguese cooking can be found in this characterful shop: pungent bacalhau, pulses including Brazilian black beans, sausages and trayfuls of pickled and salted pig's trotters, snouts, tails and ears. A back room contains a selection of Portuguese wines and spirits, including port.

Chicken Satay

The London Cookbook
METRO PUBLICATIONS
2008

Proper satay sauce, with its rich spicy nuttiness, is a world away from a dash of soy sauce stirred into peanut butter. The specialist ingredients – lemon grass, galingal, candlenuts and tamarind pulp – can be found in Chinatown or Thai food shops.

500 g chicken breast fillets

16 wooden skewers

½ cucumber

Marinade

1 tsp cumin seeds

1 tsp fennel seeds

1 onion

2 garlic cloves

1 thumb-sized piece of galingal

2 stalks of lemon grass

1 tbsp ground coriander

1 tsp ground turmeric

1 tbsp unrefined golden caster sugar

1 tsp salt

1 tbsp oil

Satay Sauce

5 candlenuts

200 g roasted salted peanuts

1 onion

4 garlic cloves

1 thumb-sized piece of galingal

4 stalks of lemon grass

1 tsp ground turmeric

1 tsp chilli powder (optional)

75 ml oil

100 ml tamarind water

300 ml water

5 tbsp unrefined dark muscovado sugar

Cut the chicken breast fillets into small, even-sized slices.

To make the marinade, dry-fry the cumin and fennel seeds until fragrant, then cool and finely grind. Peel and chop the onion, garlic and galingal. Peel the tough outer casing from each lemon grass stalk and finely chop the white bulbous part.

In a large bowl, mix together the chicken, cumin, fennel, onion, garlic, galingal, lemon grass, coriander, turmeric, sugar, salt and oil. Cover and marinate overnight in the refrigerator. Set 16 wooden skewers to soak overnight in cold water.

To make the satay sauce, soak the candlenuts for 10 minutes in cold water; drain and finely grind. Finely grind the peanuts and reserve. Peel and chop the onion, garlic and galingal. Peel the tough outer casing from each lemon grass stalk and finely chop the white bulbous part.

Using a food processor, blend together the onion, garlic, galingal, lemon grass, candlenuts, turmeric and chilli powder into a paste.

Heat the oil in a wok or large, heavy-based saucepan. Add in the paste and fry for 10 minutes, stirring often, until fragrant. Add in the tamarind water, water, ground peanuts and brown sugar, stirring well. Bring to the boil, then reduce the heat and simmer gently for 10 minutes. Set aside and serve warm or at room temperature.

To cook the satay, preheat your grill at its highest setting. Thread the chicken pieces onto the skewers, dividing evenly. Grill the satay until cooked through, around 10 minutes, turning often. Meanwhile, chop the cucumber into chunks.

Serve the chicken satay with the satay sauce and cucumber chunks.

Arabella Boxer

Arabella Boxer is half Scottish, half American. She was married for twenty-four years to cartoonist Mark Boxer. In 1964, when she was thirty, she began to write about food and became *Vogue*'s food writer for nineteen years. She has published many books, including *First Slice Your Cookbook*, devised and designed by her husband. *A Visual Feast*, with renowned food photographer Tessa Traeger, won an André Simon Award in 1992, and *Arabella Boxer's Book of English Food* won a Glenfiddich Award in the same year.

Eggs

A Visual Feast
EBURY 1991

All eggs are edible, and have probably been eaten at one time or another. Swans' eggs were once used for wedding cakes, while plovers' and quails' eggs have been considered a delicacy for hundreds of years. All domestic birds' eggs may be eaten; this includes those of geese and ducks as well as hens. Duck eggs are supposed to be especially good for making cakes, while pullets' eggs, like those of bantams, are full of flavour despite their small size. Quails' eggs have become fashionable again, just as they were sixty years ago. They are sold raw, a dozen at a time, in tiny boxes. Simply hard-boiled and shelled, they make an excellent canapé, served with a larger (hen's) eggshell filled with celery salt. They are always served boiled, either hard or soft, and are often used as a decorative garnish. They can also be bought smoked.

Doves' eggs were once much used, for the dovecote was not merely a decorative addition to a country house, but had a sound practical value. With all the facilities of modern life, we tend to forget the exigencies of feeding large families through the winter months. With a dovecote, a supply of fresh eggs and the occasional bird was assured. Dovecotes were never filled by man; they were simply built and left empty, whereupon flocks of wild doves would arrive, on the principle of the nesting box. Nowadays their eggs are protected, with the exception of the collared dove in Scotland.

Almost all wild birds' eggs are now protected by law, with a few exceptions. The eggs of the lapwing, or green plover, may be gathered from the nest, but only up until April 14th, and then only for home consumption; their sale is prohibited. Those of the black-headed gull fetch high prices during their short season in late May, but those of the black-backed gull, the herring gull and the common gull are not good enough to eat, except in dire emergency. Pheasants' eggs are supposed to be very good, but are too valuable to be eaten.

Eggs vary widely in shape, size and colour. The owl's egg, like the dove's is so spherical as to be almost round, while the guillemot's egg is long and pointed, like an avocado pear. This is a form of protection, for the guillemot lays its eggs on precipitous ledges on cliffs; when caught by the wind, this egg swings round on its axis, and does not fall.

Although English cookery books from the fourteenth century onwards contain many recipes for cooking eggs in pastry, with vegetables, in omelettes, fritters and custards, they are rarely mentioned in accounts of meals. Perhaps they did not figure in the grand meals that were considered worthy of recording, but they were certainly used in large numbers in puddings, both savoury and sweet, in sauces and in stuffings. Up until the seventeenth century, hard-boiled egg formed the basis of most stuffings in the way that breadcrumbs do today.

Yet I can find only three mentions of egg dishes as part of a meal. The first was in an account of a grand dinner in 1730; among a list of sixty-eight dishes was a reference to a roast pheasant dressed with its eggs; another to a dish called Portugal Eggs. Thirty years later, in the *Diary of a Country Parson*, Parson Woodforde records a simple dinner of roast mutton, veal cutlets, a selection of cold meat, and eggs boiled in their shells.

In the nineteenth century the egg made its first appearance at the breakfast table. Until then a heavy meal of meat dishes with cheese and beer had been the custom among country folk, while more sophisticated people had taken to a light breakfast of rolls with hot chocolate.

Now the traditional English breakfast as we know it became established: a meal consisting of porridge, eggs and bacon, and fish, followed by toast and marmalade, accompanied by coffee or tea.

In this country our consumption of eggs doubled just before the First World War; then it doubled again shortly before the Second World War. It seems that the restrictions imposed in wartime interrupted what would otherwise have been a pattern of steady growth. In the interwar years, for the first time in centuries, the English started to eat less. The heavy meals of the eighteenth and nineteenth centuries gave way to a totally new approach to food, encouraged by the emergence of smaller households, with fewer children and servants alike. In this era of lighter meals the egg took on a new importance. Certainly by the 1920s and 1930s an egg dish was considered acceptable as the first course at a luncheon, while a few years later it would be thought of as a possible meal in itself. Nowadays egg dishes have become almost a way of life, especially for people living on their own. As Cole Lesley recorded in his biography of Noel Coward, all the Master wanted to eat in the evening was "a little eggy something on a tray".

Poached Eggs on Celeriac Purée

Serves 4 as a first course, or 3 as a light main dish, with a green salad.

1 celeriac, peeled and cut in chunks

350 g potatoes, peeled and cut in half

75 ml single cream

50 g butter

sea salt and black pepper

4 eggs, poached

3 tbsp grated Gruyère cheese

Put the celeriac in a pan, cover with lightly salted cold water, and bring to the boil. Cook until just tender when pierced with a skewer, then drain very well and dry out over gentle heat.

Repeat the process with the potatoes, then push both vegetables through a medium food mill into a clean saucepan.

Stir over low heat until well dried out, then add the cream and butter which you have warmed together, gradually, stirring as you do so. Season with plenty of sea salt & black pepper, then tip into a shallow dish and lay the poached eggs on it.

Sprinkle the grated cheese over the surface of the dish and brown quickly under the grill.

Egg Croquettes

Serves 4 as a first course, or 3 as a light main dish, with a green salad.

300 ml milk

½ bay leaf

a pinch of mace, or nutmeg

1 small onion, chopped

25 g butter

2 tbsp flour

6 eggs, hard-boiled

2 tbsp chopped parsley

sea salt & black pepper

flour

1 egg, beaten

dry white breadcrumbs

frying oil

Start a day, or several hours, in advance. Heat the milk with the bay leaf and mace, or nutmeg. When it reaches the boil, cover the pan and remove from the heat. Stand for 15 minutes, then discard the bay leaf and re-heat gently.

Cook the onion slowly in the butter until lightly browned, about 4 minutes. Then stir in 2 tablespoons of flour and cook for 1 minute, stirring.

Pour on the re-heated milk and bring to the boil, stirring. Cook gently for 3 minutes, then remove from the heat.

Chop the eggs coarsely and stir into the sauce, adding chopped parsley, sea salt and black pepper. Turn into a shallow dish which you have rubbed with butter and chill for several hours, or overnight, to firm.

When ready to cook, use a dessertspoon to form oval shapes like eggs, or large rolls like corks. Roll them lightly on a floured board, then dip, first in beaten egg and then in breadcrumbs.

Fry in a 2.5 cm layer of oil until golden brown, turning once. They will take about 2–3 minutes on each side.

Drain on soft paper before serving, with a tomato and pepper sauce.

Henrietta Green

Henrietta Green has made the encouragement of small speciality food producers one of the mainstays of her career as a food writer, journalist and broadcaster. This has won her several awards, including a Guild Award for the Greatest Contribution to British Food, BBC Radio 4 Food Programme's Campaigner and Educator 2000 and The *Good Housekeeping* Award 2006 for Outstanding Contribution to Food. In her search for the best – be it a place to buy, eat or learn – Henrietta has criss-crossed Britain several times, accompanied by her trusty dog. The results were first published in her award-winning *British Food Finds* in 1987 and then in two editions of her *Food Lovers' Guide to Britain* and is now available online on www.foodloversbritain.com.

Rocombe Farm Fresh Ice-Cream

Food Lovers' Guide to Britain
BBC Books 1993

ROCOMBE FARM
FRESH ICE-CREAM
123 Union Street, Castle
Circus, Torquay, Devon

Rich, luscious, creamy, pure and infinitely moreish, this is ice-cream at its most magnificent. Containing the best – and only the best – ingredients, the basic mix is made with organic (to Soil Association standards) full-cream Jersey milk, double cream, unrefined cane sugar and organic free-range eggs. In other words, everything you'd hope for in ice-cream.

Peter and Suzanne Redstone have been running a Jersey herd in Devon for nearly 20 years. They had always had a dream to make the 'best-ever ice-cream' but it was not until 1987 that it came to fruition. Making on the farm was impossible (then they could not afford to install the necessary 3-phase electricity), so they rented a shop in Torquay. 'We made it like it is made in a kitchen. What you'd throw in is what we'd throw in. One of our first flavours was banana, so we thought let's throw in bananas – and out came nectar'. The holidaymakers obviously agreed as it was a sell-out. Everything was freshly made every day in the shop, and each day they 'invented' a new flavour. Some, like Cinnamon 'n Biscuit, Thunder & Lightning (treacle and clotted cream), Honey & Toblerone, and Sparkling Cyanide (champagne, brandy and toasted almonds) sound scrumptious; others, including Marmite & Peanut Butter, Peter is the first to admit were not exactly triumphs.

The quest for new combinations still continues in the shop and every day they launch a new one. To date they have come up with over 1,500 flavours. Sean Hill of Gidleigh Park contributed Prunes in Armagnac and Joyce Molyneux of the Carved Angel gave them Orange Cardamom. It is the freshness, the home-madeness, the 'real' ingredients of Rocombe ice-cream that makes it stand out a mile. If they want to add caramel, then they make the caramel, 'a lot of extra work, but worth it' and 'because it is difficult to incorporate whole fruit into a continuous machine, we make in batches'.

Since that auspicious start, the Redstones have gone from strength to strength. They run another shop at 7 Torbay Road, Paignton, and they now wholesale their ice-cream all over the country as well as in such top shops as Harrods, Harvey Nichols and Selfridges. Manufacturing has returned to the farm but – and it is a very important but – they have not compromised the standards one iota. Everything is still fresh; no flavour-house ingredients are used, so there are no cloying or synthetic aftertastes; the clarity and purity are startling. With a minimum butterfat content of 16.5% and an over-run (added air) somewhere between 35 and 40%, this a super-premium ice-cream in a class of its own, way up there with Häagen-Dazs. Moreover, when I recently blind-tasted it with Häagen-Dazs for a Radio 4 Farming Today programme, Rocombe won hands-down.

Now you may have noticed that no mention has been made of emulsifiers and stabilizers. This is because the Redstones do not use any, 'People don't believe us' Peter told me, 'but it's rather like Roger Bannister. No one thought a 4-minute mile was possible until he came along'. Emulsifiers and stabilizers are generally put in to hold the mix together and to give it texture and shelf-life; but if you have as high a fat content 'and for the right texture it must be cream' and use eggs as Rocombe ice-cream does, you just don't need them. The fact that these additives are not there not only makes Rocombe a purer product but also means it has a purer, cleaner, fresher flavour.

Their wholesale range includes such miracles of delight as Lemon Meringue, a sharp lemon base softened with melting meringue; Bananas 'n Cream with the taste of the fruit shining through; Bailey's Toasted Almonds, which succeeds in a nutty, alcoholic haze; and a Super Chocolate Chocolate Chip that is densely deeply chocolatey; and lots more – about 20 in total. Believe me, if you are an ice-cream freak, you have to taste them. Enjoy, I'm certain you will.

'Farmhouse' ice creams

Seemingly hundreds of farms make and sell ice-cream. The reason why is simple: farmers want to "add value" to their milk and we, the general public, are only too happy to buy a "farmhouse" product. Closer inspection reveals that these ice-creams are not any different from those made in a factory. Granted some do have a higher dairy-fat content, but most contain the same stabilizers and emulsifiers added to prolong shelf-life and to make the ice-cream hold together – not a very "farmhouse" approach. Equally, most are not as you might hope, flavoured with the real thing – be it fruit or nuts or whatever. Instead tins bought in from flavour-houses are used. Yes, I know the farmers proudly claim "No artificial flavourings or colourings", but don't be fooled. Because of a quirk in our food labelling laws, if a flavouring is human-made but chemically identical to the real thing, it does not have to be called "artificial". Now I am not necessarily suggesting that these chemically identical flavours are harmful, but they are misleading; and, more to the point, they taste synthetic. If I buy a farmhouse ice-cream, I want it to taste fresh and to be made with fresh ingredients that come from a farm not a laboratory. When you've tried as many as I have, you'll realize that – with few exceptions – it is an impossible dream.

Sri Owen

Sri Owen was born in Sumatra and moved to Britain in 1964 with her English husband. She is now an internationally renowned author, lecturer and cook , whose admired and authoritative books include *The Rice Book* (winner of the André Simon Award), *Indonesian Regional Food and Cookery* (winner of the Langhe Ceretto Prize for Best Recipe Book) and *Healthy Thai Cooking*. Since she was first published in 1976, Sri has become the foremost authority on Indonesian food in Britain, and her most recent book *Sri Owen's Indonesian Food* was published in 2009. She and her husband Roger are now at work on the forthcoming *Oxford Companion to Southeast Asian Food*.

Rice in the West

The Rice Book
DOUBLEDAY 1993/
FRANCES LINCOLN 1998

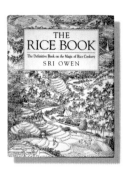

For a long time, western Europe regarded rice as another kind of spice. It was certainly reaching England before the middle of the thirteenth century; the *Oxford English Dictionary's* first citation for the word is from the household accounts of King Henry III in 1234, and we know that between Christmas 1264 and the following Easter the Countess of Leicester's household got through 110 pounds (50 kilos) of rice, costing 1.5 pence a pound, a high price which explained the careful book-keeping and the fact that the rice was locked in the spice cupboard. At about the same time, the accounts of the Duke of Savoy show that rice 'for sweets' cost 13 Imperials a pound, whereas honey was only 8 Imperials. In Milan, rice was heavily taxed as 'spice brought through Greece from Asia'.

The Black Death, which ravaged Italy from 1348 to 1352, and then recurred at irregular intervals as bubonic plague, has been credited with the introduction of rice to the northern Mediterranean. The workforce had been reduced by perhaps one-third, and the low yields of wheat and barley were hardly enough to keep people alive. Rice was a high-yielding, energy-giving crop that required far less labour per sack of grain harvested. Gian Galeazzo Sforza sent a sack of rice to the Duke d'Este of Ferrara in 1475, with a letter telling him that one sack of seed would produce twelve sacks of food grain.

According to present-day Italian writers, however, large tracts of the Piedmont and Lombardy plains had been turned into paddy fields several decades before this famous letter, with the export of seed grain already strictly prohibited as a state secret. The Venetians may have brought rice from Turkey; an early Italian variety was called *Nostrale*, which suggests that this was 'our' rice, as opposed to whatever anyone else might later have imported. According to the Italian historian Aida de Maddalena, the Milanese governors of Lombardy in the fifteenth century ordered a merchant, who was travelling to South Asia, to bring back a sack of unhusked paddy; this was sown in three places, then transplanted over a large area. Early north Italian rice fields were watered from *fontanili*, little springs whose water was in fact too cold for the rice to bear well. But a particular advantage of rice was that the harvest came much later than the wheat harvest, so there was no shortage of labour. The harvest was also more reliable.

In England, in 1585, rice steeped in cow's milk with white bread-crumbs, powdered fennel seed and a little sugar was thought good for increasing the flow of milk in a nursing mother's breasts. But by the seventeenth century rice was no longer a magical luxury. Dorothy Hartley quotes Gervase Markham, who died in 1637: 'If you will sow rice you may do it, but it is like to prouve a work of curiositie rather than of profit ...' He explains how to grow rice in an English field, where there is plenty of water but not enough sun to bring it to harvest. Then he discusses it as food. 'If you boyle rice in milk adding thereto sugar and cinnamon, it will provoke unto venerie. Many do think it maketh fat; but seemingly that (according to the physitions) it is not digested in the stomach but verie hardly, it must need nourish but little – How can it possibly make one fat?'

A century or so later, it was being imported to Britain in large enough quantities to be considered quite an ordinary item of diet – usually in milk puddings. Hannah Glasse's *The Art of Cookery Made Plain and Easy* in 1747 contains some twenty rice recipes. Most are puddings, one or two still using almonds as a flavouring as they had been used five hundred years earlier. But the new age is here as well, in a recipe 'to make a Pellow the India way'. Then the availability of cheap rice from new possessions overseas drove this former luxury food further and further down the British market. Nineteenth-century food writers become patronizing about rice. In 1842, the *Domestic Dictionary* says that 'it grows abundantly in the East Indies and in Egypt, and there forms the chief food of the poor ... There is a deep-rooted belief in England that the frequent and abundant use of rice will bring on blindness; but this opinion is not borne out by experience.' I should think not, indeed.

By this time, rice was being taken to countries very remote from where it grew. Farm workers in nineteenth-century Norway ate a porridge of water and barley on working days, milk and barley on Sundays, but milk and rice for feasts and celebrations. In Finland, rice porridge was served as dessert on Christmas Eve, and Christmas lunch began with the leftover porridge, sliced thick and fried.

When I first came to England, I remember being very surprised to find kedgeree on the breakfast menu of the hotel we stayed in – rice for breakfast I was used to, but not with toast and butter. After thirty years, my English husband will still only eat rice at breakfast if there is really nothing else; but his generation did not spend their working lives 'up country' in India or Malaya.

Oriental dishes which became popular in eighteenth- or nineteenth-century Europe were usually, and quite understandably, very different from their originals. *Khichri* was recorded by an English writer in the 1660s as 'Beans pounded, and Rice, which they boile together ... Then they put thereto a little Butter melted.' Madhur Jaffrey, in *Eastern Vegetarian Cooking*, points out that there are 'wet' khichri, which are really rice porridges similar to those that are found in all rice-growing countries, and 'dry' ones. Europeans in the East took to khichri for breakfast and supper, because, like the local people, they found it digestible and soothing, good for invalids or those with hangovers. The French chef Charles Francatelli, writing in the 1870s, included in his book a recipe for kedgeree which he called *Riz à la Soeur Nightingale*. Whether he had Florence Nightingale's permission to use her name in this way, I don't know.

Fish is not an ingredient of khichri but in India often comes to table with it; the English regard kedgeree as basically a fish-and-rice dish. This is fine, as long as kedgeree does not become an excuse for serving up any old tired leftover fish. I give here my favourite kedgeree, which I like to eat for lunch rather than breakfast – I would certainly dispense with the toast and butter. I have chosen smoked mackerel with coarsely ground black peppercorns, which you can buy ready-prepared from supermarkets, but you can of course use whatever fish you like best.

Please see recipe overleaf ●◆

Kedgeree

Preparation: 10 minutes

Cooking: 20 minutes

Serves 4-6

340 g (12 oz) long grain rice (Basmati, Texmati, Sunlong, etc.)

2-2.5 litres (3-4 pints) water

340 g (12 oz) smoked peppered mackerel, or smoked haddock

56 g (2 oz) butter

2-3 hard-boiled eggs, finely chopped

½ tsp chilli powder, or 1 chilli, deseeded and finely chopped (optional)

salt

1 tbsp flat-leaf parsley

1-2 tbsp Crisp-Fried Onions (Prepared in advance; see below)

Soak the rice in cold water for 30 minutes and then drain. Skin the smoked fish, remove any bones and flake finely.

Heat the water with ¼ teaspoon of salt in a large saucepan. When it boils, put in the rice and stir so that the rice will not stick to the bottom. Bring the water back to the boil and cook for 6-8 minutes, so that the rice is tender but not soft. Drain the rice in a colander. Leave it to cool for a few minutes.

Put the rice in a large bowl and carefully mix it with the flaked fish and chopped eggs. Season with a little salt, and some chilli if you like it hot.

Melt the butter in a wok or saucepan and stir the kedgeree into it. Keep tossing and stirring for about 3 minutes, until it is heated through.

Serve straight away, on well-heated plates, with the Crisp-Fried Onions and parsley sprinkled over it.

Crisp-Fried Onions

Preparation and cooking: 40-45 minutes

Makes about 500 g (1 lb)

1 kg (2 lb 3 oz) shallots, thinly sliced

285 ml (½ pint) sunflower oil

It is easier to make theses fried onions in a wok, but a frying pan will do. Heat the oil until a sliver of onion dropped into it sizzles immediately. Fry the shallots in 3 or 4 batches, stirring all the time, for 3-4 minutes each time or until they are crisp and lightly browned. Remove with a slotted spoon to drain in a colander lined with absorbent paper. Let them cool, then store in an airtight container; they will keep crisp and fresh for about a week.

1995 TO 1999

A *focus* on ingredients Old & New

Colin Spencer

Lindsey Bareham

Peter Gordon

Claudia Roden

Mary Berry

Antonio Carluccio OBE

Carla Capalbo

Sara Jayne-Stanes OBE

Richard Ehrlich

Colin Spencer

Colin Spencer is a distinguished novelist, playwright, painter and portraitist, as well as being one of the country's leading food historians and specialists in vegetarian food. His many books on vegetarian cooking established him as one of Britain's most eloquent proponents of vegetables. His renowned book of vegetarian dinner party menus, *Cordon Vert* was said by Derek Cooper back in 1985 to 'lift vegetarianism out of its sackcloth and sandals, and move it into haute cuisine'. Colin was Food Editor of the *Guardian* for thirteen years and also wrote a column for *Country Life*. His many food books include *British Food: An Extraordinary Thousand Years of History*, winner of a special commendation from the Trustees of the André Simon Memorial Fund in 2002 and of the Guild of Food Writers Michael Smith Award in 2003. Colin has served as both Chair and President of the Guild.

Rocket
Eruca sativa

Colin Spencer's Vegetable Book
Conran Octopus 1995

Of all the salad plants and their leaves, this is my own favourite by far. When small, the plant has green leaves which are slightly reminiscent of radish, dandelion or an oak-leaved lettuce, but the taste is singular – peppery and growing more mustard-like as the plant ages. The leaves bequeath enormous zest to a mixed salad, though in my opinion the flavour is better without dressing. I use it extensively as part of a first course, its striking flavour a marvellous foil as a base for grilled chèvre, sliced avocado, or a variety of purées and salads.

Yet there is a great puzzle surrounding this edible and almost addictive plant. Why did it disappear entirely from Britain's gardens and thence our table for almost three hundred years? Further, one might ask, does the belief that the leaves have erotic properties have anything to do with that disappearance?

There is no doubt that the Ancient World considered it as possessing aphrodisiac properties; it was sown around the base of statues consecrated to Priapus and believed to restore vigour to the genitalia. Ovid terms the herb 'salacious', while Martial links it with spring onions as 'lustful'. Apicius uses both the seeds and the leaves, grinding the first as an ingredient in aromatic salts to be added as flavouring (it appears in a sauce for cold boar), while the latter is part of a sauce for boiled crane, and the pounded leaves with other herbs are used as a dressing for salt grey mullet. In one recipe Apicius acknowledges rocket's salacious reputation and teams it with bulbs 'for those who seek the door of love, or as they are served with a legitimate wedding meal, but also with pine kernels or flavoured with rocket and pepper.'

The plant has a long history, for in the Middle East between 9000 and 7000 BC rocket was one of the first plants to be cultivated. It originated as a weed with both rye and oats, infiltrating the very first cultivated plants, wheat, barley, rice, soya beans, flax and cotton. As cultivation stretched upwards from the river into the higher regions, or travelled north to harsher climates, the so-called weeds were better adapted to these conditions and so took over the fields. Thus the weeds became the crop and the crop the weed. (In the same way, the tomato plant was a weed which spread northwards from Peru through the New World tropics to Mexico as a weed of both maize and bean fields.)

Unaware that rocket was one of the first cultivated plants, the early Christian church only knew of its supposed erotic properties and frowned upon its use and cultivation. Numerous writers spoke of its 'hotness and lechery' and the Church, at one point, banned its cultivation in monastic gardens.

Its common name is derived from the Latin 'eruca', which denotes a downy stem like a caterpillar. Giacomo Castelvetro in 1614 delights in its use as part of an early spring salad (see below). John Evelyn's rocket is derived from Spain to be planted in his calendar in March. In the late 1690s Evelyn refers to it as both 'hot and dry', but 50 years later in 1747 Hannah Glasse omits rocket from her list of salads. Had it, by then, fallen out of favour? It would seem so.

Its decline is traced quite clearly in Sturtevant's Notes on Edible Plants (published 1919). Here he says, 'in 1586 Camerarius says it is planted most abundantly in gardens. In 1726 Townsend says it is not now very common in English gardens, and in 1807 Miller's Dictionary says it has been long rejected.' It is interesting to note that this decline was not paralleled elsewhere; it continued to flourish in gardens and cooking all over the Mediterranean countries and it appeared in American gardens in 1854 or earlier.

John Evelyn shared the seventeenth-century passion for novelty in gardens; new varieties of fruit and vegetables were grown with great enthusiasm, yet were they eaten with the same enthusiasm? One doubts it. Pepys hardly mentions vegetables, except as ingredients for broths. For people were suspicious of vegetables, believing them (quite rightly) to be a source of unwanted wind. They were also thought to cause melancholy. Though it is doubtful that rocket was ever eaten here cooked (as it was and still is in the Mediterranean), but as part of a salad it would have been well-seasoned with oil as this was thought an antidote to flatulence. All raw, undressed food was much frowned upon.

What could possibly be the reason, then, for the sudden disappearance of rocket from the British salad bowl, kitchen and herb garden? After Evelyn it stops being eaten in these islands, until it reappears in seed catalogues around 1980. Within this short time it has risen astonishingly quickly in popularity, so that every enterprising gardener and cook grows it, and the large multiple stores stock it.

It would seem that the disappearance of rocket and other salad vegetables in this country was due to the rise in market gardens. The rapid growth and prosperity of towns favoured the development of market gardens situated nearby. The vegetables and fruits grown in these gardens were chosen from the stock in the great houses and they tended to be the most popular, which could be sold off easily: peas, beans, potatoes, carrots, celery, cabbages, cauliflowers and Savoys and the root vegetables, turnips and parsnips. Some of these vegetables became field crops; others gradually came to be grown, but not until a hundred years later, as part of the garden produce around the house to eke out the family diet. The rule or selection favoured what could be cultivated and sold easily. This would seem to apply to rocket, at first glance, as this salad plant seems too wild in appearance and habit to fit into the well-ordered market garden. Rocket can, after all, be found wild and other salad leaves could certainly have been picked easily from the countryside.

A countryman with a small plot of land early in the nineteenth century could grow his own vegetables. Cobbett at Singleton in Sussex in 1823 notes, 'the gardens are neat and full of vegetables of the best kinds. I see very few of 'Ireland's lazy root' (meaning the potato)'. The vegetables all tend to be the ones mentioned above with emphasis upon the brassicas. By this time, if rocket had strayed into such a garden it would have been plucked out as a weed. This conservatism is still rife today in the rural gardener, who looks upon my own garden of salad leaves, radicchio, endive, chicory and mustard greens as being alien, and filled with plants not worth giving room to in his own plot of cabbages, beetroots, leeks and onions.

The evidence for rocket's downfall and obscurity is even more striking if one consults A Modern Herbal by Mrs Grieve, published in 1931 with an introduction by Mrs Leyel, and long considered a modern classic. Here there is an entry for 'Rocket, Garden', which refers to Hesperis matronalis, sweet rocket, but which then lists Eruca sativa as a synonym. It also goes on to make another profound mistake by saying that the rocket found in the wild in Britain and Russian Asia are escapes from gardens. Mrs Grieve gives no separate entry for the great culinary rocket, E. sativa, an omission which is very odd in such a comprehensive work some 900 pages long. It is even more astonishing when one realizes that a small volume by Lady Rosalind Northcote, The Book of Herbs, published in 1912, gives a nervous appraisal of the herb, but refers back to the 1629 work of Parkinson (herbalist and apothecary to James I), Paradisi in Sole, who believed rocket 'causeth headache and heateth too much'. Lady Northcote ends her half-page reference by commenting 'it gives little encouragement to those who would make trial of rocket'.

Well, no, she is right. What a pity both Mrs Grieve and Lady Northcote did not take more notice of John Evelyn. Could it be that the ancients' love and admiration for rocket as an aphrodisiac made later writers nervous of it? Especially those who might be influenced by the severe admonitions of the medieval church, such as Edwardian gentlewomen like Mrs Grieve, who cast it completely out of her mind and from thence the botanical world entirely.

COOKING   Rocket is seldom cooked here, though it is always part of the wild greens called *horta* which are gathered and cooked in Greece in the autumn. They are simply boiled for 5 minutes, then well drained and served with oil and lemon. Patience Gray uses rocket with pasta in *Honey from the Weed*:

'Orecchiette con la Rucola' – 'Little ears' with rocket (Orecchiette are the traditional pasta of Apulia, shaped like little shells, particularly useful for holding the sauce.)

A Salentine Dish. Use wild rocket, Eruca sativa (or broccoli heads or heads of rape). Gather the plants when small, wash them well and throw into a pan of salted boiling water. Cook the orecchiette in another pan and drain when they are al dente. Cover the bottom of a frying-pan with olive oil, add 2 hot peppers, 2 peeled cloves of garlic, sliced, and cook for a few minutes. Put the well-drained pasta and the rocket in the pan, stir with a wooden fork, mixing all together, and serve very hot with a piquant grated cheese.'

However, rocket is best when used in a salad or by itself, perhaps Castelvetro's 'excellent mixed salad' is the most beguiling of all.

'Of all the salads we eat in the spring, the mixed salad is the best and most wonderful of all. Take young leaves of mint, those of garden cress, basil, lemon balm, the tips of salad burnet, tarragon, the flowers and tenderest leaves of borage, the flowers of swine cress, the young shoots of fennel, leaves of rocket, of sorrel, rosemary flowers, some sweet violets, and the tenderest leaves or the hearts of lettuce. When these precious herbs have been picked clean and washed in several waters, and dried a little with a clean linen cloth they are dressed as usual, with oil, salt and vinegar.'

No writer that I have yet to discover mentions that the wonderful peppery flavour of rocket will be diminished once it is dressed with oil and vinegar. If you want to retain that crisp taste, almost of green peppercorns, then keep some of the leaves undressed. This is my method: lay the rocket leaves on a platter, then mix the other salad ingredients with the dressing and pile that on top of the rocket in the centre. That ensures that some leaves around the edge remain undressed.

Rocket, Mushroom and Flageolet Salad

generous handful of rocket leaves

4 or 5 spring onions, chopped

5 or 6 chestnut mushrooms, sliced

2 or 3 tbsp cooked flageolet beans

4 tbsp walnut oil

1 tbsp lemon juice

pinch of unrefined golden caster sugar

sea salt

shreds of lemon zest, to garnish (optional)

Lay the rocket leaves over a serving platter.

In a bowl, mix all the other ingredients with salt to taste and let them marinate for an hour.

Then pile the mixture in the centre of the rocket-lined platter and serve garnished with some strips of lemon zest, if using.

Rocket and Avocado Sandwich

This is my favourite summer sandwich. Rocket and avocado go marvellously well together, but I confess I like a touch of other flavourings in it as well, as a kind of background track to the two stars.

This amount will make two fairly large and hulky sandwiches, which provide an excellent and satisfying lunch for two people.

2 tbsp soft goats' cheese

4 slices of your favourite brown bread, buttered

smear of Marmite, Vegemite or Vecon

about 10 thin cucumber slices

1 ripe avocado, peeled, stoned and sliced

20 or so rocket leaves

tiny drop of Tabasco (optional)

sea salt and freshly ground black pepper

Smear the goats' cheese on the buttered side of 2 slices of the bread and smear the Marmite or whatever on the other 2 slices.

Lay the cucumber slices over the cheese, season with pepper, then lay the avocado slices on top of that, followed by the rocket leaves. Season with salt and Tabasco, if using.

Then cover with the other pieces of the brown bread. Press the tops gently down and slice the sandwiches in half with great care.

Lindsey Bareham

Lindsey Bareham made her name as restaurant critic and food writer for *Time Out*. She went on to write a daily recipe for the *Evening Standard* and then to become the *Times* cook and to write for *Saga Magazine*. Of her first cookbook, *In Praise of the Potato*, Elizabeth David wrote: 'I love the book. It's full of delicious recipes and good information'. Lindsey helped Simon Hopkinson write *Roast Chicken and Other Stories*, which won the 1994 André Simon Award and the 1995 Glenfiddich Award for Food Book of the Year. Lindsey's *The Big Red Book of Tomatoes* was shortlisted for the Glenfiddich Food Book of the Year.

Tomatoes and Bread

The Big Red Book of Tomatoes
MICHAEL JOSEPH 1999

Probably the most universal refreshment in summer among working men in Greece, Italy and Catalonia is a slab of bread onto which are crushed some ripe tomatoes with a garlic clove, sea salt, bathed in olive oil. It relies on the rusticity of the bread, the fragrance of the ripe tomatoes, the taste of olive oil for excellence, and the accompanying wine.

PATIENCE GRAY, *Honey From a Weed, Fasting and Feasting in Tuscany, Catalonia, The Cyclades and Apulia*

When a ripe tomato is squashed against bread something magical happens. The magic works with all kinds of bread – it is just different magic – and it doesn't matter whether the bread is fresh or stale, toasted or turned to crumbs. You see the combination again and again in different guises in the cuisine of every country where tomatoes grow. In Italy, France, Greece, Spain and Portugal, for example, the simple pleasure of rubbing the flesh of a tomato into a piece of bread, until the bread is soaked red with tomato juices, is a daily routine of summer. With a twist of salt and a splash of olive, this is food for the Gods. It is also a building block for other ingredients: anchovy, roasted peppers and aubergine, rocket, onions, fresh herbs, olives, ham and cheese.

The British, who have their own tradition of things on toast, make a version of tomato bruschetta or pa amb tomaquet, as they call it in Catalonia. We like fried bread or buttered toast covered with grilled tomatoes and we like it best of all for breakfast. Different though all these simple tomato and bread snacks might be, all are related to the Neapolitan pizza. At its best, as it is still served at Michele's, one of the original pizza parlours of Naples, the pizza is made with a thin misshapen piece of dough. It is baked in a brick, wood-burning stove, and cooks until it puffs and bubbles, like nearby Vesuvius, sending the intensely flavoured tomato sauce swimming all over the pizza.

The Italians also make wonderful tomato sandwiches. There is something about the combination of slightly chewy and very crusty ciabatta loaded up with slices of sun-ripened tomato, mozzarella and rocket, that is particularly good. Many people despise tomato sandwiches because they go soggy. In Nice, they put this soggy factor to good effect in a giant sandwich called pan bagnat. It looks impossible to eat, loaded as it is with most of the ingredients of a salade Niçoise. The best ones have been weighted so that the tomato and olive oil combine as a sort of vinaigrette that seeps into the dough. As you bite it squelches over the thick slices of tomato, the black olives, and anchovy, and whatever else has been piled in.

But don't let us forget that tomatoes on their own, in buttered French bread, can be worth shopping specially for. Think of it now: chunky slices of sun-ripened tomatoes, freshly baked crusty bread, unsalted butter, and a little salt. It couldn't be much different than the traditional British tomato sandwich. This is far more refined. We like our tomatoes neatly sliced, layered up in thin slices of buttered bread (with the crusts removed) then cut into dainty little triangles.

Tomatoes work well cooked into bread, specially when the juice is separated from the flesh and used to make the dough. However, the most pronounced tomato flavour in baked bread comes from sun-dried tomatoes. In Spain and Italy, in particular, there is a peasant tradition of soaking yesterday's bread in chopped tomato. The addition of olive oil and one or two other choice ingredients, such as onion, garlic and vinegar, maybe celery and basil too, results in surprisingly luscious soups-cum-salads. And, stale bread crumbs, layered up with sliced tomato and fresh herbs, and maybe a little onion or garlic, cook into elegant, and surprisingly light gratins. These are, of course deconstructed versions of tomatoes Provençal, an appealing dish of tomatoes stuffed with garlic and parsley breadcrumbs.

THE ULTIMATE
TOMATO SANDWICH

When I first floated the idea of writing a book about tomatoes my editor was unmoved. A tomato, she said is a tomato. They aren't like potatoes, she went on, is there really a book in it? Then, one Saturday, after her usual outing with the Dummer Beagles, the beaglers were entertained for tea at the Wiltshire farm of one Robert Wharton. It was a wonderful spread, she told me, but little did she realise that she was about to receive tomato enlightenment. The tomato sandwich she inadvertently picked out was so extraordinarily good that she couldn't wait to tell me about it.

Intrigued, I wrote to Mr Wharton explaining that I was writing a book about tomatoes and asked if he would share his recipe with me. The surprising upshot was an invitation to lunch at Vong in Knightsbridge. Waiting for me on the bar was a pile of pretty regular looking sandwiches: thin slices of white bread, crusts removed and a hint of red between the slices. Mr Wharton and his nephew Oliver, who it transpired is Vong's general manager, watched bemused as I bit into a sandwich. It was the texture that hit me first. The tomatoes were neither sliced nor diced but the flavour was the very essence of tomato. Extraordinarily, the bread had no hint of sogginess and the mixture didn't squelch out of the buttered slices as I bit. This, I had to agree, was tomato sandwich perfection.

It turns out that Mr Wharton's brother, Oliver's father, is a New York restaurateur and Oliver a trained chef, so with food in the blood, as it were, it is no surprise that Robert Wharton decided to perfect the tomato sandwich. 'I wanted to make something that would spread nicely and wouldn't slip off the bread. A tomato sandwich that wouldn't make the bread soggy.' There was no actual recipe, he said, he did it by eye and, of course, taste. It is difficult to be precise because the quality of the tomato is paramount and the extra seasonings – red wine vinegar, tomato ketchup, sugar, Worcestershire sauce, Tabasco – are a matter of taste. Here, then, is a guideline recipe based on my experimentation. The secret ingredient: gelatine.

The Ultimate Tomato Sandwich

250 g vine-ripened tomatoes, cored, scalded and peeled

1 tsp tomato ketchup

½ (half) tbsp red wine vinegar

pinch unrefined golden caster sugar

4 drops Tabasco

3 tbsp olive oil

5 cm square piece leaf gelatine or 1 heaped tsp gelatine granules

optional extra: Worcestershire sauce

Cut the tomatoes into quarters. Place a sieve over a bowl. Scrape the seeds into the sieve. Press the seeds with the back of a spoon against the side of the sieve to extract as much juice as possible. You should end up with about 50 ml of tomato water.

Add the ketchup, vinegar, sugar and Tabasco. Whisk in the olive oil.

If using the leaf gelatine, stir it into the vinaigrette and leave for five minutes before stirring vigorously until it completely dissolves. If using the granules, stir them into the vinaigrette. Both should noticeably thicken the vinaigrette immediately.

Chop the tomato (you should end up with about 145 g) very finely or press it through a large-holed sieve. Stir the tomato into the gelled vinaigrette.

Taste and adjust the seasoning, perhaps adding a few drops of Worcestershire sauce, more Tabasco, or more sugar.

Cover and leave in the fridge for about 30 minutes. It will keep, covered, in the fridge for several days. It is delicious, incidentally, spooned over hard-boiled eggs or stirred into hot pasta that has been moistened with a little cream and chives.

Peter Gordon

Peter Gordon, co-owner and Head Chef of London's Providores and Tapa Room, is renowned as the leading proponent in the UK of the Antipodean 'fusion' style of cooking. Peter began his career at the age of seventeen as an apprentice in Melbourne, then travelled around Southeast Asia, India and Nepal – an experience that was the catalyst to his development of fusion cuisine. Back in New Zealand in 1986, he became Head Chef of the original Sugar Club in Wellington. Its success convinced the owners to transplant it and its Head Chef to London's Notting Hill in 1995. It quickly became one of the hottest tickets in town and picked up a Time Out Award only a year later. The best-selling *Sugar Club Cookbook* followed, alongside monthly columns for glossies and several TV appearances.

Introduction

Sugar Club Cookbook
HODDER & STOUGHTON
1997

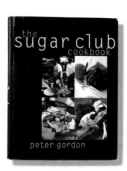

For most of my childhood in New Zealand I lived with my grandmother, so it's only natural that I came to adopt her approach to food and its purpose: sustenance, conversation and adventure. Molly would send us kids traipsing off to the beach to collect seaweed. Some ended up in the soups or stews she made from cheap joints, while the rest slowly turned to mulch in the garden. She had tubs of it fermenting away ready to dilute and feed to her pumpkins. These entwined themselves through the Macrocarpa trees – allowing her to pick a pumpkin without having to stoop. In the garden were all sorts of herbs, which she used to flavour, to heal, or both. The flowers of the comfrey went into salads, but when any of us had a sprain she made a poultice from its leaves – she knew, of course, that its popular name is 'Knit Bone'. For a boy growing up in New Zealand in the 60s and 70s it all seemed the norm. If Gran did it, then surely everyone else did too!

The things I learnt in my youth have stayed with me ever since: the generous use of fresh herbs and how a cheap cut of meat or the fleshless bone from a ham can transform a soup. My first cooking memory is helping my mother Timmy to cook an apple pie when I was about four: she did all the work while I just put the peeled and sugared pieces into the pie crust. My cousin Lynette introduced me to mushrooms uncooked – marinated in olive oil and garlic. What a revelation! At home in Wanganui we never used vegetable oil. After Dad and his mates had cut up the carcasses of slaughtered beasts in the garage we'd turn the beef fat into soap by adding caustic soda and who knows what else. Almost all the food we ate was cooked in rendered fat. Scary.

I made my first scrapbook of recipes when I was five and then, at the age of seven, while cooking a dinner of fish and chips, I fell off my cooking stool and pulled the entire pot of boiling oil on to myself. Hospital, skin-grafts and more hospital followed. The family were convinced I'd lose my interest in food, but I didn't. After a short stint doing

Horticultural Science at university I packed my bags for Melbourne, where I cooked and ate for five years. Melbourne – with its rich ethnic mix, numerous styles of food and a very high standard of living for most – must be one of the finest culinary centres in the world. As an apprentice I ate out once or twice a week, enjoying Vietnamese, Japanese, Greek, French and Thai cuisine. At the time Rogalsky's, Stephanie's, Berowra Waters and You and Me were all cooking 'New Australian' food, a reinvention of classical European cuisine. It was a minefield of ideas and a fantastic time. Once three friends and I drove 1,000km to Sydney just to have lunch at Berowra Waters! I still remember the bone marrow with brioche and baby chicken in salt crust with green sauce.

In 1985 I went to Bali and spent the next year travelling through Asia on my way to Europe. I was amazed by the food, religions, smells, colours, pace of life and, above all, by the brilliant people I met. Travelling through Indonesia, Malaysia, Singapore, Thailand, Burma, Nepal and India, I developed a great fondness for chillies, coconut, bamboo, spices, vegetables, relishes and anything warm and sunny. It was the most wonderful year of my life. After a brief spell in London I returned to Wellington, New Zealand, to set up the kitchen of the original Sugar Club. I'd been contacted in London by the owners, Vivienne Hayman and Ashley Sumner, who had heard of me through my cousins. They wanted to set up a place where one could go for interesting, eclectic and tasty food. Would I be interested in coming over and consulting for ten weeks to get it all going? The site they had was in the red-light district, in Vivian Street – an area known more for the transvestites and hookers who worked it than for diners. But the venture was a success and I had a great time – so much so that I stayed for two and a half years! During my time at the Wellington Sugar Club I introduced our legendary beef pesto, various laksas, home-made goat's cheese, prawns in ginger and garlic, nori rolls, Bur Bur Cha Cha and much else besides.

In 1989 the Sugar Club was sold and I returned to London with the intention of opening another Sugar Club with Vivienne and Ashley, who were already scouting for suitable premises. The food in London restaurants was not what I was used to: it was either one style or another. There wasn't the pick and mix I had come to love from my travels and my childhood. By now I appreciated almost everything – from offal and green curries to buffalo yoghurt and deep-fried breads. As there didn't seem to be any places cooking eclectic food we were convinced we had a good idea and set about opening a place of our own.

We tried for nearly five years, but an assortment of obstacles prevented us from securing either a venue or the necessary finance. The closest we came was through discussions with a brewery, but they felt

please turn to page 124 ◗◆

Grilled Scallops with Sweet Chilli Sauce and Crème Fraîche

This dish – one of my all-time favourites – is now synonymous with the London Sugar Club. I first put it on the menu in July 1995, and it has only come off when storms prevented divers collecting scallops. It's also the dish that most reviewers choose when they visit! The crème fraîche softens the strong flavours of the sauce, which in turn cut through the richness of the scallops. The chilli sauce recipe makes more than you need, so keep the surplus in the fridge for other dishes.

Serves 4

12 large diver-caught scallops, trimmed

sesame oil

salt and pepper

watercress leaves

½ cup crème fraîche

Sweet Chilli Sauce

10 cloves of garlic, peeled

4 large red chillies, stems removed

3 thumbs of fresh ginger, peeled and roughly chopped

1 thumb of galangal, peeled and roughly chopped

8 lime leaves

3 lemon-grass stems, remove the two outside leaves, discard the top third of the stem and finely slice the remainder

1 cup fresh coriander leaves

1½ cups unrefined golden caster sugar

100 ml (5 fl oz) cider vinegar

50 ml (3½ fl oz) Asian fish sauce

50 ml (1¾ fl oz) tamari

Put the first seven ingredients of the chilli sauce in a food processor and purée to a coarse paste.

Put the sugar in a saucepan with 4 tablespoons of water and place on a moderate heat, stirring well until the sugar dissolves. When it has, remove the spoon and turn the heat up to full.

Boil for 5–8 minutes and do not stir until it has turned a dark caramel colour (but don't allow it to burn). Now stir in the paste, bring the sauce back to the boil and add the last three ingredients.

Return to the boil and simmer for 1 minute. Leave it to cool before eating.

Lightly oil the scallops with sesame oil and season, then grill each side on a char-grill, overhead grill or skillet for 90 seconds.

Sit them on a bed of watercress, put a dollop of crème fraîche on top and drizzle generously with sweet chilli sauce.

❧ *continued from page 121*

we were a risk as our views on food and service differed from theirs and the offer was withdrawn at the final meeting. We had worked on the deal for nearly a year and I found it very disheartening. I decided to pursue an independent career so that I could get into cooking without further delay. Ashley, Vivienne and I parted for two and a half years.

In January 1995 the site of the present Sugar Club was a run-down Asian restaurant on All Saints Road in Notting Hill. We were advised that the street was a no-go area, as had been said of the original site in Wellington. Still, we felt it was perfect: it was a good size, and it had a courtyard and lots of light. The planning and development were an exciting time. Where would the ovens go, and the bar and banquettes? After lots of hard work and effort, and much anxiety for Ashley and Vivienne, it was with a great feeling of achievement that the London incarnation of the Sugar Club finally opened its doors in June 1995. The first two weeks were a gradual build-up with friends – and friends of friends – filling the tables. At the end of the second week we received two excellent reviews and have never looked back since.

During the previous five years I'd worked at many restaurants and tried to do what I'm best at and feel comfortable with. I call this the 'magpie' approach to food – the mixing and matching of textures and tastes from the east to the west, sweet and sour, salty and spicy, soft and crunchy. If it tastes good it works.

My approach to food is that simple. It works or it doesn't. The careful mixing of sweet and savoury can really enhance a dish. Many people have difficulty appreciating the concept until they realise that chutneys are exactly that. As I have a mild allergy to dairy food I try to avoid it, but serve me a dessert without cream and I go to pieces. I love offal for the intensity of its texture and flavour. Chillies are tops – a judiciously placed bit of spiciness may go undetected yet will magically enhance a dish – even in desserts such as poached pears in red wine. I find it difficult to cook without an abundance of fresh herbs. Garlic, olive and sesame oils, tamari and Asian fish sauce are indispensable in my kitchen. Last year I discovered Spanish smoked paprika – both sweet and spicy. It transforms an aïoli, risotto, roast potatoes and so much else. Currently in the kitchen at the Sugar Club we have a string of dried aubergines hanging up – I'm not sure what they do with them in Turkey but no doubt they'll be on the menu before long! There is so much to learn about food and that's what is so exciting.

My style of food is loosely called 'Pacific Rim' or 'fusion', and it draws its influences from all over the world. It's simple to prepare and quick to make. I suggest you try it out and use the magpie technique to take from it what you want.

Claudia Roden

Claudia Roden was born to a cosmopolitan Jewish family in Cairo. She completed her formal education in Paris and then moved to London to study art at St Martins. She had grown up eating food from all over the Middle East, and began collecting recipes at a young age. 'Food was,' she explains, 'a way of re-connecting with my culture – my lost heritage.' Claudia's meticulously researched first book, *A Book of Middle Eastern Food* (1968) introduced the aromatic ingredients of Middle Eastern food to a large, new audience. Several books later, her encyclopaedic and sensuous *Book of Jewish Food*, referred to as a masterpiece and a classic, won many major food awards, including the Glenfiddich, the André Simon and the Guild's Book of the Year Award.

Cold Fried Fish in the Jewish Style

The Book of Jewish Food
ALFRED A KNOPF 1996/
PENGUIN BOOKS 1999

In *Children of the Ghetto* (1892), Israel Zangwill writes of a young man in the East End of London who held a Christian girl he fancied to be cold of heart. 'Perhaps,' he wrote, 'though he was scarcely conscious of it, at the bottom of his revulsion was the certainty that the Christian girl could not fry fish. She might be delightful for a flirtation of all degrees, but had not been formed to make him permanently happy.'

The Jews in London had a very particular way of frying fish in batter and eating it cold which has become a classic of Jewish cooking in Britain. It was a legacy of the Portuguese Marranos (crypto-Jews) who came to England in the 16th century, many via Holland. Manuel Brudo, a Portuguese Marrano, wrote in 1544 that the favourite diet of Marrano refugees in England was fried fish. They sprinkled it with flour and dipped it in egg and in breadcrumbs. Lady Judith Montefiore, the anonymous editor-author of the first Jewish cookbook in English, published in 1846, referred to the frying oil as 'Florence oil', which meant olive oil. At that time an important community of Marranos in Livorno (where her husband came from) exported olive oil to England.

Thomas Jefferson, the third President of the United States and a famous epicurean, discovered 'fried fish in the Jewish fashion' when he came to England. When his grand-daughter Virginia put together a collection of his favourite recipes, she included a recipe for fried fish in the Jewish manner to be eaten cold from Alexis Soyer's *A Shilling Cookery Book for the People*, published in 1855. Soyer, who was the chef at the Reform Club, explained that the fish was simply salted and either dipped in a flour and water batter or, as in some Jewish families, dipped first in flour, then in egg and fried in oil. He added that frying in oil was superior to frying in fat or dripping, but more expensive.

Cold fried fish in the Jewish style was much praised by gourmets and featured in early English cookbooks. Hannah Glasse was the first to include a recipe in her *The Art of Cookery Made Plain and Easy* in 1781. Eliza Acton gave one in *Modern Cookery for Private Families* in 1845.

In a piece on the 'Culinary Aspects of Anglo-Jewry', John Shaftesley notes that in 1968 the National Federation of Fish Friers presented a commemorative plaque to Malin's of Bow as the oldest enterprise to sell fish and chips together in Britain. Joseph Malin, a Jewish immigrant newly arrived from Eastern Europe, founded a fish business in Bow in 1860 and began selling chips with fried fish. It was a combination of Ashkenazi, Sephardi and Irish ways in an East End which was a mix of Eastern European and Irish immigrants (this was after the potato famine) with some long-established Sephardi families. Dozens of fish and chip shops opened in the East End, and all around the country the Jewish fried fish trade joined with the Irish potato shop.

Whereas fish and chips became the English national dish, cold fried fish became the most popular method of cooking fish for Jews in Britain. My mother-in-law told me that when her family had the fish shop in the East End, they used to fry fish every Friday and distribute it to relatives.

Pickled Fried Fish

This marinated fried fish has a rich, spicy, sweet and sour flavour. It will do very well as a cold snack.

Serves 6

750 g (1 lb 10 oz) fish fillet, cut into 6 serving pieces

salt

flour, for dusting

1 egg, lightly beaten

fine breadcrumbs or matzo meal, for coating

light vegetable oil, for deep-frying

250 ml (9 fl oz) cider vinegar

2 tbsp unrefined light muscovado sugar

2 bay leaves

3 garlic cloves, sliced

¼ tsp ground ginger

5 peppercorns

½ tsp whole coriander seeds

a pinch of mace

Sprinkle the pieces of fish with salt and leave for an hour, covered, in the refrigerator.

Drain off the water that has been drawn out.

Dip each piece in flour, then in lightly beaten egg, then fine breadcrumbs or matzo meal, turning them so that they are well coated all over.

Deep-fry in about 2.5cm (1 inch) of light vegetable oil. The oil must be sizzling but only medium hot, or the coating will burn before the fish is cooked. Put the fish pieces in carefully and fry, turning them over once, until brown on both sides.

Drain on kitchen paper. Arrange the fried fish in a dish.

Put the vinegar in a pan with the sugar, 2 bay leaves, garlic, ginger, peppercorns, coriander and mace.

Simmer for 5 minutes and let it cool.

Pour over the fish and leave to marinate for 48 hours in the refrigerator. It keeps very well for at least a week.

Mary Berry

Mary Berry is one of the best-known and respected cookery writers and broadcasters in the UK. She started her career as Cookery Editor of *Housewife* magazine and later moved to *Ideal Home*. She has presented seven TV series for Thames TV and more recently for BBC 1 with Mary Berry's Ultimate Cakes and Mary Berry at Home. For many years she was a contributor to BBC radio. She has written more than 40 cookery books, including *The Aga Book*, and is revered by both experienced cooks and novices for her down-to-earth approach to food presentation and meal planning. *The Mail On Sunday's You Magazine* said: 'Mary Berry is to Aga what Pavarotti is to opera.' In June 2009, Mary was presented with a Lifetime Achievement Award by the Guild.

Strawberry Meringue Roulade

Serves 8

sunflower oil for greasing

4 egg whites

250 g (8 oz) unrefined golden caster sugar

45 g (1½ oz) flaked almonds

icing sugar for dusting

Filling

300 ml (½ pint) double or whipping cream, whipped until thick

250 g (8 oz) strawberries, quartered

23 x 33 cm (9 x 13 in) Swiss Roll Tin

Mary Berry's Complete Cookbook
DORLING KINDERSLEY
1995

Lightly oil the Swiss roll tin and line with a sheet of baking parchment.

Whisk the egg whites until stiff but not dry. Add the sugar, 1 tsp at a time, and continue to whisk, until all the sugar has been incorporated and the mixture is stiff and glossy.

Spoon the meringue into the lined tin and tilt to level the surface. Sprinkle over the flaked almonds.

Bake near the top of a preheated oven at 200°C (400°F, Gas 6) for about 8 minutes until the top is golden brown.

Reduce the oven temperature to 160°C (325°F, Gas 3), and continue baking for 10 minutes or until the meringue is firm to the touch.

Remove the meringue from the oven and turn out on to a sheet of baking parchment. Peel the lining paper from the base and leave the meringue to cool for 10 minutes.

Spread the whipped cream evenly over the meringue, and scatter the strawberries over the cream.

Roll up the meringue from a long side, using the lining paper to help lift it. Wrap the roulade in baking parchment and leave to chill in the refrigerator for about 30 minutes. Lightly dust with sifted icing sugar before serving.

Antonio Carluccio OBE

Antonio Carluccio recently celebrated fifty years of championing genuine, regional Italian food and wine. In Piedmont, at the age of seven, Antonio started his life-long past-time of collecting fungi with his father, a railway station master. He began his varied career as a journalist in Turin but moved to London in 1975. He took over the Neal Street Restaurant in Covent Garden in 1981, opened a deli next to the restaurant in 1991 and in 1998 started the first Carluccio's Caffè. In 1983 Antonio made his first appearance on BBC 2 talking about Mediterranean food. He has written many best-selling books and made numerous television programmes. *Carluccio's Complete Italian Food* was shortlisted for both a Guild of Food Writers Award and an André Simon Award in 1998. In the same year, Antonio was awarded the Italian equivalent of a British knighthood and made Commendatore OMRI by the President of Italy for services to Italian gastronomy, and in 2007 he was awarded an honorary OBE by the Queen.

Fresh & Cured Meats
Carni e salumi

Carluccio's Complete Italian Food
QUADRILLE 1997

Italians eat 70 kg of meat per person per annum, and more than a third of that is eaten in the form of pork. This is, of course, balanced by a large quantity of fresh vegetables and fruit. As is to be expected from the heartland of the Mediterranean diet, the average Italian meal, divided into anything from three to five courses, rarely includes large lumps of meat. A notable exception is the famous bistecca alla fiorentina, a huge T-bone steak that weighs at least 500 g per portion. The beef used for this dish comes from special beef cattle raised in a valley near Florence, the Val di Chiana. The steak is so tender that it is usually grilled and eaten rare, an exception for Italians who prefer their meat to be slightly more thoroughly cooked.

In Piedmont, cattle are raised to make other local specialities like bollito misto (mixed boiled meats), brasato al barolo (topside braised in red wine), insalata di carne cruda (a special salad of raw beef) and carne all'Albese, a raw meat salad served with white truffle from Alba. The cattle used to provide meat for these dishes are known as sanato or vitellone, which although more mature and developed than veal calves are still fairly young, with very tender flesh.

The rearing practices for some animals, especially that of veal calves, causes much controversy. I must say that, while I agree that humans have to be fed, I think it is possible to be more scrupulous about the manner in which the rearing is done. Veal has always been popular with chefs for its short cooking time and blandness, qualities that allow the meat to act as a backdrop to the flavours cooked with it. Personally, I prefer a firmer meat with a more pronounced taste.

In Italy there is no indication that veal calves, which have an appreciably pale meat while still milk-fed, are kept in narrow crates to avoid

please turn to page 132

Bollito Misto Mixed Boiled Meats

Piedmont and Lombardy both claim to be the birthplace of this gargantuan dish. Boiled meats have always been eaten everywhere in Italy after being used to make soup. For Bollito Misto the different types of meat are cooked specifically to produce something really succulent. This dish is only worth doing for lots of people on special occasions.

Serves 10–12

4 celery stalks, cut into chunks

3 carrots, cut into chunks

1 large onion, peeled and spiked with 4–5 cloves

a few peppercorns

1.5 kg (3¼ lb) beef brisket

1 veal tongue, weighing 600–800 g (1¼–1¾ lb)

1 boiling chicken, weighing 2 kg (4½ lb)

1 kg (2¼ lb) veal brisket

piece of veal cheek, weighing 500 g (1 lb)

2 cotechino sausages, weighing about 300 g (10½ oz) each

salsa verde and mostarda di Cremona, to serve

Put the vegetables and peppercorns in a very large pot of lightly salted water and bring to the boil.

Add the beef and cook gently for 30 minutes. Then add the tongue, chicken, veal brisket and cheek and simmer for 2 hours, skimming regularly to remove any scum from the surface. (If you don't have a large enough pot for all the meat, divide the vegetables and meat between 2 pans.) Top up with boiling water if necessary to make sure the meat is always covered.

Prick the skin of the cotechino sausages with a needle, put them in a separate pan and cover with cold water. Bring to the boil and cook gently for 1–1½ hours.

When all the meats are cooked and tender, remove them from the water. Peel and trim the tongue. Slice the meats and arrange them on a large serving plate.

Serve hot, accompanied by the sauces, vegetables and a little stock.

◆● *continued from page 130*

exercise. Calves are still kept with their mothers in the majority of cases. The 'industrialization' of meat production is avoided, if possible, because Italians like good meat – even if it is a little more expensive. The best beef animals are fed with hay or with a mixture of grains and corn-based fodder in winter, and in summer on fresh grass.

Pigs are a different matter as, unfortunately, to fatten them up they are raised in barns. They are, however, fed on a mixture of whey (a by-product of Parmesan cheese) and a mixture of grains. In Emilia-Romagna, some of the best pigs are fed on acorns to achieve particularly flavoured meat that distinguishes Parma ham from others.

Many Italians still keep animals if they can and the pig is the most popular, both for its taste and because the whole animal can be used – either for fresh meat and sausages, for salamis or for lard. When I was a boy during the War, my family were given two suckling pigs. We housed them in a specially made hut at the end of a disused railway line and when they were fully grown and fattened my father called in the local norcino or pork butcher. One of the pigs had to be offered to everyone in the village, a rule made by all the villagers when war broke out. With the remaining pig, my mother made salamis, lard and hams.

From Bolzano in Alto Adige, where speck is produced in the Austrian tradition, to Sicily where a dessert is made with pork blood, every region has its customs and recipes for pork. Pigs are usually slaughtered in winter, with much local celebrating.

One region that has made pork famous is Emilia-Romagna where Parma ham and many other preserved meats are made, including salamis, mortadella and culatello di zibello. These products, especially mortadella di Bologna, pancetta and zampone (stuffed pigs' trotters) are enjoyed all over Italy. Calabria also has some specialities, including salsiccie piccanti (spicy sausages), while Piedmont has salam d'la duja, salami preserved in lard. Another speciality is porchetta (stuffed piglet), a dish much loved by the Romans – ancient and modern.

As well as pork, beef and veal, Italians also eat lamb and goat and, sometimes, horse and donkey meat. Lamb and goat are most popular in Southern Italy. Some people believe that horse meat is particularly healthy and that the best mortadella is made with donkey meat.

Choosing fresh meat is a skill, but one that should be developed by anyone who wants to eat just a little of the very best meat. I remember being sent to buy meat when I was a child. I returned home with it proudly, only to be sent straight back to the butcher as it was not a good enough cut. I learnt an important lesson then, to know what constitutes a good cut. It is worth finding a good butcher to help you. Pay more and eat less, that is my recommendation.

Carla Capalbo

Carla Capalbo is one of the world's leading writers on Italian food and wine. Born in New York, she was brought up in London and Paris, and has been based in Italy for twenty years. She divides her time between writing personal, detailed food and wine guides to Italy – illustrated with her photographs – and producing articles about food and wine for newspapers and magazines on both sides of the Atlantic, including *Decanter*, *Bon Appetit* and *olive*. She has spent the last decade as a nomad, living in fishing communities, mountain villages and more recently, in Friuli, to research her books.

Venanzio Restaurant

Piazza palestro
3 Colonnata 54030 Carrara Massa

The Food and Wine Lover's Companion to Tuscany
CHRONICLE BOOKS 1998

Driving from Carrara to Colonnata is exciting: the road winds steeply up through the imposing, cavernous quarries that for centuries have given the world its finest marble. Even Michelangelo got his stone here. It is overwhelming to think of the human labour that has gone into taming these monumental mountains. The tiny stone village of Colonnata is tucked into this dramatic landscape. Its only restaurant is now synonymous with a special food: *lardo di Colonnata*, salt cured pork back fat.

"Our *lardo* is as old as the quarries," explained Venanzio Vannucci, who brought Colonnata's *lardo* into the gastronomic spotlight. "For a thousand years this village has conserved slabs of *lardo* in *conche*, troughs or bowls carved in marble. Recipes for the *salamoia*—curing salt, herbs, and spices—are generations old." Using this *salamoia* for six months in the marble results in a pure white, aromatic *salume*—nothing like its yellowed, rancid, and tough air-dried counterpart.

Venanzio's is exquisite. My lunch began with pieces of hot bread topped with fine, ribbon-like slices of *lardo*, with only a tiny streak of pink meat within the white. A sprig of rosemary lay on the piping hot plate; its warmed, aromatic perfume hit me first. The heat of the bread, the light, buttery softness of the *lardo*, its delicate yet exotic fragrance and balanced seasonings were extraordinary. An unusual carpaccio followed: a fillet of Chianina beef was marinated in the *lardo*'s *salamoia* for three days, then sliced paper thin. The tender coral meat, whose flavour just hinted at the spices and herbs it had been kept with, came surrounded by *mentuccia*—a vibrant wild mint. These pure foods had the clarity of birdsong.

A freshly-made omelette was filled with just-picked sprigs of fragrant *vignalba*, a wild clematis, and topped with slivered gray truffle, whose heady perfume complemented the herb's sweet bitterness. A sensual, brilliant dish. Tender ravioli with a light meat stuffing came in a fresh tomato and basil sauce. Sliced *tagliata* of beef arrived on a searingly hot plate and cooked as I watched. A frozen chocolate *semifreddo* was decorated with flowers Venanzio had gathered himself. There are wonderful wines (Sergio Manetti's ladies smiled down from his Pergole Torte labels) and a relaxed atmosphere in this small room, where quarry workers eat alongside foreign visitors. After lunch Venanzio showed me his garden. I left with my hands full of wild herbs and violets.

Sara Jayne-Stanes OBE

Sara Jayne-Stanes is Director of the Academy of Culinary Arts and the author of *Chocolate: the Definitive Guide*, which won the Guild's Jeremy Round Award for Best First Book, and *Chocolate* (2005). Sara is also a chocolatier and chocolate evangelist, and Chairman of the Academy of Chocolate, launched in 2005 to encourage chocolate lovers to 'look beyond the label'.

Truffe Gâteau

This is one of my favourite recipes as it is a timeless example of 'elegance in its simplicity' and, once mastered, it is relatively quick to make. It keeps for at least 7 days in the 'fridge – some people like it even more 'mature' – and if you have any over, it freezes like a dream!

Serves about 15

450 g dark chocolate (70% is a good guide but not always a guarantee of quality – the better the chocolate the better the result)

500 ml whipping cream – use at room temperature 16/20°C

3 tbsp rum (optional)

cocoa powder, unrefined golden icing sugar and/or cinnamon to dust.

Line a 25.5 cm (10 in) flan ring or an oblong container – like a bread tin – about 21 cm x 7.5 cm x 10 cm (8½ in x 3 in x 4 in deep).

Melt the chocolate in a bain marie - don't let the water rise above 40°C.

While you are waiting for the chocolate to melt, in a large bowl lightly whip the cream and rum (if using). Stop when the whisk leaves a trail.

Pour about half the chocolate into the cream and fold in. Then fold in the rest of the chocolate until completely amalgamated.

Pour the mixture into the container, smoothing the top. Refrigerate for at least three hours or longer for a really firm finish.

Turn out and dust with cocoa powder or icing sugar or a touch of cinnamon (go easy on this or it will overpower – you can use a mixture of cinnamon and cocoa or unrefined golden icing sugar).

VITAL POINTS TO REMEMBER:

The cream must be at room temperature. If it is too cold the mixture 'sets' the chocolate as soon as they make contact and it goes grainy. If it too hot it doesn't set properly. The chocolate must be about 35°C (within a margin of a degree or two). Again if it is too cold it won't amalgamate with the cream properly – and if it is too hot, it won't set.

DO NOT OVERWHIP the cream – however tempting this may seem. It does not make a good truffe. The correct consistency is gauged the moment the cream begins to thicken but still pouring texture and whisk leaves a faint trail.

I love it on its own but it works well with all sorts of custards and ice creams and fruit purées

Chocolate: the Definitive Guide
GRUB STREET 1999

Richard Ehrlich

Richard Ehrlich has been writing about food and drink since the late 1980s, when he served as Food and Drink Editor of *Cosmopolitan* and *She* magazines. He wrote about food for the *Guardian* and *The Times* and served as drinks columnist for the *Independent on Sunday*. He has written for *Time Out* for many years and has contributed to several other newspapers and Radio 4's *Food Programme*. He is currently the wine columnist for *Good Housekeeping* and a regular contributor to the *Guardian*'s 'Word of Mouth' blog. Winner of two Glenfiddich Awards, he has written five cookbooks.

My Night Behind Bars

INDEPENDENT ON SUNDAY
JANUARY 1997

It's my big night, and I am prepared for it. Sensible shoes. Swiss Army Knife in my trouser pocket. Gary Reagan's Bartender's Bible under my arm. Yes, it's my first night as a bartender.

I figure that bartenders will become as trendy as chefs. And face it, everyone wants to be a chef. That is, they want to watch chefs on TV, buy their books, and hallucinate (after a few drinks) about being able to cook like Rick or Gary. Chefs have the high-glamour image once accorded to lead guitarists.

So why, I wonder, shouldn't bartenders be next? They're in the catering biz; they're cool, young and immensely skilled; they perform a kind of theatre. And what they do, they do far better than the folks at home.

Convinced that I had a ground-floor idea here, I considered enrolling at the London Academy of Bartending. Learning on the job seemed a better idea, so I rang mix-master Dick Bradsell of London's ultra-cool Detroit (35 Earlham Street, London WC2). What Bradsell doesn't know about cocktails is not worth knowing. He seemed the perfect tutor.

"Dick", I said, "I want to learn how to be a bartender."

To my astonishment, no laughter sounded down the line. Dick told me to come on a Tuesday night, which is not one of the busiest. Armed with my accoutrements, I rode the Tube with a head full of fantasies. Shmoozing with the regulars. Performing incredible feats with a cocktail shaker. Perhaps inventing and naming my own cocktail. Splendour in the Glass? Pineapple Paradise Regained? Ehrlich's Energiser?

When Dick started talking, my dreams quickly evaporated. The first thing he'd do if I were a real beginner, he told me, was teach me how to use the till. Then he'd find out whether I knew how to wash and polish glasses, since that's what I'd be doing for my first month on the job. (Some aspirants fade away at this point.) If I made the grade, and showed the necessary social skills, after a while I'd be allowed to open bottles of beer. Maybe even pour them into glasses. Along the way I'd learn basic rules: no smoking, no drinking, no touching my hair or face. Watch all the time, never be still, clear away glasses, wipe spills, check ice. Put things back where you found them. Learn to spot trouble before it happens.

That would all come with my education in bartending. And after a couple of months, he'd train me to become a cocktail bartender. The distinction is an important one.

At around seven, I was furiously taking notes when in walked my first lesson in the art of trouble spotting. Eight suits, and all of them pin-striped. One slapped down a credit card and ordered a round of Labatt's Ice beers. "Eight Labatt's", replied Dick. (That's another rule: repeat the order back to the customer.) Then he turned to get the bottles and whispered, "We're going to hate him, but we have to love him." What did this mean?

Within 20 minutes, all became clear. Another round of beers followed, and then a round of Lemondrops (a shooter based on Absolut Citron vodka). More beers. More Lemondrops. Margaritas. Bottles started breaking. Voices got louder. The staff developed worried looks. I expected to see a few lunches deposited in the ashtrays.

"It's always the suits," Dick said later. "They're the ones who cause trouble." The no-suit policies of some of London's trendier bars began to make sense. A place called RikiTik acquired instant fame when it turned away Quentin Tarantino for wearing a suit. Maybe they thought he'd whip out a .45 after sinking a few Lemondrops.

While keeping an eye on the Suits Behaving Emetically, and helping barman Bill De hOra when things got busy, Dick instructed me in one of the basic skills: measuring. Measures are a big deal in bartending for legal, economic and psychological reasons. When you're serving shots or mixed drinks, you must give no less than the legal measures (25ml). Somewhat surprisingly, you're also forbidden to give anything more (something to do with drink-driving: they don't want over-the-limit drivers pleading innocence because they thought they were drinking ordinary measures).

The economic importance of measuring is obvious. Bars make money selling drinks, and the more they put in each one, the less money they make. Careful measuring is one way round this, but it's time-consuming and lacks theatricality. Bartenders learn to measure by counting instead. Dick showed me how. For a double measure (which is all they serve at Detroit), you count 1-2-2-1-2. The bottle has to be turned straight down for this to work. Dick emptied a bottle of Wyborowa (the house vodka), filled it with water, and let me practise while he attended to business.

Reader, I blew it. My first 10 tries were short, the next 10 slopped all over the bar. I emptied my 50ml into a large water glass after each failure, and since the glass filled up, I drained it as I went along. After a few glasses I noticed a woman watching me. She looked alarmed, and with reason: what she saw was a guy pouring clear liquid from a vodka bottle then drinking it by the half-pint. I grinned at her as if to say, "Don't worry, it's just water". She looked away, and left soon after.

At Detroit measuring is done accurately and honestly. Other places use cheater's tricks. Dick showed me a few. In a mixed drink, like a G&T, the bartender might pour gin over the ice, squirt in the tonic, then add gin to top up. That usually means you're getting one quarter-measure and one half-measure, but the final shot (less diluted) makes it seem strong. Dick has also been in places where the bartender poured into the bottom of the measuring cup, which holds about a teaspoon. "You have to let the customer see what's going into the drink," he says.

Apart from the endless glasses of non-vodka, I poured no drinks. Dick made the offer — a gesture born of kindness, not confidence — but I wanted more practice. We ate dinner — Detroit serves good food — and talked, and at 11.30 I left. On the Tube, I experienced pangs of self-doubt. Was I ready for the big time? Could I count to 1-2-2 1-2? Is the Pope Jewish?

At least I had my book. If I ever got to mix drinks and someone asked for a Presbyterian or a Joumbaba, I'd be ready for them.

2000 TO 2004

FROM Street *food* TO Brain *food*

Clarissa Hyman
Kevin Gould
Fuchsia Dunlop
Nicola Graimes
Xanthe Clay
Sue Lawrence

Clarissa Hyman

Clarissa Hyman, the current Chairperson of the Guild, comes from a family dedicated to eating. Her parents owned a Jewish deli in Manchester and she confesses to being brought up in a pickle barrel, with 'schmaltz in my veins'. Clarissa began her career as a researcher and producer at Granada TV, specializing in factual and lifestyle programmes. She went on to become a highly respected freelance writer on food and travel, writing for publications as diverse as *The Times*, *Country Living*, *The European*, and the *Egon Ronay Guides*. She won the Guild's Food Journalist of the Year Award in 2000 and the Glenfiddich Food Writer of the Year Award in both 2002 and 2007. *Cucina Siciliana* won the Guild's Jeremy Round Award for Best First Book.

Palermo Street Food

Cucina Siciliana
Conran Octopus 2001

At the entrance to the teeming Capo market, near the newly renovated Teatro Massimo opera house of Godfather fame and symbol of Palermo's rebirth as a great European city, a street seller with a prickly pear stubble was doing a roaring trade. Surrounded by an appreciative male audience, he slipped his hand inside a straw basket covered with a cloth, to produce, like rabbits from a hat, steaming fistfuls of offal to slap onto sesame seed buns. From afar, his customers looked as if they were genuflecting, bending forward to avoid grease spots on their jackets and ties.

The souk-like alleys of the market, one of four in central Palermo, are theatrically hemmed in by gangrenous, decaying tenements: buildings randomly display missing rooms, absent ceilings or the loss of an entire floor. Impossible tangles of wires and cables dangle like festive decorations.

Yet, in Autumn, there are fresh green olives, bright and hard, pink flushed garlic, potatoes stacked in perfect size and order or sold boiled along with roasted onions for salads. And all the fruits of Sicily as depicted on the Roman mosaics of Piazza Armerina. The richest of produce in the poorest of settings, and a reminder that the Sicilian artist Renato Guttuso drew the original stark, unsentimental illustrations for Elizabeth David's 'Italian Food'.

The picture of a favourite saint is wrapped around scales on a fish stall. The heavy makeup of the brassy assistant is accentuated by the naked light bulbs of stalls, packed so tight, the awnings filter out the morning light. You pass a shrine encircled by fresh flowers, then a building with its innards exposed to view. The guts of the city. As well as its heart.

At the Mercato di Porta Garini, which segues into the Capo, we passed stalls selling skinned ox feet with nails intact, boiled tongues and bunches of sausages tied with raffia. Baby goats in their furry coats hung by their necks. A man was excising the brains out of a skull. The cheapest of cuts, the obscurest and most esoteric parts of every animal, are boiled together and served to local shoppers. The best place, however, to sample the Palermo speciality, pani cuí la meusa, beef lung and spleen sandwiches, is the Antica Focacceria di San Francesco in the heart of the old Kalsa district, founded in 1834. Once patronised by Garibaldi, Pirandello and Lucky Luciano, it is located opposite the lovely Gothic church of the same name; high ceilings, bow windows, original marble fittings, coloured glass doors and wrought iron chairs give it a Spanish feel. The great cast iron and brass range roaring away under the central counter was, until recently, wood-fired, but now runs on bottled gas.

Behind the counter the soft bread rolls, guastelle, are filled with warmed ricotta (in the microwave, another sign of the times), slivers of offal scooped from a vat filled with simmering lard, a little salt and, as a final touch, caciocavallo grated with what looks like a two-handed hacksaw. The rolls are expressively termed schietti or single when filled with offal only, maritata when accompanied by the cheese; they are chewy and greasy, though not unpalatable, an acquired taste you could learn to crave once a year.

A little later, on our way to the coast, in search of freshly boiled octopus, the colour of Englishmen left too long out in the sun, we screeched to a halt somewhere in the Palermo suburbs. At a makeshift roadside stand kebabs, another legacy of Arabic rule, were glowing over a charcoal brazier. The vendor whipped them off the skewer onto a piece of greaseproof paper, added some salt and a squeeze of lemon. It smelled good, looked like chunks of chicken breast but tasted more savoury, chewier and slightly fatty. "Brava!" roared Michele, who had been watching my reaction closely, "Now, you eat like a real Palermitana!" Real Palermitani, of course, eat stigghiole, veal or lamb intestines.

Back in the city centre, the first hint of winter had come with the appearance of the chestnut sellers on the street. Each had a tall, chimney-like contraption with charcoal in the bottom and a pan on top billowing steam. Michele said they used slow-burning, old wooden railway sleepers for fuel. As we walked through the Piazza Castelnuovo, newly made over with a pavement studded with tiny, inset lights – "Like walking on the stars", exclaimed Rosy – her attention was distracted by another fast food vendor. "That's wonderful! Something I'd never thought I'd see in Palermo – I have to go get one." It was a New York Hot Dog stand.

Panelle Chickpea Fritters

Panelle are popular Palermo street snacks of Arab origin. They are also traditionally eaten, along with arancine and cuccia, a pudding made from whole wheat berries, on December 13th, the feast day of Santa Lucia. On that day, Sicilians avoid all food made with wheat flour in memory of the time they were miraculously saved from famine by the unexpected arrival of a ship laden with wheat. Too famished to wait for the grain to be milled, they cooked it whole.

Makes about 20

250 g (9 oz) chickpea flour

600ml (1 pint) water

salt

a handful of finely chopped parsley

oil for deep-frying

lemon juice

soft bread rolls (optional)

Pour the water into a heavy pan, then steadily whisk in a stream of chickpea flour. Lumps are undesirable.

Add salt and parsley and cook over a medium to low heat, stirring constantly, until it thickens and pulls away from the side of the pan.

Pour the mixture onto a cold surface, ideally a marble slab, and use a wooden spoon or spatula to spread it out wafer thin.

Leave to cool, then cut the paste into small triangles and deep-fry until golden brown.

Sprinkle with lemon juice, and eat at once. Or, sandwich in a bread roll to make pane con panelle.

Kevin Gould

Kevin Gould is one of Britain's most original and passionate food experts, writers and photographers. In 1991 he opened his first shop, Realfood, followed by the retail outlet Joy, an events-catering business, and restaurants The Love Café and The Love Bar. In 2001 his first book *Dishy* was published to great acclaim as a 'retro but revolutionary' new type of cookbook, using flow-charts for recipes; it subsequently won the *Design Week* Best Editorial Design Award. A consultant for many multinational food retailers and manufacturers, Kevin is also a full-time writer on food and food trends, loved for his tongue-in-cheek humour. He writes for many publications, including the *Daily Telegraph* and *Time Out* (as Dr Dishy), as well as several websites. At the Guild's 2003 Awards, Kevin was named Food Journalist of the Year for his work in *Waitrose Food Illustrated*.

Introduction

Dishy
Hodder & Stoughton
2000

Thank you for choosing dishy

All DISHY writing, graphics and recipes are carefully designed to give you confidence around the kitchen.

Dishy ingredients

MUSIC

You need to have your favourite sounds in the kitchen. Like your music, DISHY cooking is about rhythm, relaxation and emotion. Hearing your beats is going to help you cook with balls, style and enjoyment.

A SUPERMARKET

All of the ingredients in DISHY, apart perhaps from fresh truffles and bottarga, which are mentioned twice, are available from any decent supermarket. And there are supermarket alternatives given for truffles and bottarga, anyway, so that's that.

CHOICE SKILLS

You have to choose quality. Quality is not the same as luxury, although there is sensual pleasure in choosing the best ingredients you can find.

You wouldn't choose to go out in a coat that dissolves in the rain, because that would be a waste of money, and you'd get wet. So, for the same reason, you shouldn't choose a rubbish battery chicken if there's a free-range or organic one easily available. Nobody really knows what effect chemicals in food production have on the human body, so choosing ingredients in their most natural state shows that you're interested in looking after number one.

Your body's a machine that needs you to choose quality ingredients (and regular servicing) if it's to give you long-lasting pleasure, so DISHY food helps you look after it. You tiger, you.

READING SKILLS

DISHY people get the habit of checking ingredients labels in the supermarket – all the ingredients you need to get hold of shouldn't contain nasty E's. Too many E's can turn you into your parents. Avoid products where the ingredients read like a chemical formula. Most chemicals are put in foods for the convenience of the producer and the supermarket, not for your convenience.

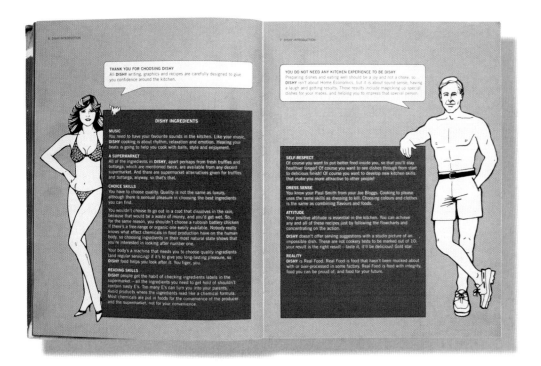

You do not need any kitchen experience to be dishy

Preparing dishes and eating well should be a joy and not a chore, so DISHY isn't about Home Economics, but it is about sound sense, having a laugh and getting results. Those results include magicking up special dishes for your mates, and helping you to impress that special person.

SELF-RESPECT

Of course you want to put better food inside you, so that you'll stay healthier longer! Of course you want to see dishes through from start to delicious finish! Of course you want to develop new kitchen skills that make you more attractive to other people!

DRESS SENSE

You know your Paul Smith from your Joe Bloggs. Cooking to please uses the same skills as dressing to kill. Choosing colours and clothes is the same as combining flavours and foods.

ATTITUDE

Your positive attitude is essential in the kitchen. You can achieve any and all of these recipes just by following the flowcharts and concentrating on the action.

DISHY doesn't offer serving suggestions with a studio picture of an impossible dish. These are not cookery tests to be marked out of 10: your result is the right result – taste it, it'll be delicious! Gold star.

REALITY

DISHY is Real Food. Real Food is food that hasn't been mucked about with or over-processed in some factory. Real Food is food with integrity, food you can be proud of, and food for your future.

Quality Smoked Salmon with Cos Lettuce, Caperberries and Fresh Limes

Option

Serves 4

½ lime
200 g slices of wild smoked salmon
handful of caperberries
black pepper

About 12 small leaves of a cos lettuce, or a little gem (if you like).

Squeeze the juice from the lime and season with freshly ground black pepper. Place it in a mister like the one you use to spray plants or your ironing.

Using the mister, spritz the salmon lightly with the lime juice and arrange on serving plates.

Alternative option

Place a slice of smoked salmon inside each lettuce leaf – if you're into the lettuce.

Using the mister, spritz the lettuce and salmon lightly with the lime juice and arrange on serving plates.

Garnish with the caperberries and tell your posse that you're getting jiggy with it.

IMPORTANT NOTICE

Avoid the cheapo smoked salmon if you can – it's almost guaranteed to be greasy, dyed crap. Many of the farmed fish lead awful lives, and are fed a daily diet of antibiotics, anti-fungals and E numbers to colour them pink. A real salmon's normal diet includes tiny shellfish, which pink them up nicely, and lots of exercise, which keeps them lean. Most fish farms find that their salmon are so crammed into cages, and get so flabby as a result that they have to be starved for two or three days before being lifted. Otherwise, when they're smoked, they drop up to five litres of oil per fish, an inconvenience that puts out the smoking fires and makes the salmon taste like hand cream ...

Real wild salmon is increasingly rare and very expensive. It tastes kind of gamier than the farmed variety, and costs kind of ten times the price. Lottery winners should apply to Harrods Food Hall, where they should ask for a side of Mr Forman's best wild, two dozen Belon oysters, and some vinegar for the inevitable chip on their shoulder. Salmon 'ranched' in Scottish sea lochs is a good substitute, especially if they've been fed organic food.

Capers are flower buds that grow against walls in hot, sunny countries. They're usually pickled in brine or vinegar and left on the side of finished pizzas, together with the chewy, burnt crusts.

Caperberries grow if the bud of the caper is not picked, and the resultant flower is fertilised. Caperberries taste more subtle than capers, and their interesting shape and texture makes them useful as a kind of posh olive.

Fuchsia Dunlop

Fuchsia Dunlop read English Literature at Magdalene College Cambridge and later studied at Sichuan University and the School of Oriental and African Studies in London. She trained as a chef at China's finest cooking school the Sichuan Institute of Higher Cuisine. In 2002 her *Sichuan Cookery* won the Guild's Jeremy Round Award for Best First Book. Fuchsia writes about Chinese cuisine and culture for various publications. In 2006 she was named Journalist of the Year by the Guild, and in 2009 *Shark's Fin and Sichuan Pepper* won the Jane Grigson Award.

Sichuan cooking

Observer Food Monthly
10 June 2001

The affair began one September day in 1993. My friend Zhou Yu invited me to lunch on my first visit to Chengdu, the capital of China's Sichuan Province. We ate in a modest restaurant near the bus station, a small place tiled in white like a bathroom, with a few tables and chairs and nothing on the walls. I can still remember every taste of that delicious meal. The preserved eggs, with their green-and-yellow yolks and amber whites, cut into segments and arranged around a pile of chopped green peppers like the petals of a flower. Cold chicken chunks, tossed in a piquant dressing of soy sauce, chilli oil and Sichuan pepper. A whole carp, braised in a sauce of chilli-bean paste laced with the heady fragrances of ginger, garlic and spring onions. And fish-fragrant aubergines, a dish which remains my personal favourite, the golden, buttery fried aubergines cooked in a deep red spicy sauce with hints of sweet and sour. Later, as we sat in a riverside teahouse sipping jasmine blossom tea, the sunlight danced through the leaves of sheltering trees, I realised I had fallen in love. I would have to return to Chengdu.

A year later it was my fond memories of eating in the city which brought me back to Chengdu. I was there ostensibly to study at the university but I had only to step outside the campus to be overwhelmed by the hubbub of sprawling teahouses, bustling restaurants and vibrant lanes. Every morning I would be seduced anew by the scent of frying *guo kuei*, pinwheel pastries with a spicy pork filling and a scattering of toasty sesame seeds. A hundred yards or so from the door of my room, just beyond a side gate of the university, was a market overflowing with fresh and seasonal produce. Fish leapt and eels wriggled in tanks of water, ducks and chickens squawked in their pens. Vegetables and fruits were piled up in great bamboo trays: water spinach and bamboo shoots, garlic stems and bitter melons, seasonal treats like three-coloured amaranth leaves, loquats and 'spring shoots', the tender leaves of a local tree. One stall sold a dozen different types of beancurd; others displayed great sackfuls of glossy red chillies and pink Sichuan pepper.

The restaurants around the university offered delicious food at incredibly modest prices. At lunchtimes I often sat outside a tiny noodle shop paying about 20p to slurp a bowlful of 'sea-flavoured noodles' in a scrumptious soup of dried shrimps, mushrooms and bamboo shoot, or gulp down the infamous 'dan dan noodles' in their fiery sesame sauce. In the evenings I devoured twice-cooked pork and pock-marked mother Chen's beancurd with plenty of stir-fried vegetables and plain steamed rice. At first it was hard to get used to the visible cruelty of Chinese cooking. In the markets, rabbits would be skinned alive, live paddy eels impaled on a nail and stripped of spine and innards, chickens and ducks plucked when scarcely dead. Chinese cooks would prepare living ingredients as if they were vegetables, with no thought of any suffering. Interestingly, the Chinese word for animal, *dong wu*, simply means 'moving thing'; it seems to carry no connotations of breath or spirit like the English 'animal' and its European relations. Some of this cruelty still disturbs me, but at least it's honest: and much less hypocritical than the cruelty of the British food industry where consumers buy their meat safe and sanitised while the animals languish in battery pens.

Every day brought new gastronomic discoveries: perhaps a street vendor specialising in a type of traditional dumpling I hadn't encountered before, or a peasant with a basket filled with some unusual seasonal fruit. It wasn't long before I decided I had to learn how to cook some of the local dishes, and I was delighted to find out that Chengdu was the home of one of China's finest cooking schools. I set out on my bicycle one day to find it, and knew I had arrived when I heard coming from a window above me the sound of fast, regular chopping, and the gentle hum of china spoons in china bowls. I wandered in and found myself in a room filled with dozens of apprentice chefs, all engrossed in learning the art of sauces. Some pounded Sichuan pepper to a powder with iron pestles, others fine-chopped pale garlic and golden ginger stems. A teacher sat nearby, sniffing and tasting the dark liquids in their crucibles, jotting down marks in a little notebook. By the end of the day I had come to a deal with the staff of the school. They would provide a cooking teacher and an interpreter as well as all the raw ingredients, and I would pay them the equivalent of about £5 each for a class.

For the next month I took twice-weekly private classes at the school. The class teacher, Gan Guojian, a brilliant cook took me through the methods for several famous local dishes, such as 'fish-fragrant' pork slivers and Gong Bao chicken. In every class I would tackle a couple of recipes, learning the basics of cutting and marinating, and trying my hand at the wok. The cooking classes were the highlight of my week and so I was delighted when, some months later, I was invited to enrol as a regular student on a full-time chef's training course. This was a great privilege as no foreigner had ever done this. The school's leaders

please turn to page 152 ●◆

Fish-fragrant Aubergines *yu xiang qie zi*

The following recipe is a Sichuan classic and one of my personal favourites. More than any other dish, for me it sums up the luxuriant pleasures of Sichuan eating. The sauce is sweet and sour and spicy, with a reddish hue and a visible scattering of chopped ginger, garlic and spring onion. The dish is equally delicious hot or cold. I usually serve it to guests with a meat or beancurd dish and a stir-fried green vegetable, but it makes a fine lunch simply with brown rice and a salad.

Serves 4 – with three other dishes

600–700 g aubergines (2 decent-sized aubergines, or a good handful of slender oriental aubergines)

salt

groundnut or corn oil for deep-frying

1 ½ tsp Sichuanese chilli bean paste

3 tsp finely chopped fresh ginger

3 tsp finely chopped garlic

150 ml chicken or vegetable stock

1 ½ tsp unrefined golden granulated sugar

½ tsp light soy sauce

¾ tsp potato flour, mixed with 1 tbsp cold water

1 ½ tsp Chinkiang or Chinese black vinegar

4 spring onions, green parts only, sliced into fine rings

1 teaspoon sesame oil

Cut the aubergines in half lengthwise and then crosswise. Chop each quarter lengthwise into 3 or 4 evenly sliced chunks. Sprinkle with 1 ½ teaspoons of salt and leave for at least 30 minutes to draw out the bitter juices. If you are using oriental aubergines, simply slice them in half lengthwise and then into 7–8cm sections – there is no need to salt them.

In your wok, heat oil for deep-frying to 180–200°C (at this temperature it will just be beginning to smoke). Add the aubergines in batches and deep-fry for 3–4 minutes until slightly golden on the outside and soft and buttery within. Remove and drain on kitchen paper.

Drain off the deep-frying oil, rinse the wok if necessary, and then return it to a high flame with 2–3 tablespoons of oil. Add the chilli bean paste and stir-fry for about 20 seconds until the oil is red and fragrant; then add the ginger and garlic and continue to stir-fry for another 20–30 seconds until they are fragrant. Take care not to burn the flavourings – remove the wok from the heat for a few seconds or turn down the heat if necessary.

Add the stock, sugar and soy sauce and mix well. Season with salt to taste, if necessary.

Add the fried aubergines to the sauce and let them simmer gently for a few minutes to absorb some of the flavours. Then sprinkle the potato flour mixture over the aubergines and stir in gently to thicken the sauce. Next, stir in the vinegar and spring onions and leave for a few seconds until the onions have lost their rawness. Finally, remove the pan from the heat, stir in the sesame oil and serve.

❧ *continued from page 149*

were particularly kind in allowing me to pay the same price as the other students – a little more than £100 for a three-month course. I think they were intrigued and rather touched by a foreigner's passion for their cuisine. On my enrolment I was issued with chef's overalls, two textbooks (in Chinese) and a personal cleaver, which I was expected to keep razor sharp by frequent visits to the enormous whetstone in the yard.

For three months I studied cookery every day with 45 young Sichuanese men and three young women. Professional kitchens in Sichuan are very male-dominated: women are rarely trusted with a wok, and if they are allowed to prepare food it is usually the cold dishes, which are assembled and seasoned in a separate room. None of my classmates at the cooking school had ever previously met a foreigner and most weren't quite sure how to deal with it. In the beginning they avoided addressing me directly, and if they did pluck up the courage to talk to me, they would call me 'foreigner'(*lao wai*). It took a couple of weeks before I could persuade some of them that I actually had a name.

Every morning I'd cycle across the city from my flat to the cooking school, picking up a couple of hot steamed buns or dumplings for breakfast on the way. The first part of the day, which began at about 8.30am, was spent in the classroom, listening to a lecture on the dishes of the day. Our teacher would take us through the minutiae of ingredients and cooking methods, scribbling diagrams and Chinese characters on the blackboard, answering our questions about cutting methods and oil temperatures. All our classes were taught in Sichuan dialect, and I struggled to keep up in the beginning. Fortunately some of my classmates would help me out when I got stuck, translating things I didn't understand into Mandarin, and jotting down vital Chinese characters in my notebook. Every student would be casually carrying around a lethally-sharp cleaver, which took some getting used to. To begin with I retained my European view of the cleaver as a murderous knife – it was only later that I began to appreciate it as the subtle, versatile instrument that it really is. (The cleaver is usually the only knife in a Chinese kitchen, and it is used for every kind of cutting, from peeling ginger and garlic cloves to chopping through meat and bone; the flat of the blade is also used for crushing pieces of ginger to release their juices, and for scooping up cut foods and transferring them to the wok.)

After the morning break we would reassemble in the demonstration room. Our teacher would start by tackling the raw ingredients, showing us precisely how they should be chopped and marinated. Our teachers' skills with the cleaver were mesmerising. I remember watching one teacher, Long Qingrong, showing us how to remove the bones and innards from a duck. She made a small incision through the neck and spine and then proceeded to undress the bird, casually removing the entire skin and flesh as she chatted, coaxing out the leg- and wing-bones, wielding the huge knife as delicately as if it were a scalpel.

For stir-fried dishes, every pair of eyes was riveted on the smoking wok. Sichuanese cooks are famous for their skill of *huo hou* (the control of degree and duration of cooking heat). Every dish would have its own *huo hou* requirements. 'Dry-fried' foods like beef and paddy eels would be stir-fried over a moderate heat until they yielded up their moisture and became partially dry and exquisitely fragrant. Sichuanese chilli and broad bean paste would always be 'fried fragrant' (*chao xiang*) in oil just hot enough to extract its deep red colour and sumptuous taste.

In the afternoons it was our turn to try. In groups of 10 we would prepare our raw ingredients, and then each of us would take our turn at the wok. As we worked, our teachers walked around the room, ticking us off for careless or irregular cutting. The art of cutting is fundamental to Chinese cooking. We had to learn all the different knife techniques, and the myriad of different shapes into which food can be cut. There were 'horse-ear' slices of pickled chilli; slivers, cubes and chunks of meat and poultry, 'fish-eye' slices of spring onion, wafer-thin 'ox-tongue' slices of radish and lettuce stem. The cooking itself was a very public affair. The person actually cooking would be surrounded by the rest of the team, who would jeer or giggle if anything went wrong. 'Too much oil!' 'It's all dried-out!' 'The sauce has gone all sticky!' I was always under particular scrutiny, and it was a great satisfaction when my dishes turned out well and impressed my classmates.

Researching Sichuanese food has been a ceaseless pleasure. But it has also had its complications. Like everyone else, I started out in China with my own cultural prejudices, my own food preferences and taboos, which all had to be dismantled, one by one. But the more I learn about China's food culture, the more fascinated I become. Nothing written about Chinese food in the West gives any idea of the grand scale, diversity and sophistication of Chinese cuisine. We might have heard about the four great regional cuisines of China, but we don't realise that almost every country town seems to have its own culinary speciality. We might know that the Cantonese 'eat anything that moves', but we don't really appreciate the cutting, flavouring and cooking techniques which can create innumerable different taste experiences from even the most common ingredients. There's a restaurant in Leshan, the southern Sichuanese city famed for its giant Buddha statue, which serves over 40 different dishes made with the fine local beancurd. And that's by no means extraordinary. So next time you dine on sweet-and-sour pork and egg-fried rice in a British Chinese restaurant, please don't forget that that is just the tip, the merest, tiniest tip of the iceberg.

Nicola Graimes

Nicola Graimes has been an editor, journalist and author for over twenty years and has written numerous books based on health, nutrition, organic food and children's diets. She has been editor of *The Vegetarian*, *Vegetarian Living* and *Good Food Retailing*. In 2002 her *Great Healthy Food for Vegetarian Kids* won the World Gourmand Best Children's Cookbook in the UK. In 2004 her *Brain Food for Kids* also won the same award as well as Best Family Cookbook. Most recently, in 2008 her *Children's Healthy and Fun Cookbook* won the Best Family Cookbook in the UK.

Meal Times

Brain Foods for Kids
CARROLL & BROWN 2004

BREAKFAST

For mental clarity, sustained energy levels and concentration, it's not just what children eat that matters but when. Children are particularly vulnerable to dips in blood sugar levels that can lead to mood swings, irritability and poor attention. Regular healthy meals, supplemented by nutritious snacks and sufficient fluids are crucial throughout the day to maintain steady blood sugar levels.

It is now widely recognised by nutritionists, and supported by research, that children who eat a decent breakfast perform better at school. Breakfast is seen as the most important meal of the day since it replenishes vital brain nutrients and blood sugar (glucose) levels that have become depleted overnight. Research also shows that skipping the first of the meal of the day can lead to an unhealthy pattern of snacking on high-fat, high-sugar foods.

Many studies show that, compared to children who do eat breakfast, those who skip this meal do not perform as well in areas such as numeracy, problem solving, information recall, and language skills. This is because the body needs fuel on waking and when it doesn't get the sustenance it needs, it switches to survival mode and only releases energy for emergencies. Lack of concentration and poor memory are both indications that the brain is struggling due to a lack of fuel.

In the main, it is believed the positive influence of breakfast on brain function is because the meal is usually based on carbohydrates – breakfast cereals and toast are good examples. Cereals are often fortified with vitamins and minerals, including B vitamins and iron, which help with energy production. They also provide glucose, which is the main fuel for the brain, while the milk poured over cereals is a good source of calcium, B-group vitamins, zinc and magnesium.

Controversially, there is also research to suggest that a protein-based breakfast is more successful in stimulating the brain and satisfies the appetite quicker and for longer than a carbohydrate meal. This may be because a protein-based meal encourages the release of chemicals that increase alertness and boost reaction times so foods such as eggs,

milk, yogurt, beans and fish may play a greater role in getting the brain fired up in the morning. The best policy, since the ratio of protein to carbohydrate is unknown, is to make sure you include both in each meal, and that includes breakfast.

LUNCH   A wholesome lunch, whether it be home-cooked, a packed or school lunch is vital for maintaining energy levels, sustaining memory, concentration and learning for the rest of the day. School meals have been the target for criticism for some time and, while many local authorities have addressed these concerns by ensuring there are healthy options, it has been found that where children are able to select their own lunch, particularly at secondary school level, these are often ignored.

When time is short, it is often difficult to be inspired about packed lunches and easy to get stuck in the 'sandwich, crisps, chocolate bar and an apple' rut. Variety is key; try offering different types of fruit, half an avocado, kiwi fruit, cubes of melon or dried fruit, for example. There are plenty of different kinds of bread to choose from such as tortilla, mini rolls, bagels, ciabatta or muffins. A flask is perfect for holding soup for a warming winter lunch, or try rice, potato or pasta salads.

Following on from the controversial research that suggests breakfast should include a higher ratio of protein food to carbohydrate, some nutritionists believe that lunch should adopt similar guidelines. Protein foods are believed to be better for mental stimulation and alertness and will help to avoid the mid-afternoon dip in energy that many children experience.

SNACKS   In the past, dieticians have discouraged eating between meals but there is mounting evidence to suggest that children need little amounts of food and often. In fact it's good for children to have a couple of snacks – albeit healthy ones – during the day to keep blood sugar levels steady. Avoid the short-term kick given by high-fat, high-sugar snacks and drinks. The sugar-high is followed by a sugar-slump, often resulting in mood swings and irritability. It may also be beneficial to provide a carbohydrate-based snack such as toast, muffin or crumpet, an hour or two before bedtime since carbohydrates facilitate the production of the calming brain chemical serotonin. A snack will also keep hunger at bay during the night since dips in blood sugar levels may be the reason for a child waking in the night.

DINNER   Originating from the same study that suggested we should eat more protein at breakfast and lunch is the finding that dinner should include a higher proportion of carbohydrates to protein. Carbohydrates such as pasta, rice, couscous and potatoes, trigger the release of the brain chemical serotonin, which is said to induce feelings of calm and encourage sleep. If your child is particularly active at the end of the day it could be well worth increasing the amount of carbohydrates they eat at this time. However, don't forget the importance of protein too. It's vital to eat a variety of protein foods to get a balance of the essential amino acids that have to be provided by diet and that are necessary for building the brain's messengers. Opt for good quality organic meat, fish, eggs, beans, lentils, cheese, nuts and seeds. For many children, this is the main meal of the day and it can be an opportunity to encourage your child to top up their intake of fruit and vegetables to reach the recommended daily intake of five portions.

Fruit and Nut Clusters

Most breakfast cereals contain excessive amounts of sugar and perhaps surprisingly salt – a bowl of corn-flakes contains more sodium than a packet of crisps! Try making this crunchy cereal – it's a type of granola that's a mixture of fruits, nuts, oats and seeds that will provide plenty of sustained energy for the day ahead. You can easily adapt this recipe to include favourite dried fruits and nuts.

About 20 portions

100 g (¾ cup) whole hazelnuts

60 g (scant ½ cup) blanched almonds

3 tbsp omega blend oil or sunflower oil

6 tbsp honey

250 g (1¼ cups) whole porridge oats

70 g (½ cup) sunflower seeds

35 g (¼ cup) sesame seeds

100 g (¾ cup) chopped dried dates

100 g (¾ cup) ready-to-eat unsulphured dried apricots, roughly chopped

milk or live bio yogurt, to serve

Pre-heat the oven to 140°C (275°F). Place the hazelnuts and almonds in a plastic bag and crush with a rolling pin until roughly broken. Place the crushed nuts in a bowl with the oats and seeds.

Heat the oil and honey gently in a saucepan until the honey has just melted. Stir the mixture into the oats, nuts and seeds.

Spoon the mixture in an even layer on two baking sheets and bake in the oven for 25 minutes, stirring occasionally, until golden and slightly crisp (the mixture will become more crispy as it cools).

Transfer to a bowl and mix in the dates and apricots, then leave to cool. Store in an airtight jar until ready to eat. Serve with milk or bio natural yogurt.

Xanthe Clay

Xanthe Clay studied at Leith's School of Food and Wine before setting up and running the kitchen in Bath's fashionable Raincheck Bar. Since 1999 she has written a popular column in the Weekend section of the *Daily Telegraph*, testing and commenting on readers' recipes. She also contributes to *Olive* and *Good Food* magazines. In *It's Raining Plums*, Xanthe compiled the best contributions to her Readers' Recipes columns based on seasonal fruit and vegetables. It was voted one of the most useful cookbooks of all time by *Waitrose Food Monthly*.

Strawberries

It's Raining Plums
MARTIN BOOKS 2002

For all that strawberries seem quintessentially English, evocative of Wimbledon, Eton mess, strawberry jam with cream and scones, they're actually of exotic parentage. A hybrid of the large but otherwise undistinguished yellow South American pine strawberry and the tiny intensely flavoured wood strawberry, the strawberry which we know was developed in England in the early nineteenth century by Mr Keens of Isleworth. So the strawberries which Jane Austen's Emma gathered at Mr. Knightley's were the little woodland varieties, coaxed and cultivated to be a little larger, or the slightly bigger Alpine wild strawberry imported from the continent, but nothing like the apricot sized strawberries we eat now.

The best strawberries of all are a variety called "Mara des Bois". Dark red and on the small side, they have the intense flavour of wild strawberries and the texture of cultivated ones. In the market at the Var town where we stay in the summer the mara des bois are piled separately from the rest of the strawberries. Even amongst so much excellent produce, these have a special status, and despite being more expensive, I know I must arrive early to have a chance of finding them. Although mara des bois have a long season, from July to October, the tiny amount imported into this country goes to the restaurant trade. So pester your greengrocer to pick up a box when he sees them at market: as the Michelin guide might say "*il vaut l'effort*".

Part of the joy of strawberries is the look of them: this is why we still buy early or out of season strawberries which are unscented and unlikely to taste of much. Of course, we hope to be lucky, as one sometimes is, and win the flavour lottery. But I doubt we would risk it were they less seductive looking, plump and shiny and lipstick red, promising sweetness and soft juiciness. If you do have a haul of rich tasting fruits, pile them in a deep blue glass bowl, and place them on the table where their voluptuous shape and colour can be enjoyed for a few hours, along with the sweet perfume drawn out by the warmth of the room. Cheaper than a bunch of flowers and far more enticing.

Rosewater Cake, Strawberries and Cream

This easy cake with its slightly crunchy glaze is lovely by itself for tea, or like this, piled with strawberries for pudding.

Serves 8-10

6 oz (170 g) butter

6 oz (170 g) unrefined golden caster sugar

3 eggs

½ lb (225 g) self raising flour

6 tbsp rosewater

½ lb (225 g) icing sugar

1 tbsp lemon juice

1 ¼ lb (600g) or so strawberries, sliced in half if large

300 ml double cream, whipped until softly billowing

Pre-heat the oven to 180°C (350°F, Gas 4)

Grease and base line an 8 x 10 in (20 x 25 cm) cake tin.

Cream the butter and sugar until pale, then beat in the eggs one by one. Mix in the flour, then 4 tbsp rosewater. Turn into the tin, spread out and bake for 35-40minutes.

Leave in the tin while you mix the icing sugar, remaining rosewater and lemon juice to make a glaze. Prick the still warm cake all over with a fork and pour over the glaze.

Remove from the tin when cold and cut into squares or fingers. Serve the cake with strawberries and cream, or for a more dramatic effect, stack the pieces in a pyramid, dollop on a little of the cream and tumble over the strawberries.

Scatter with rose petals, either fresh from unsprayed, garden roses, or crystallized, and serve with the rest of the cream.

Pimms Jellies with Orange Cream and Strawberries

A British summer in a glass, the orange cream balances the alcoholic bite of the Pimms.

Serves 6

175 ml Pimms

3 sheets gelatine

400 ml lemonade

juice of half a lemon and half a lime

½ pint double cream

grated rind of an orange

2 tbsp unrefined golden caster sugar

½ lb strawberries and peeled segments of two oranges

mint sprigs and borage flowers

Soak the gelatine in cold water until soft. Heat half the lemonade until just about boiling, remove from the heat and stir in the gelatine.

When the gelatine is dissolved, add the Pimms, lemon and lime juice, and the rest of the lemonade.

Pour through a sieve into a bowl and refrigerate until set.

Lightly whip the cream and stir in the sugar and orange rind. Slice the strawberries.

To serve, dollop some jelly in a glass, and top with strawberries and orange segments. Finish with a blob of the orange cream and a long sprig of mint tucked in the side.

Sue Lawrence

Sue Lawrence, who served as the Guild's President from 2003 until 2008, began her cooking career in 1991 when she won Masterchef. She now writes in magazines, journals and books, championing the food of her native Scotland, and can regularly be seen talking about Scottish food and traditions on British and Australian TV. Her latest book, *Taste Ye Back*, features interviews with prominent Scots all over the world, talking about their childhoods and the strong bonds they developed with the food they ate as children.

Tablet

Scots Cooking
HODDER HEADLINE 2000

The scene is a large garden somewhere in Scotland on a warm summer afternoon, circa 1965. The occasion is the church garden fête. I remember queuing up (probably in my best cotton frock) at the cake and candy stall with my 3d [240d in a pound] to buy a bar of tablet before the fête had even been opened. And I was not alone. Tablet, neatly wrapped in waxed paper, was first to sell out at any fête, and the people in the queue stretching past the bric-a-brac and tombola stalls invariably ignored the lady in the big hat who was officially opening the fête, as they politely attempted to edge up the queue a little more.

These days, when invited to help at my church fair or coffee morning, I am often asked to help on the cake and candy stall. It might be inside a hall instead of outside on rolling lawns, but the spirit is the same. The tablet is always first to go – and there is never enough.

Almost unknown south of the border, tablet is one of Scotland's oldest types of confectionery. It is rather like fudge with a bite to it. Marion Lochhead refers to it in her book, The Scots Household in the Eighteenth Century: 'Barley-sugar, tablet, crokain [from the French croquant = crunchy] are all old and honourable Scots confections. Tablet might be made simply by boiling a pound of sugar in two gills of water until it candied; with cinnamon or ginger added for flavouring.' By 1929, when F. Marian McNeill wrote her book, milk had been added, for her recipe requires granulated sugar, thin cream or milk and flavouring. For the latter, she suggests cinnamon, coconut, fig, ginger, lemon, orange, peppermint, walnut or vanilla.

Having been brought up on plain tablet, I like it with just the merest hint of vanilla, pure and simple. If ever there was a childhood memory to evoke happy thoughts of sunshine, laughter and lush green gardens, it is an indulgent bite of tablet. I leave the rather more rarefied confections such as madeleines to Proust.

see recipe overleaf ◗◆

Tablet

Makes 16–20 bars

125 g (4½ oz) unsalted butter

1 kg (2¼ lb) unrefined golden granulated sugar

300 ml (10 fl oz) full-fat milk

pinch of salt

200 g (7 oz) tin of condensed milk

1 teaspoon pure vanilla essence

Place the butter in a large heavy-based saucepan (only a reliable pan should be used, otherwise the tablet mixture will stick) and melt over a low heat.

Add the sugar, milk and salt and heat gently until the sugar has dissolved, stirring occasionally.

Bring to the boil and simmer over a fairly high heat for 8–10 minutes, stirring often (and making sure you get into all the corners with your wooden spoon).

Add the condensed milk, stir well, then simmer for 8–10 minutes, stirring constantly. The mixture should bubble, but not too fiercely. After 8 minutes, test if it is ready. It should have reached the 'soft ball' stage, which means that when you drop a little of the mixture into a cup of very cold water, it will form a soft ball that you can pick up between your fingers. On a sugar thermometer; it should read 115°C (240°F).

Remove from the heat at once and add the vanilla (or other flavourings). Using an electric hand-held beater, beat at medium speed for 4–5 minutes, just until you feel the mixture begin to stiffen a little and become ever so slightly grainy. You can, of course, do this by hand but it will take at least 10 minutes and it is hard work!

Pour immediately into a buttered 23 x 33 cm (9 x 13 in) swiss roll tin and leave to cool. Mark into squares or oblongs when it is almost cold. When completely cold, remove and store in an airtight tin or wrap the pieces individually in waxed paper.

2005 TO *present day*
Sugar & Spice, Pies *and* Puddings

Hugh Fearnley-Whittingstall

Richard, Earl of Bradford

Mridula Baljekar

Lewis Esson

Patrick Anthony

Mark Hix

Hugh Fearnley-Whittingstall

Hugh Fearnley-Whittingstall, who began his career in food as a sous-chef at The River Café, is widely known for his uncompromising commitment to seasonal, ethically produced food. In 1997 his first TV series, A Cook on the Wild Side: TV Dinners, in which he famously feasted on human placenta, established him as a unique commentator on the food scene. Hugh started living in the original River Cottage in Dorset in 1998, and *The River Cottage Cookbook* has won several awards. *The River Cottage Meat Book* won the André Simon Food Book of the Year Award and *The River Cottage Fish Book*, jointly written with Nick Fisher, won both the André Simon Food Book of the Year Award and the Guild's Michael Smith Award for Work on British Food.

Hit the Sweet Spot

The Guardian Weekend
28 march 2009

This morning, when you lazily stirred a spoonful into your tea or scattered a little over your cereal, you were toying with something once so precious it was known as 'white gold'. Millions were enslaved to feed our craving for the stuff, and at one point it was so rare it was used only as a condiment or even a medicine. Then, in the 18th century, as sugar started to pour in from our tropical colonies, we Brits became dizzy with a sugar rush unrivalled by any other nation. It was whipped, moulded, shaped and sculpted into sweet, sophisticated fantasies to mark the climax of every class-conscious feast. Sugar was the very hallmark of elegant living. And talking of hallmarks, we staked our claim in the social hierarchy of sugar-lovers with a fetishistic range of silver nips, sifters, casters, sieves and tongs.

But now, incredibly, the very word 'sugar' is so debased, reviled even, that "sugary' is synonymous with insincerity and phoneyness. Well, there's nothing fake about this week's recipes in the fourth part of my Cupboard Love series. I'm celebrating sugar. It's uplifting, cheering and, as builders everywhere know, energising. It adds sweetness, certainly, but it rounds out other, more complex flavours, too.

Organic golden caster sugar is the one I use most, both at home and in the River Cottage kitchen. Less refined than regular white caster sugar, it's still super-fine and can be speedily whipped into butter or egg whites to create the lightest of cakes and meringues, or swiftly dissolved into liquids to make everything from cocktails to cordials and sorbets to syllabubs. Granulated gives more of a crunch, as does the toffee-ish demerara, making them perfect for sprinkling on to fruitcakes or biscuits to create a toothsome topping. Light muscovado has a creamy, caramely quality, and its honeyed sweetness is great in baking and a good addition to crumbles. But it also adds an extra depth of flavour to roast vegetables, particularly those, such as carrots and parsnips, that are inherently on the sweet side. Sprinkle on a teaspoonful or two about 10–15 minutes before the end of their cooking time and you'll see what I mean. Dark muscovado, meanwhile, is the big hitter, adding a huge whack of fudgy, rummy flavour to gingerbreads and fruit cakes. It's rich in natural molasses, moist and fragrant, and – an added bonus – it gives a better keeping quality to cakes.

Sweet is one of the five fundamental tastes (along with bitter, salty, sour and umami, that complex one best described as savoury), so sugar is added to all kinds of things to balance and round out flavour to make things taste more 'of themselves' – rather than simply to add sweetness. Think of the classic sweet-sharp flavours of rollmop herrings and chutneys, and the impact of adding a pinch of sugar to vinaigrette or tomato sauce to bring it into the realms of perfection. This week, I'm falling for the bitter-sweet charms of potatoes in a classic Italian agro-dolce dressing.

When you're shopping for sugar, go for the real, unrefined, preferably fairtrade, deal when you can: Billington's (billingtons.co.uk) and the Co-op have good ranges – look for 'golden caster' and 'golden granulated'. And don't be fooled when buying brown sugars: not all brown sugars are equal – some are brown on the outside and white on the inside, in other words little more than refined white sugar given a paint job with a bit of caramel or molasses. So look for the words 'unrefined' and 'muscovado': this is the good stuff, rich in its own complex, natural flavours. Sweet.

Brown Sugar Meringues

Don't be nervous about making meringues: just ensure that both bowl and whisk are scrupulously clean and dry, and add the sugar slowly, beating like fury after each addition, until the mix is wonderfully glossy and stiff. These are crisp on the outside and chewy inside, just as meringues should be.

Makes 10–12

3 egg whites, at room temperature

90 g unrefined golden caster sugar

90 g unrefined light muscovado sugar

Pre-heat the oven to 110°C (225°F, Gas ½). Line two baking trays with parchment paper.

Whisk the egg whites to stiff peaks. Add the sugars a tablespoon at a time, whisking well after each addition, until the mixture goes thick, smooth and glossy. This thorough beating ensures that the sugar is properly incorporated and you get perfect, light meringues without a hint of graininess. Spoon mounds of meringue mix – around a tablespoonful each – on to the baking trays, spacing them well apart, and bake for about 2 ½ hours, until the meringues have dried out.

Lift them carefully off the parchment and cool on a wire rack.

Serve sandwiched with whipped cream or ice-cream, broken up and folded into Eton Mess or fools, drizzled with melted chocolate, sprinkled with nuts...

Jamaican Ginger Cake

Serve this warm as a pudding or cold as a cake, in good, thick slices. It will keep in an airtight container for up to a week.

Serves 8–10

50 g unsalted butter

80 g unrefined dark muscovado sugar

100 g black treacle

100 g golden syrup

50 ml dark rum

50 g preserved stem ginger, finely chopped, plus a little of its syrup

1 egg, lightly beaten

150 g self-raising flour

1 tsp ground allspice

1 tsp ground ginger

1 pinch salt

Pre-heat the oven to 180°C (350°F, Gas 4). Grease a loaf tin, round baking tin or oven-proof frying pan that's about 22 cm in diameter, and line with baking parchment. Lightly grease the paper.

Put the butter, sugar, treacle and syrup into a medium saucepan and heat gently until melted and combined. Leave to cool a little, then stir in the rum and chopped ginger, followed by the egg.

Sift together the flour, allspice, ginger and salt, then add to the pan. Stir until smooth.

Pour into the lined tin and bake for 40-45 minutes, until a skewer inserted into the centre comes out clean.

Leave to cool in the tin. Once cool, brush some syrup over the top of the cake for extra, delicious stickiness.

Richard, Earl of Bradford

Richard Thomas Orlando Bridgeman, 7th Earl of Bradford is a creative restaurateur with a passion for great food. Porters English Restaurant opened in 1979 and in many ways anticipated the current vogue for putting traditional British dishes back on the nation's tables. The restaurant has enjoyed critical acclaim for a generation and aims to sustain the values of honest pricing and high-quality food. Richard wrote *The Eccentric's Cook Book* and, with Carol Wilson, *Porters English Cookery Bible* and *Porters Seasonal Celebrations Cookbook*. Lord Bradford is a former President of the Master Chefs of Great Britain.

Pie in the Sky

SAVOUR
THE GUILD OF FOOD
WRITERS' MAGAZINE
APRIL 2009

Once upon a time I had a dream, to open a reasonably priced, real English restaurant in central London, not aimed at the posh end of the market, but to create somewhere with the fun atmosphere and friendly service of an American style eatery, ensuring at the same time that it was family friendly as well.

In 1978 I owned and helped to run a delightful and thriving French restaurant, Bewicks in Walton Street. But, after two years of considerable success, including gaining a star in the prestigious Egon Ronay Guide in 1977 – 'young, eager and enthusiastic management has transformed this Chelsea restaurant' – I had realised that, with a mere 48 covers, it was too small to make serious money. Therefore I put it on the market, and looked for a site to realise my English dream.

At that time the Covent Garden area was in a fair state of turmoil, as the fruit and vegetable market, where Eliza Doolittle had sold her flowers in My Fair Lady, even though the film was actually all shot in a studio in Hollywood, had closed down and was being redeveloped.

However, its location seemed brilliant to me, in the heart of Theatreland, with Fleet Street, in those days where most of the major newspapers had their offices, just down the road, well served by London Underground and bus services and plenty of businesses around, and so I concentrated my search there.

When details came through for a large premises in Henrietta Street, a mere 100 yards from the main market, with a glorious frontage of Victorian tiles and polished wood, it seemed more than perfect, absolutely ideal.

The natural English product to concentrate on, trying to compete with the Italian pizza or the American hamburger, in my view, was the pie – an infinite variety of possible fillings and toppings, capable of being prepared in bulk and easily served as an individual dish. The pies would naturally be accompanied by mashed potato, and the menu would also contain a wide choice of those wonderful British 'nursery' puddings.

Not one to leave things to chance, I engaged a company to conduct a feasibility study into the public acceptability of such a concept, using focus groups.

Unfortunately we discovered that it was thought by many to be too restrictive, and we therefore adapted it to include starters and non-pie dishes main courses as well.

So what was I to call this restaurant that was going to transform the image of real English food into something popular and accessible for families on an eating out budget? Many permutations were put forward, until the very simple suggestion of Porters seemed perfect to everybody, especially in relation to the close proximity of Covent Garden Market.

In my view, the only time that you can promote a restaurant successfully is when it opens, and therefore we devoted consideration to both press and radio advertising and an active PR campaign, as a result we got off to a reasonably busy start.

However, exactly a year later, Covent Garden Market re-opened, and we were completely swamped with business; our footfall went up over 60 per cent in the first week, and didn't stop there, because we got used to working at a quicker pace, and, as we learnt how to speed everything up, we were able to get even more customers through.

As a consequence of the level of trade, we decided to drastically alter the menu, going for exactly what the focus groups had apparently told us wouldn't work – all pies and puddings - and within a short time we didn't look back, as everything was massively simplified by that. Some days we were doing over 1,000 customers, absolutely unbelievable and a huge success.

The greatest mistake that any restaurant can make is to coast along, thinking that everything is working perfectly. Hopefully we have never been guilty of that at Porters, even though there were difficult times; especially in the five years after 1981 when my much loved father died, at the comparatively young age of only 69.

Porters has altered a lot from those early days, as we have adapted to circumstances, including changing the name to Porters English Restaurant – something deceptively simple that has reaped far ranging and unexpected benefits, as you would find if you put the two words 'English restaurant' into Google Search.

Steak, Guinness and Mushroom Pie

Still the all time favourite pie at Porters since Porters opened in 1979.

700 g (1 ½ lb) chuck steak, cut into 4 cm (1 ½ in) cubes

2 medium onions, 1 finely chopped, 1 thinly sliced

25 g (1 oz) butter

50 g (2 oz) seasoned flour

1 tbsp sunflower oil

150 ml (5 fl oz) Guinness (or red wine)

300 ml (10 fl oz) beef stock

bouquet garni

salt and black pepper

275 g (10 oz) button mushrooms

275 g (10 oz) puff pastry

beaten egg to glaze

Melt 25 g (1 oz) butter in a casserole dish, add the onions and cook gently for 10 minutes, until soft and golden brown. Remove from the dish and put to one side.

Toss the steak in the seasoned flour patting off excess.

Add the oil to the casserole dish, increase the heat and brown the meat in batches of 6-8 cubes at a time.

Drain the excess oil from the dish. Return onions and steak to the casserole, increase the heat and add the Guinness (or wine), bring to the boil and continue to boil for 1 minute.

Add the stock, bouquet garni, salt and pepper, return to boil, cover and then place in the oven, Gas 3 (170°C) for 1½ hours.

Add the mushrooms and cook for a further 1–1½ hours or until the steak is extremely tender.

Check the seasoning, remove the bouquet garni and allow to cool. For maximum flavour this process is best done the night before. Store in the refrigerator, but remove 1 hour before baking.

When ready to cook the pie, pre-heat the oven to Gas 7 (220°C). Spoon the steak mixture into a 1.2 litre (2 pint) pie dish. Roll out the pastry slightly larger than the pie dish. Moisten the rim of the dish and place the pastry on top sealing the edges well. Cut away the excess pastry and knock up the edges.

Brush with beaten egg and cook for 30–40 minutes until the pastry is crisp and golden brown.

Mridula Baljekar

Mridula Baljekar was born and raised in Assam, North East India. On moving to England she turned her childhood passion for cooking into a successful career. Her first book, *The Complete Indian Cookbook*, published in 1990, sold nearly a million copies worldwide. Many books and a television series followed, and in 2006 *Great Indian Feasts* won the Gourmand World Cookbook award as the Best Asian Cookbook in the World and Cookery Book of the Year.

Great Indian Feasts
JOHN BLAKE 2005

Makes 350 g (12 oz)

1 small ripe, pineapple

4 tbsp vegetable oil

¼ tsp each black mustard seeds, cumin seeds, fennel seeds, onion seeds

5–6 fenugreek seeds

1½ tsp ground cumin

1 tsp ground coriander

1–3 tsp chilli powder

25 g (1 oz) seedless raisins

25 g (1 oz) unsalted raw cashews

1 tbsp crystallised ginger, finely chopped

1½ tsp salt or to taste

125 g (4 oz) unrefined light muscovado sugar

1 tbsp white wine or cider vinegar

Pineapple Chutney

Quarter the pineapple, peel, then remove the 'eyes'. Remove the central core and cut the quarters into smallish chunks.

Heat the oil over a medium heat and add the mustard seeds. As soon as they start crackling, throw in the cumin, fennel, onion and fenugreek seeds. Let them all sizzle for 5–10 seconds.

Add the pineapple and the remaining ingredients, except the vinegar, stir and reduce the heat to low. Cook gently for 45–50 minutes, stirring occasionally.

Add the vinegar, stir and remove from the heat. The pineapple should remain in small soft chunks. Transfer to a hot sterilised jar. It will keep well without refrigeration for 4–5 weeks, but refrigerate once opened.

Makes about 450 g (1 lb)

450 g (1 lb) cranberries

2 tbsp olive oil

½ tsp each black mustard seeds and cumin seeds

2–3 star anise

1–2 fresh red chillies, chopped

½ tsp hot chilli powder

½ tsp ground cumin

50 g (2 oz) seedless raisins

75 g (3 oz) unrefined light muscovado sugar

½ tsp salt

Spiced Cranberry Chutney

Perfect with traditional roast turkey, kebabs, venison and pork sausages.

Using the pulse in your food processor, roughly chop the cranberries.

In a heavy saucepan, heat the oil over a medium heat. When hot, but not smoking, throw in the mustard seeds, followed by the cumin and star anise. Let them sizzle for 15–20 seconds.

Add the fresh chillies and cook for 30 seconds, then stir in the chilli powder and ground cumin.

Add the raisins, cranberries, sugar and salt. Mix everything together and cover the pan with a lid. Reduce the heat slightly and cook for 6–8 minutes. Remove from the heat and fill in a hot sterilised jar. Refrigerate once opened.

Lewis Esson

Lewis Esson, one of the country's most experienced editors, worked for various publishing companies in both London and New York. After an interlude running the Pan Bookshop in Chelsea and a high-class deli in Mayfair, he returned to publishing with an increasing focus on food, as editor of several partworks and as Editorial Director at Octopus Books and then Macdonald Orbis. Working freelance, he has since edited and project-managed many award-winning food books and was Contributing Editor of the English language-edition of *Larousse Pratique* and of *The Good Cook's Encyclopedia*. Lewis, author and co-author of several books, including *Breakfast at the Wolseley* with AA Gill, was Chair of the Guild from 2004 to 2005.

Eggs

Breakfast at the Wolseley
QUADRILLE 2008

THE PERFECTLY SCRAMBLED EGG

Check the use-by date of the eggs as, if they are not that fresh, adding any milk or water to them may make the results too watery. Ideally have the eggs at room temperature (or temper them in some warm water from the tap for a couple of minutes, if straight from the fridge).

In a mixing bowl, lightly beat 2–3 eggs per person (depending on their size) with salt and pepper to taste. You can – if your eggs are fresh enough – add a couple of tablespoons of water or milk or cream at this stage. As it turns to steam, it is said to lighten the result; the milk or cream can make the eggs creamier, but purists say that the cooked milk solids toughen the results and can add an unwelcome flavour.

Gently heat 15–30 g butter per person in a heavy-based (preferably non-stick) pan until melted. Try to match the size of the pan to the quantity of egg; you don't want too high a proportion of the mix to be in contact with the bottom, or the eggs will cook too rapidly. A 20 cm pan is ideal for 3–4 eggs; 25 cm for 6–8 eggs.

Add the eggs and briefly increase the heat, then lower it again after a count of ten. Start stirring the eggs as they turn opaque. Continue to cook gently, stirring fairly constantly (leaving intervals between stirs allows the formation of larger curds, which some prefer) until the eggs are just short of the ideal creamy texture and are not in any way set.

Remove the pan immediately from the heat, still stirring, as you want the residual heat in the pan to finish the cooking of the eggs.

A spoonful or two of double cream stirred in at this stage not only adds texture but will also lower the temperature and help stop the eggs overcooking. If you think it necessary, you can also put the bottom of the pan in some cold water.

Season again, if necessary, serve and eat immediately.

Note One way of ensuring really fluffy scrambled eggs is to beat an extra egg white per person until it stands in soft peaks, then fold that into the whole-egg mixture before cooking.

If necessary, the poached eggs will keep in the bowl of cold water for several days. When you are ready to use them, just lower them into another pan of gently simmering water for up to 2 minutes to re-heat.

Eggs need ideally to be really fresh for good poached eggs, so that the egg keeps its shape in the water. If your eggs aren't that fresh, one good trick is to pop them in the freezer for about 15 minutes, so that the whites get much more viscous.

Bring a large, heavy, shallow pan of water to a steady gentle simmer and add 1 or 2 dessertspoons of distilled vinegar. As with boiled eggs, the amount of vinegar placed in the water will allow a 'tight' form and presentable shape: the white will not wander or separate from the yolk. Do not add salt, as this will toughen the egg. The best vinegar to use is a distilled clear vinegar. Avoid all malt or herb vinegars as the flavour will dilute the flavour of the egg and could also be transferred to it.

Crack the eggs into heatproof teacups or saucers, then lower into the water and slip them out onto the simmering surface. Once they are all in (don't poach more than 4 eggs at a time or they reduce the water temperature too much), cover with a lid and leave undisturbed for 3 minutes. It is important that the water is still moving; this stops the eggs from sinking to the bottom or cooking unevenly and will facilitate their removal. Some people advocate swirling the water around in a vortex to help shape the eggs, but this only works for 1 or 2 eggs, and it shouldn't be necessary if the eggs are fresh enough and the handling and cooking sufficiently gentle.

At the end of this time, check on the eggs. If they are properly cooked, the whites will all be opaque and the yolks just visible through a veil of white. If not, put the lid back on for another 20 seconds or so until the eggs are cooked. Because the contents of the eggs are in more direct contact with the hot water, the timing of poached eggs is not as affected by the size of the eggs as in the case of boiling.

Lift the eggs out quickly with a perforated spoon. If not serving them immediately, carefully place them into a bowl of iced water to stop the cooking process. If serving them straight away, a quick dip in fresh warm water can help lessen any vinegar flavour, if that is important.

Once they are cold, you can, if you like, lift the eggs carefully out of the water and neaten their appearance by trimming off any ragged bits of white.

Omelettes at The Wolseley are very simple: only eggs and seasoning are used. The best are made by cooking with gas as you have more control over the heat. If using an electric hob, be prepared to take the pan off the heat as necessary.

Beat the eggs together, but not too much, or they will be heavier and more watery. Pour into a very clean and dry pan coated with just a film of melted butter. It should be hot enough for the butter to have stopped foaming, but should not be smoking.

As the curds cook, use a spatula to draw the outer edges into the middle, allowing uncooked egg to flow into contact with the hot pan. Add any seasoning at this stage. Any earlier, and the salt will cause the eggs to toughen and become watery.

The aim is to get a nicely set and coloured underside and a top that is still just slightly liquid, so that the finished omelette will be what the French call baveuse, or 'dribbling', when you dig an impatient fork into it. When sufficiently cooked, add any filling and fold one-half of the omelette over the other.

As well as the inner consistency, there are two types of finish, depending on the degree of overall cooking: the golden brown and the pale, light and fluffy.

There are many other variations on these final stages. The omelette can be folded inward in thirds, or have one-third folded in and then the omelette tipped out on a plate to fold the remaining third underneath, producing a long, narrow omelette.

When plated, allow your omelette to stand for a minute or two, depending on the temperature of the room.

Patrick Anthony

Patrick Anthony was born in Dublin, trained in catering management but went into the theatre. This led eventually to a career in television where, on a thin news day, he demonstrated the making of Irish coffee, which resulted in a regular Friday night live recipe spot, 'Patrick's Pantry'. Sky TV poached him to co-host a daily magazine programme with Tony Blackburn, after which he joined the inaugural Ready Steady Cook team for one series but remained for eight years, usually paired with fellow Guild member Richard Cawley. Other activities include six years of a daily recipe column for *Express Newspapers*, a monthly column for *Eastern Daily Press*, ten books, including several *Ready Steady Cook* books, and a weekly radio show for BBC Eastern Counties.

The Rye Royal Scallop Festival

THE SATURDAY TELEGRAPH
24 FEBRUARY 2007

From the battlements of the 900 year old St. Mary's Church tower in the beautifully preserved Sussex town of Rye, the view below and all around reveals a treasure trove of medieval, Tudor and Georgian buildings lining the quirky, often cobbled, narrow streets which have enchanted visitors and travellers for generations. Even Elizabeth I, when she graciously agreed in the summer of 1573 to be entertained in what is known today as the Old Custom House, was said to be so delighted by her visit, on departing, she renamed the town 'Rye Royal'.

Today the royal presence that contributes to the town's economy is the King Scallop taken from Rye Bay in the season from November to April and enthusiastically celebrated by the annual Rye Bay Scallop Festival enabling around 16 local restaurants over ten days in February to display their skill and ingenuity in presenting this great delicacy. Interestingly, the classic chef and cooks handbook *Le Repertoire de la Cuisine* lists but a scant half-dozen recipes for the mollusc and perhaps it's yet another indication of how adventurous cookery has become in the UK to note that there are some forty different dishes on offer during the festival, including what I think must be the most far-reaching expression of fusion cuisine I've ever seen – 'Darjeeling-infused Scallops served with Bok choi, Venere rice and Pistachio oil' – giving us India, China, Italy and Asia Minor together on one plate!

Former marine diver and now fish and shellfish merchant, John Botterell supplies many of the local restaurants and considers scallops to be 'sexy – one of those ingredients which brightens up the whole approach to spring'. More seriously, in reply to the question concerning the current emphasis on sourcing 'hand-dived' scallops he declares 'there is no way scallops can be hand-dived in Rye Bay: apart from the hazard of shipping traffic, there is a huge volume of tide that sweeps up and down along this area of the eastern channel which goes through a bottleneck at a rate of knots and it's this highly active nutrient-rich flow rushing through the scallop beds which promote their successful growth….unlike some sensitive areas elsewhere, up at this end of the country the sea bed tends to have a sort of shale and stony bottom and there isn't much life there other than basically scallops, the only other notable features being a lot of ordinance from the last war.'

Asked about sustainability, he explained that the fishermen in Rye have a voluntary code under which if the catch rate per tow drops below a certain amount up to the month of May they cease dredging until the middle of November, which enables the breeding season to function successfully and ensure the continuing supply.

Of all the Rye Bay scallops caught in a season 80 per cent of the total catch goes directly to Boulogne market and it's hoped that events like the festival will encourage appreciation here at home, even though they will always be expensive. The high investment costs required to land them plus the fact that every 32 kilo sack yields just about 5 kilos of edible meat will ensure that they remain a luxury treat.

The recipe below is my variation on a dish served in the formerly great Maxim's of Paris; it's very simple to achieve and utterly delicious.

Scallops with Saffron Cream

8–10 prepared scallops

1 dsp oil

50 g butter

1 shallot, finely chopped

good pinch of crushed saffron stamens, steeped in 3 tbsp of hot water

1 dsp cognac

2 tbsp dry vermouth

2 tomatoes, skinned, seeded and chopped

4 closed cap mushrooms, trimmed of stalks and finely sliced

4 tbsp double cream

1 tsp soy sauce

salt and pepper

plain boiled long-grain rice to accompany

1 tbsp finely chopped parsley

Rinse the scallops under cold running water, pat dry and slice in half to create discs. If the coral (roe) is present, remove before slicing.

Heat a wok or sauté pan; add the oil and about 20 g butter followed by the scallop discs plus roe if using. Briskly stir-fry for about 1 minute then tip into a waiting bowl.

Wipe out the wok or pan with kitchen paper and return to a moderate heat. Add the remaining butter and the chopped shallot, and allow to cook gently for a couple of minutes, then introduce the saffron liquid, the cognac, the vermouth, tomato, mushrooms, cream and soy sauce. Gently stir together and allow to bubble up and thicken slightly (2–3 minutes).

Add the reserved scallops (plus any coral) and lightly season. When warmed through (about 30 seconds) serve with the boiled rice and, with your usual flair, sprinkle the finely chopped parsley over the scallops and saffron-scented sauce.

Mark Hix

Mark Hix trained as a chef under Anton Edelman and Anton Mosimann and, aged just 22, became Head Chef of The Candlewick Room restaurant, the only one in the City to be awarded a Michelin Red M. From there he went on to become Executive Chef for the Caprice Group and, in 2008, he opened two restaurants of his own. Mark has won several awards for his column in the *Independent on Saturday Magazine* and in 2005 his *British Regional Food* won a Special Commendation at the André Simon Awards and the Guild's Michael Smith Award for Work on British Food. In 2009 *British Seasonal Food* won the Guild's Cookery Book of the Year Award.

Elvers in crisis

British Regional Food
QUADRILLE 2006

You may well have heard of the elver-eating competitions in and around Frampton in Gloucestershire, but sadly those celebrations have long since died away, as the tiny elvers, or glass eels (so called because they are almost translucent), have become an increasingly rare commodity. The life story of the eel is a mysterious one, and completely opposite to that of the salmon. The eel begins its life as larvae in the Sargasso Sea – a lens of warmer water on the surface of the Atlantic off the American coast – and then makes a long (up to 3 years') journey piggy-backing on the Gulf Stream to our rivers. There it matures and then heads back across the ocean to spawn and begin the cycle all over again. After their astounding transatlantic journey, the baby elvers, still only about the length of a matchstick, arrive in the rivers like the Severn around May to June each year.

Richard Cook and his father Horace have been in the elver business for some years now and from their stories, it's been a cut-throat one too. On our visit to Westbury on Severn, the season was just under way and the elvers were few and far between. For two evenings, we joined Dave, a hardened elverman, on his fire-lit tump (patch) on the banks of the Severn during one of the highest spring tides of the year. We waited until full high tide, about 9.30pm. Elvers have to be caught at night because they are negatively phototactic, meaning that only the lack of light will bring them to the surface and close to the banks.

Dave had a good fire ablaze, made from a couple of old wooden pallets, to keep us warm, and he had a few tins of cider for his expected guests. In a couple of hours, he had caught about 30 elvers, which amounts to about 100 g. Because they're now so scarce, the price is high and the guys on the bank could get as much as £300 per kilo for their catch. In the height of the season, a good fisherman can weigh in a few kilos, which makes a pretty good living for part-time fishing.

In case you are worrying about such fishing when the elvers are in such desperate decline, it is all well controlled and the majority of the catch from here goes live for breeding in China, Japan and parts of

Europe, including Lough Neagh in Northern Ireland, where Father Kennedy runs a cooperative, restocking the loughs with the Cooks' elvers. Richard then buys them back at their adult stage for smoking at the Severn and Wye Smokery. This final stage completes the eels' life cycle. Isn't it mad to think that you'll pay up to £300 for a kilo of elvers, yet you can go and buy the smoked eel at a fraction of the price!

The elver station that Horace has set up in Chaxhill is crucial to the future of the eel. He has about 12 tanks in which elvers are housed once they weighed in. In fact, demand for the tiny eels was so high a few years ago that they bought a plane to transport the things to their destination. I could write another book on the elver stories and, sadly – or perhaps thankfully, in the circumstances – the demand for them, at least here, is diminishing. At that price, what do you expect?

We've always served them in the restaurants simply with olive oil, garlic and a hint of chilli, but Horace showed me the local way, which I've since got rather hooked on. I did add a little something to the local recipe, though, that Horace welcomed, especially when I told him how much they pay for it in London. That little addition was some wild garlic leaves, the season had just started, and Horace and Richard drove us to the local woods in search of them before we had our elver feast.

The first thing you need is some good fatty bacon, and Gloucester Old Spot pigs produce just that. I cut it into thin strips, leaving all the

please turn to page 182 ●◆

Bakewell Pudding

Makes one 20 cm pudding

150 g puff pastry

250 g butter, melted

1 egg, beaten, plus 7 extra egg yolks

250 g unrefined golden caster sugar

1 tbsp ground almonds

3 tbsp raspberry jam

Pre-heat the oven to 190°C (Gas 5). Roll the pastry out to a thickness of about ⅓ cm and prick it all over with a fork to prevent it rising, then use to line a 20 x 3 cm deep, preferably sloping-sided, tart tin (I use an ovenproof non-stick frying pan, as this seems to be as close to the original as you can get). Leave to rest for 1 hour in the fridge.

Meanwhile, in a mixing bowl, mix the butter, egg and extra yolks with the sugar and almonds, and stir over a pan of simmering water for 3–4 minutes until it reaches a honey-like consistency.

Spoon the raspberry jam evenly over the bottom of the chilled pastry case, then pour the almond filling into the pastry case and bake the pudding for 45 minutes, or until the top is golden and the filling just set. If it's browning too much, turn the oven down halfway through.

Serve the pudding warm or at room temperature, with or without some cream.

❧ *continued from page 181*

fat on, and gently cooked it in a frying pan for a few minutes to release the fat. I then turned the heat up, dropped the elvers in with some torn garlic leaves, seasoned them well, then added a couple of beaten eggs. You just stir in the egg to lightly coat the eels and bacon. I dished this up for Horace with some local Weston's cider, and he was in heaven.

BAKEWELL
AND ITS FAMOUS
PUDDING

My journey last year to Bakewell managed to kill two birds with one stone, as I managed to catch some nice wild brown trout while we were there. A semi-culinary party were invited by Lord Edward Manners to stay in the delightful Haddon Hall for the weekend above the old original fourteenth-century kitchens and to fish the Wye. As you've probably noticed, most of my research trips involve a spot of fishing, and when there is a highly sought-after river involved, why not?

We returned most of our catch, except for a couple of nice fish on the last day, which fellow chef Raymond Blanc and I cooked with some locally gathered wild herbs like sorrel and wild garlic. Raymond knocked up a classic *truite au bleu* in the fishing hut with fish straight out of the water, which is the whole idea of the dish. I had only ever eaten *truite au bleu* a couple of times, and that was with farmed fish, so it was a treat to have the dish caught by me and cooked by Raymond.

After everyone left to return south, we went in search of the famous Bakewell Pudding, even checking into the Rutland Arms Hotel, once the White Horse, where the pudding was supposedly first created.

The story goes that the Bakewell Pudding was first made by accident in the White Horse in 1860. Although, strangely enough, a book I have on my bookshelf by Eliza Acton, dated 1845, has a recipe for Bakewell Pudding and describes it as being a popular dish throughout the North, not only in Derbyshire, so the story may well be a bit of a myth. Whoever devised it, the recipe became so popular that, in 1860, Mrs Wilson, wife of a tallow chandler, set up a business making these puddings in her home, which is now the Original Bakewell Pudding Shop.

Although we think we found the original Bakewell Pudding Shop in the square, there were also a couple more also claiming to be the original. I bought a pudding from each and they all seemed to have modest traces of almond essence, although all were quite tasty.

One thing is clear, early recipes don't mention almonds. Acton uses citrus peel but no pastry, whereas modern Bakewell Puddings do, and that suggests the recipe has been altered over the years with ingredients that were possibly then in short supply or not available. However, the Bakewell Tart, which seems the popular variation outside of Bakewell, is quite far removed from the pudding, and more of a frangipane tart, unlike the pudding, which is more of a clafoutis cum custard tart.

On the future *of* Food & Food *writing*

Jenni Muir

Emma Sturgess

Carla Capalbo

Caroline Stacey

Lulu Grimes

Jenni Muir

Jenni Muir, a graduate of Le Cordon Bleu cookery school and former student of the Culinary Institute of America, is a freelance journalist and editor, writing regularly on food, restaurants, shops, hotels, and food-related health issues. A regular contributor to *Time Out* magazine and guides, she is also Editor of *Time Out London Eating & Drinking Guide*, for which she reviews in excess of 150 restaurants a year. When not writing about restaurants, the Australian-born writer can be found travelling the UK investigating hotels, spas, cookery schools and food producers, and editing the cookbooks of various well-known chefs. Jenni has also written *A Cook's Guide to Grains* and *The Guest List*, an inspirational guide to destination hotels around the UK and Ireland, selected by Channel 4's Richard and Judy as one of their top Christmas books.

Colleĉtable Food Books
TIME OUT
NOVEMBER 2007

Flashback 1994. I'm nosing around popular Cambridge bookshop Galloway & Porter when I come across a pile of cookbooks at knock-down prices. One is by a chef I'd seen recently in *Sainsbury's Magazine*. Maybe there'd been an overrun at the printers, or a problem with storage space in the warehouse. Maybe the book simply wasn't selling as well as the publishers had hoped and they decided they had to get rid of some. In any case, here was a stack of them on sale at £7.95 instead of the published price of £17.99. More than a tenner off and a pristine hardback, too. I'll have that, I thought.

Within a few months that same book, *Roast Chicken and Other Stories* by Simon Hopkinson with Lindsey Bareham, had won the Glenfiddich Award for Food Book of the Year. A couple of years ago, *Waitrose Food Illustrated* claimed it was the 'most useful recipe book ever written' and sales of the newly designed paperback edition leapt into the *Bookseller* Top 50 chart. Suddenly there was interest in the original hardback.

As I hadn't found it especially useful, my copy spent much of its life slumbering along with several other cookbooks in dusty boxes at the Big Yellow Self-Storage Company. But it turns out all that beauty sleep was worthwhile; copies of the first edition now change hands for £125–£155 and mine's in very good nick. The yellow sticker that's still on the front, '£7.95', just makes it more valuable, to me at least.

Back in 1994, the book trade was very different to today. Amazon was unheard-of, and a supermarket was the place to buy baked beans, not the latest bestselling novel or autobiography. Sainsbury's and other supermarkets published their own brands of cookbook from time to time, but no one headed there, as they can now, in expectation of being able to snare the latest Delia Smith or Nigel Slater at 50 or 75 per cent off the cover price. But while the publishing industry seems intent on devaluing its brand-new releases, so that the public perceives them as only slightly more valuable than plain paper stationery, the market for well-written, well-kept secondhand cookbooks is steadily rising.

I've no intention of selling my copy of *Roast Chicken...*, but, like those punters on 'Antiques Roadshow', I find myself compelled to consult secondhand dealer Jonathan Tootell. His company, Gardener & Cook, which specialises in books on food and gardening, has just opened a concession on the lower-ground floor of Foyles on Charing Cross Road. Not only has he sold two *Roast Chicken...*s for well over £100 each recently, he's found increasing demand for the book Simon Hopkinson has subsequently revealed is his favourite, Richard Olney's *French Menu Cookbook*. But even given the nature of media hype a secondhand copy of this work will set you back just £30, even if it is in good condition.

Also on display are books by Hopkinson's *Roast Chicken...* co-writer Lindsey Bareham, a former food editor of *Time Out* magazine. *Onions Without Tears* and *In Praise of the Potato* are priced at £50 and £65 respectively. 'Most of the rare and expensive stuff tends to be very good writing,' Tootell explains. 'Lindsey Bareham hardbacks are now very hard to find and she's an extremely good writer. You've got her *Big Red Book of Tomatoes* too? Gee!'

I'm delighted, and make a mental note to speak to my husband about rewriting our will. Enthusiasts like me, who won't sell their good stuff, inadvertently help keep the prices of the most desirable books at a premium. They don't even have to be hardcover editions. There's a fat paperback called *Cuisine Bon Marché* currently on Amazon at £120. Tootell spent four years hunting for his beloved copy, and has subsequently had it signed to him by the author; there's no way he's selling. I (as usual) picked mine up for a song in a discount shop because, at the time, hardly anyone was interested in little-known *Telegraph* contributor, Hugh Fearnley-Whittingstall.

Tootell first began collecting cookbooks around 15 years ago and has been running Gardener & Cook for almost two years. The shelves at Foyles hold only about ten per cent of his stock, so it's worth enquiring, as many chefs do, if there is something you are looking for.

Twentieth-century cookbooks make up the bulk of the food range, as Tootell knows most about that field, but there are also antiquarian titles (many more in the gardening section), and books discussing food-related social history, restaurants and agriculture. His special favourite is an American book called *Manifold Destiny: The One! The Only! Guide to Cooking on Your Car Engine!* Yes, that is actually while driving.

He also has a soft spot for vintage paperbacks by Elizabeth David featuring illustrations by John Minton. Tootell pulls out *French Country Cooking* and *Mediterranean Food,* which were originally priced at 3/6 and 2/6, as the covers show: 'They make great presents if you don't want to spend a great deal. We have lots of them and they're in such good nick.'

The condition a book is in can have a greater effect on the price than its scarcity. Many homes in Britain have copies of classics such as Reader's Digest's original *The Cookery Year*, and *The Times Cookery Book* by Katie Stewart, but they will be battered, torn and stained with oil and stock, because they are so useful. Naturally when a much-loved family reference finally gives up the ghost, people want a clean replacement, but they're not easy to find. Victorian favourite *Mrs Beeton's Book of Household Management* is readily available, but which edition, what condition and at what price? Tootell has various copies: a first edition for £900 ('but it's not a great copy; a really good one would be about £1,500'), a second edition for £350 or so, and a 1968 leather-bound facsimile of the first edition for £100.

As with all aspects of retail, the internet is changing the way people buy secondhand books. Whether you're looking to sell or buy, there are potential pitfalls. The web's inflated some prices, says Tootell, because it's made people more aware of the scarcity of some cookbooks. Titles that a dealer or expert buyer would pay a fiver for in secondhand shops not too long ago are now advertised at 'ridiculous' rates. On the other hand, the fact that a book is offered at a high price doesn't necessarily mean it will sell for that, and – as Tootell explains – the next person to come along with a copy will try to undercut it.

There's the hype factor to take into account, too. Since Marco Pierre White's appearance on 'Hell's Kitchen' this year, prices for his books have gone a bit bonkers. *White Heat* – an iconic work the world over, in which Bob Carlos Clarke's photographs of Marco and his brigade in the kitchen at Harvey's are as important as the recipes – has always been a bit of a collectors' item, and a signed hardback first edition now costs £200–£250. Suddenly, too, *The Mirabelle Cookbook* has been advertised on eBay for £100–£150. And, he adds, if you're looking for something to use in the home kitchen, Marco Pierre White's *Canteen Cuisine* (from the former Chelsea Harbour restaurant co-owned by actor Michael Caine) has far more accessible recipes than the tricky Michelin-star-calibre dishes of *White Heat*. This kind of advice shows that Tootell is more enthusiast than dealer. When asked what titles would make a great wedding or special birthday present, he doesn't just roll off a list of impressive names at premium prices, but wants to know what type of cook the recipient is, whether they like to read about food or would prefer reliable recipes for the kitchen. He wants the books to be used and enjoyed. 'We select books partly because they're rare and valuable,' he says, 'and partly because they're just great books.' It's proof that, just as 'Antiques Roadshow' and all those boot-sale programmes on daytime TV advise, the most satisfying things to collect and invest in are the things you love.

Emma Sturgess

Emma Sturgess began writing about food for her university newspaper and developed a relish for restaurants that led to a column in *Metro* newspaper. She trained with Darina Allen and Rory O'Connell at Ballymaloe Cookery School in Cork and has worked in enough professional kitchens to know she's isn't cut out for it, but can't quite bring herself to get rid of her whites. She believes that food is one of the most fascinating, diverse and enjoyable subjects a writer can have. Emma writes on food for books, the trade and consumer press, and online, including *The Guardian* and *Metro*. She won the Guild's Restaurant Reviewer of the Year Award in 2009.

The Restaurant Experience

FRAME MAGAZINE
SPRING 2009

Great eating-places have never just been about the food. The most conventional measure of restaurants, the Michelin Guide, judges only what's on the plate, but it can be no coincidence that what's on the plate generally comes with a side order of atmosphere, razzmatazz or pomp. Unless you live in a thrilling megawatt-lit otherworld, the chief appeal of most restaurants is that they have more atmosphere than your house.

As the frequency with which we eat outside the home has increased, so have the chances of getting a decent feed. And, as good food slowly becomes the minimum qualifying standard (there will always be exceptions, and sometimes only bad food will do), our attention turns to the wider experience. As the old restaurant proverb really should have it, you can only build the giant goldfish wall once the dim sum is good.

The restaurant experience starts not with the guest sitting down at their table, but with them securing that table in the first place. Devoted restaurant-goers either find this anticipation intoxicating or infuriating; either way calling at an allotted time, exactly one or two calendar months ahead of the desired booking, is part of the accepted ritual of high-end dining. El Bulli, in Roses, Spain, is regarded as the best restaurant in the world and opens for a fleeting time each year. In 2009 there will be only 136 services, between June and December, for around 50 covers a time. Hopefuls emailed their requests for tables during one week last year, and a stack of El Bulli rejections is a badge of honour for enthusiastic restaurant collectors.

This kind of exclusivity is an inevitable consequence of the way in which chef Ferran Adria develops and serves his menu, and he seems genuinely regretful that more customers can't enjoy it. But brazenly elitist reservations policies, operated via unlisted booking lines and two-tier walk-in systems, can also add greatly to the potency of the experience. Having beaten the system, the customer will be fully primed to enjoy their lunch. People who are spending their own money on a hard-won table will fight incipient disappointment all the way.

The idea of restaurant as theatre may have its roots in the golden days of guéridon service, when salads were dressed and desserts flambéed tableside. Crepes suzette have apparently been flamed with a flourish since being invented at Monte Carlo's Café de Paris in 1894. On the high street, the flambé trolley's successors are teppanyaki hotplates and conveyor-belt sushi, but fine dining junkies can now get their fix at a chef's table. Once, kitchens were secret places where, it was imagined, coarse and sweaty cooks swore and scratched; you'd no more want to see it in action than eat in a cowshed. Since television deified the men in whites, made the nitty-gritty of their jobs a matter of public record and their skills sexy, customers want to get as close to them as possible.

Gordon Ramsay's restaurants are famously tasteful, bordering on bland, so it's no surprise that his customers have reacted with particular enthusiasm to the excitement of a ringside seat. Four of his London restaurants, and several sites abroad, offer views over the pass and interaction with the chefs, along with all the comforts of your own private dining staff. It's expensive and exclusive, making money, power and privilege just as significant as the blue fin tuna carpaccio with pickled white radish. In Las Vegas, the ultimate showtown, Restaurant Charlie offers two great-looking ways to get in on the action. Downstairs at the kaiseki bar, 21st-century sushi chefs take their part in the tradition of before-your-very-eyes preparation, while celebrities in town for the night relish the privacy of the 18-seat set-up. Upstairs, there's a seating oddity, jutting out above the hobs and burners: the 'kitchen table sky-loft'. This elevated private table dispenses with the sometimes awkward dynamic of the chef's table – no accidental eye-contact between professional and voyeur – by offering a mezzanine view of the kitchen in full swing.

Whether you're pawing at the chef's veloute-soaked sleeve or studiously avoiding eye contact with anyone who professes to be there to serve, the restaurant experience is about other people. A welter of other customers create atmosphere and take the pressure off the table of two. A surprising amount of diners would rather wait for food, yell their orders and fight to pay the bill than suffer the indignity of being the only table in the place. That's why basement dining rooms, which prospective customers can't see first, can suffer even in the good times.

Service style, attitude, even uniform (designers who have dabbled in staffwear include Michael Kors, Hugo Boss and Zac Posen) can also alter perceptions dramatically. Offhandedness and idiocy strike killer blows, just as small kindnesses can breathe life into a dying dinner. But it's a mistake to assume that waiters with a superiority complex aren't doing it deliberately. Not all restaurants welcome the custom of one-off 'civilian' strangers when their reputations rest on celebrity customers and big spenders. If an ordinary Joe was to find himself in, say, London's perennially starry The Ivy, surrounded by fifty other ordinary Joes and no-one worth rubbernecking, he may well be gravely disappointed.

Stunning design has undeniable appeal. Few can argue with the statement made by fabulous washrooms or blue-glowing aquariums like the one at Al Mahara, Dubai. But these are headline fripperies. If the meal is any good, you'll be spending most of your time at the table. The view from your seat is the most important one of the night.

We are creatures of habit, and it's human nature to cleave to the wall. Being able to see what's coming may once have been a defence against predators; now a good view of the dining room offers amusement and distraction, and fair warning that the wine waiter is making an approach. But the view from the seat also encompasses the food you're about to eat. Nowhere makes a better fist of avoiding the plate than The Fat Duck, Bray, where bespoke serving-pieces are legend. The famous 'sound of the sea' dish comes suspended over a bed of sand, with an iPod, presented in a huge shell, for listening to crashing waves, while other dishes mimic cereal boxes, film canisters and sweetie wrappers.

Especially in uncertain times, there is a lasting fondness for the old-fashioned. Grand temples of excess, such as Paul Bocuse's three Michelin-star L'Auberge du Pont de Collonges near Lyon, have an appeal that goes beyond the Disney-style decor. There's something reassuring about being offered dessert from the three separate trolleys, and they have the view-from-the-seat problem solved by using ornate tableware and putting no-one near the bathroom. But great experiences don't just happen at the top end. Communal seating, noise, chaos, even a bit of mild dirt, can create memorable experiences, although not all restaurants go as far as Chicago's famously raucous Weiner's Circle hot dog stand, where it's not unusual for staff to flash customers who aren't too drunk to say the magic words.

Customers still call restaurants (apart from Weiner's Circle) and ask, hopefully, for a good table. Guides still recommend the best spots. The challenge facing restaurant architects is to make this a thing of the past. In a well-designed restaurant, there should be no such thing as a crap table. Once you've made the booking, ordered the food and chosen the wine, the edible experience all comes back to the view from the seat.

Carla Capalbo

see page 133 for biography

Cook It Raw!

How eleven of the world's top chefs went wild in Copenhagen

SAVOUR
THE GUILD OF FOOD
WRITERS' MAGAZINE
JUNE 2009

If you've been wondering where creative cooking could go after siphoned foams and molecular deconstructivism, the answer is: to Copenhagen. While countries from around the planet met there last month (May 24–26) to discuss global warming at the World Business Summit on Climate Change, eleven of the world's most talked-about chefs gathered on the Danish capital's canal at René Redzepi's Noma to explore the future of planet Earth's (high) gastronomy at Cook it Raw!, an event sponsored by the Danish government's ministry of economic and business affairs.

"Cook It Raw! (whose subtitle was Cook it Clean) was intended as a workshop where today's great thinkers about cooking could get together and explore how modern food can work within an ecological approach to living, limiting electricity and playing with the aspects of rawness, from raw and uncooked ingredients, to wild and local foods. The results were amazing," says Alessandro Porcelli, the gastronomic conceptualist who masterminded the event. Cook it Raw! was designed as a two-day event: a field trip and exploration of wild and farmed Danish ingredients on Saturday, and the 11-course dinner cooked by the chefs on Sunday. The chefs, all men, from North America, Europe and Japan, all feature highly in world ratings. Their brief was to create a recipe, ex-novo, for the event. Also invited: twelve journalists from Europe and north America, to chronicle (and eat) it all.

The foraging expedition began at Dragsholm Slot, a 19th-century castle an hour west of Copenhagen whose domain includes woods, fields and beaches. The monumental building is now also a hotel and restaurant serving Nordic dishes, many of whose ingredients are sourced from the estate.

Revived by bitter asparagus beer and home-baked asparagus rolls, we set off behind René Redzepi, armed with baskets like children on an Easter egg hunt. René stopped beside the castle's lake. Leaning out over the water, he reached into a cluster of tall bulrushes and pulled one up, cutting the root away and peeling off the outer layer of leaves, as if cleaning a leek. To everyone's surprise, he then took a big bite out of the bottom of the pale green stem. "Here, try it," he said, passing it around. It was crunchy, juicy, with a delicate grassy taste that ended on a bitter note. And it was exciting. Next he stopped by a meadow's edge to pluck the delicate white flowers of onion cress, then the coarser, sweeter flowers of the non-stinging nettle. Leaves, flowers, stems, and berries were sniffed and tasted, shared and discussed – occasionally even spat out – in the thrill of discovering this new palette of flavours and potential. The chefs were encouraged to harvest whatever they could use for their dishes of the following evening, and the baskets began to be filled with clover-like wood sorrel, sharp green pine shoots, fragile woodruff and elderflowers.

"What's the Spanish for bucolic?" someone asked.

A short ride on a tractor-drawn cart brought us out of the woods to the sea's edge, a tranquil inlet with scalloped border that revealed another set of tastes and timbres. Here, minuscule seed pods, when popped against the tongue, tasted of coriander. We combed the verge for sea beet, purslane and sour scurvygrass. The chefs, liberated from the stress and enclosures of their city kitchens, were free to play. We left with our baskets full of herbs and flowers from a list of 53 local wild edible plants.

COOKING
IT RAW The journalists were treated to a boat trip of Copenhagen on Sunday morning. Sunday afternoon was spent at Noma with the chefs as they assembled their dishes, with clusters of assistants from Noma working in every available kitchen space. The restaurant is on the water, with unfussy wooden floors, clean-lined tables, and sheepskins draped over the back of its modernist dining chairs as practically the only decoration.

The meal began with Noma's signature centrepiece: root vegetables growing in a clay flower pot. The soil – of crunchy malt and beer-roasted hazelnuts – is edible, as is the herb dip beneath. Metre-long bulrushes made a spectacular entrance as did small, jumping brown bay shrimps, there for the eating by anyone who could catch them. "This is Adam and Eve stuff," said a man on my table, "I feel like a cross between a viking and primitive man."

Ichiro Kobuta specializes in Kyoto cuisine. His beautifully choreographed dish was served as three elements. A small glass contained sweet red shrimp with fresh wasabi in spring aromas, with broad bean mousse and lily root. A spoon held lightly seared turbot, custom-made five spices, venison jus and micro-cress sprigs. (My neighbour described it as 'Finnegan's Wake in a teaspoon'). A large, sliced Danish Belon accompanied by Japanese orange dressing and citrusy ponzu was deemed by many the best oyster they'd ever tasted.

This line of delicacy continued in Daniel Patterson's "interpretation of a coastline, where ocean and shore flavours meet the earth's". Here, in what resembled a small floating island – or even a planet – a base of finely chopped cucumber was given a sea-cast with ink that had been 'milked' from a live squid (and, as I understand it, lived to tell the tale). On it, minuscule whole cooked potatoes were arranged, with sprigs of saline samphire and tiny explosions of chilli to arouse the tastebuds.

Both Italian chefs, Davide Scabin and Massimo Bottura, approached the project conceptually. Massimo Bottura's 'Pollution' came in response to a Corriere della Sera article predicting that, if fishing continues at its current rate, by 2050 the world's seas will be slimy, seaweed-filled and inhabited only by giant marauding squid and jelly fish. Visually, his dish recreated that doomsday atmosphere: a murky green liquid dotted with 'toxic' white foam was strewn with the bodies of baby clams and strips of raw squid, and punctuated by lumps of corral and occasional leaves of samphire and other iodized marine vegetation. It took some getting beyond this pessimistic picture to appreciate the complexity of the tastes. From the warm bitterness of raw monkfish liver paste and the briny, viscous depth of Belon oysters strained and folded into an extraction of sea asparagus and squid ink, the dish was lifted to high, clean notes by Amalfi-lemon foam. Bottura said. "Eating ingredients raw, you taste what they have been fed on. Raw food became a trend in the mid 1990s when sushi first arrived in Italy. Banishing ovens and burners is more politically correct, you don't always need technique."

Claude Bosi's poetic dish of pounded raw king crab topped with flowers, pickled cucumber dice and assorted aromatic leaves offered respite after Bottura's seascape. The scale of the greenery was Lilliputian, with tiny Vetch shoots, sour scurvy grass and other beach herbs floating above the pinkish crab plane. Bosi added depth by roasting the crab shell, bringing dark, sweet caramel character to his elegant composition.

David Chang's dish was clean, uncluttered, yet unmistakably exotic. "I wanted to take the raw idea as literally as possible, so I didn't really cook anything," Chang explained. He brought a favourite ingredient, Hawthorne Valley buttermilk, produced two hours north of his New York City restaurants. Lumps of the buttermilk which, after a night of being curdled by vinegar, had the texture of silky junket, sat like icebergs in a complex apple dashi broth. Aromatic accents came from resinous pine nuts, sesame oil, wild garlic flowers and the citrus sharpness of red-stemmed wood sorrel. Miso and rice vinegar added smoky, sour notes to the buttermilk's creamy sweetness. "I've never really foraged for herbs before, maybe out of laziness, but it's a skill you could learn quite quickly."

Elemental, elegant and pure: Pascal Barbot's assemblage of marinated raw Danish mackerel, raw turnip encrusted with black and white sesame seeds, lemon-peel confit and nasturtium leaf was accompanied by a cup containing Scandinavian smoked eel topped with loose wild angelica purée. It celebrated the textures and flavours of the raw ingredients by keeping them separate, so you really experienced the juiciness of the sweet turnip root, the bitter pepper of the nasturtium, the sweetness of the lemon as it cut the saturated mackerel flesh.

I found Iñaki Aizpitarte's dish to be among the most daring, in pure food terms. It explored the link between the earth, its creatures and the sea. In the centre of the plate, lobster meat was raw-poached in a lukewarm salt solution, "décollé en émulsion," as the chef described it, and served with an infusion of smoked mackerel and rice vinegar, with its intestines "to bring an iodized side to it." It was dressed with sprigs of sour wood sorrel. On one side of the plate, a smear of dark liver paste (of raw pigeon and chicken livers scented with orange) descended almost menacingly towards the pink lobster flesh, adorned with pistachios grated like fresh wood shavings. You dragged the lobster through the liver to eat it for a sweet, salty, earthy effect. "My dish is deceptively simple," he said. "In fact, I spent all day preparing it."

Davide Scabin's provocative 'B.C.' took us back to a primordial time when man sought his protein from the forest floor, searching for grubs and worms in the bark of trees. "I wanted to explore the paradox of modern society, in which the rich have enough money to buy Kobe beef but never have any time, and the poor have no money but plenty of time to create something of value," he says. To prove his point, Scabin took the poorest, toughest cut of beef – the shoulder muscle that's too stringy even for braising – and, using only man-hours, transformed it into a tartare worth 1,300 euros per kilo. "I put seven people to work with scalpels. It took them ten hours each to cut the meat lengthwise into thin strips, one muscle fibre at a time. We even created a new texture." The thin, curvy 'worms' were served with a sprinkling of black caviar 'eyes' within hollow cinnamon sticks, to be held horizontally in the fingers and licked out with the tongue.

Joachim Wissler arrived from Germany too late for the foraging excursion, and I felt his dish suffered from this missed opportunity: he might have changed his plan, as other chefs did, prompted by the discoveries of the wild Danish ingredients. His raw roebuck fillet with malt 'soil' and miniature mushrooms painted an autumnal woodland scene that felt out of step with the freshness of the spring's exuberances.

Master pastry chef, Albert Adrià, seems to have gone through some angst deciding what to prepare for the event. "He went from an initial position of saying that he couldn't make a dessert without baking biscuits or a cake, or using the freezer to make ice cream, to rethinking his whole position on energy," says Porcelli, who kept up a lively correspondence with the chefs as they grappled with the raw concept. Using as little energy as possible, Albert froze Sicilian lemons using nitrogen gas before breaking the fruit into separate kernels with a hammer. For his 'natural sponge' cake, Adrià microwaved batter in plastic cups for just 40 seconds. He turned the (very holy) cake out of the mould, then pulled it delicately open as if in hinged segments to maintain its natural sea-sponge look. In this brilliant white on white dessert, the sponge was served with delicate elderflower sorbet, and accented by the frozen lemon, a soured cream, extremely resinous Spanish pine nuts and their oil, and a dollop of pungent sun-yellow dandelion honey from Italy. "Raw is relative," he said, enigmatically. He brought an inspired finale to an extraordinary meal.

A RAW FUTURE

While some may feel that this is just elitist, frivolous stuff, what goes on at the pinnacle of gastronomic experience sends strong messages to other chefs and influences trends. Judging by these chefs' enthusiasm for the raw, energy-conscious approach, its future is assured. Cooking it raw fits the moment. It fits with Richard Corrigan's theory that the recession could stimulate cooks to work with a limited palette of ingredients while using less energy. It dovetails too with Michael Pollan's credo to eat food, not too much, mostly plants, wild if possible (obviously where their use does not damage the environment or contribute to their depletion). And it offers a new direction for the future.

What distinguished Cook it Raw! from other chefs' get-togethers was the challenge to produce cutting-edge, modern food following the reduced-energy, raw-ingredient precepts. Wild ingredients have always been used. There's nothing new in that: boiled field chicory and grilled porcini have well-earned places in the culinary galaxy. Yet Noma's example to chart and experiment every edible element in the Nordic sphere goes further. Making salads from beech leaves and bulrushes, or infusions with birch bark and tree sap explore new ways to affirm what's local, seasonal and good. It takes on biodiversity in a fresh, respectful way and does it by reducing the importance (and the eater's perception) of technique. Iñaki Aizpitarte admitted that he'd spent all day producing his dish, yet the effect was one of spontaneous, clean flavours and food that had been interfered with as little as possible. After the meal, Pascal Barbot marvelled that not one gram of butter had been used by anyone to create it, not a single reduction had been made. For too long the Scandinavians were under French culinary dominance, with its hierarchies and rules, and they were not the only ones. Today's chefs have spent a decade exploring and expanding technique, including diverting forays into molecular science, but few had considered the effects of reducing energy (or water consumption) in their kitchens. Cook it Raw! changed that, at least for this group of hugely talented cooks and friends. Together they extended the boundaries of modern food and reset the compass.

Caroline Stacey

Caroline Stacey started writing about food and chefs on *Caterer & Hotelkeeper*, then switched sides and ate her way several times round the world without leaving London as restaurant reviewer for *Time Out*. She has since been Food Editor of the *Independent* and a regular contributor to *The Times*, the BBC's food website and *Good Food* magazine, writing about education, public health and the ethics involved in shopping and cooking, as well as the pleasures of eating. Caroline won Glenfiddich Food and Drink Awards in 1996 and 2002 for her restaurant reviewing and was named the Guild of Food Writers Food Journalist of the Year in 2005.

Ethics of eating meat

Food Matters
BBC WEBSITE
MARCH 2009

Intensive animal rearing contributes to climate change and eating too much meat is bad for both human health and for the wellbeing of the millions of intensively farmed animals. So, should we give up steak to save the planet?

Driving and flying are bad for the environment. That message has been well and truly driven home to consumers. But transport isn't the worst carbon culprit: intensive animal-rearing, and associated transport costs, is. According to a report by the United Nations' Food and Agriculture Organization (UNFAO), intensive animal rearing accounts for 18 per cent of global greenhouse gas emissions, while transport of meat accounts for 13 per cent. Consequently, environmentalists are urging consumers to think hard about what they eat, particularly meat. BBC Food investigates the issues and ethics of meat-eating.

THE ENVIRONMENTAL IMPACT

In late 2008 Dr Rajendra Pachauri, a vegetarian and chair of the UN's Intergovernmental Panel on Climate Change, recommended that consumers scale down on meat-eating to cut greenhouse gas emissions, starting by giving it up for just one meal a week. His speech put steak and chops' contribution to global warming under the spotlight.

Production of meat and dairy has significantly more impact on the environment than growing vegetables, grains and other plant foods does. The UNFAO estimates that meat production accounts for nearly a fifth of the world's greenhouse gas emissions. That's more than all of the world's air and road transport combined.

A third of the world's cereal harvest and 90 per cent of soya is grown for animal feed. Soya imports now account for 40 per cent of animal protein feed in the UK, largely because animals require a great deal of feed to turn them into food for humans. It takes up to 10 kg of cattle feed to produce just one kilogram of beef, 4–5 kg of grain to produce a kilogram of pork and 2–3 kg of grain for one kilogram of chicken.

Livestock-rearing has also contributed to deforestation in the Amazon rainforest, as forests have been cleared to make way for cattle.

More than two-thirds of now-deforested Amazon Basin land is taken up by cattle grazing. Much of the rest of the deforested Amazon Basin has been given over to growing animal feed, particularly soya. In December 2008, Friends of the Earth launched its Food Chain Campaign to demonstrate to consumers how an appetite for steaks and cheese in Britain is linked to soya farming in South America.

THE BEEF
WITH BEEF

In Britain, the methane given off by 10 million cows accounts for eight per cent of the country's greenhouse gases.

Beef has an especially jumbo hoof-print. One calculation by the Animal Science Journal estimates that carbon dioxide emissions from producing a single kilogram of beef are comparable to driving a car more than 250 km (155 miles). Then there's the greenhouse gas – 23 times more powerful than carbon dioxide – that cows emit. In Britain, the methane given off by 10 million cows accounts for eight per cent of the country's greenhouse gases, calculates the Food Climate Research Network.

Transporting feed to the millions of factory-farmed pigs and chickens, added to the cost of housing and heating them, also has an environmental impact. Moving the meat around and refrigerating it to keep it fresh creates yet more greenhouse gas emissions. And back on the farms, the waste that comes from rearing animals on an industrial scale can pollute soil and water systems.

Meat production is a drain on water supplies too. Again, beef scores worst. According to Waterwise, the not-for-profit group focused on decreasing water consumption in the UK, it takes 17 times as much water to produce a kilogram of beef as it does to grow a kilogram of maize. Put another way, 13 litres are needed to grow one tomato, 200 litres go into a 200 ml glass of milk and it takes 2,400 litres of water to produce a 150 g hamburger. These are examples of 'water footprints' – the amount of fresh, and increasingly scarce, water (not including rain) it takes to produce food.

INCREASED
CONSUMPTION

British consumers are eating more meat than ever – 50 per cent more than in the 1960s. According to the UNFAO's report 'Livestock's Long Shadow', Europeans and the even more meat-minded Americans aren't the only ones eating more. Since the 1970s meat consumption in developing countries has more than doubled, although, with global average meat consumption at 100g per person a day, rich countries are tipping the scales at 200–250 g while poorer ones are lucky to get 20–25 g, revealed a Lancet report. As the world's population grows, meat consumption is expected to double within the next 50 years.

So that's the case for the prosecution. But, in the unlikely event of a mass overnight, world-wide conversion to vegetarianism, the impact on economies and environments would nonetheless be devastating.

The numerous breeds reared by humans ensures the maintenance of biodiversity, and animals can be an important part of a holistic farming system: they produce manure, are used for traction and transport in developing countries and they eat the parts of crops that humans can't. Hides and bones are used to make goods that would otherwise have to be manufactured from man-made materials. At least one billion people in the world are thought to depend on livestock for their livelihoods.

And, ethically, why shouldn't people in poorer countries have the opportunity of developing their economies through livestock production as industrialised countries have done, and have the chance to enjoy more meat in their diet?

In better-off countries the meat-eating majority have no moral or environmental objections to being responsible carnivores. Humans are naturally omnivorous and farm animals have long been an integral part of the ecosystem and landscape. Many would argue that humans have a responsibility to the domesticated breeds that depend on humans for survival.

MEAT IN MODERATION

Yet it's not just vegetarians urging people to eat less meat. Dr John Powles of Cambridge University's Department of Public Health and Primary Care believes that the only way to prevent livestock contributing to global warming is for people in rich countries to cut down on meat so that those in developing countries can have more.

Compassion in World Farming's campaign to end factory farming will only succeed if consumers make a conscious decision to eat less meat. "There's no way that animal welfare can be catered for if global meat consumption keeps growing," explains Joyce D'Silva, the charity's ambassador. "The environmental and human health arguments for eating less meat are very strong, and we believe we should eat less meat in the Western world and buy higher welfare meat."

Dr Tom MacMillan of the Food Ethics Council agrees: "The challenge is not only to eat less, but also to eat better meat – produced in more humane and environmentally sound production systems."

If the average UK household bought half as much meat, according to CIWF's calculations, carbon emissions would be cut by more than if we used our cars half as much. Is it really such a sacrifice to cut out a chop or a chicken breast here and there to decrease our animal intake to 500g of meat and 1 litre of milk or 100 g of cheese per week, if it means, in the words of CIWF's D'Silva, "healthier people, happier animals and a healthier planet"?

Lulu Grimes

Lulu Grimes is currently Food Director of *Good Food* and *olive* magazines, and was Food Editor of *olive* since it was launched. She has wide experience as a magazine food editor (*Food and Travel* and *Sainsbury's Magazine*), and as an editor for Murdoch books in Sydney, where she researched and worked on a series of internationally published food and travel books covering China, India, Thailand, Italy and France. She regularly broadcasts on the radio and has written for *The Sydney Morning Herald*.

The Blog and Food Writing in the 21st Century

2009

In the current climate food writers could be forgiven for wondering where their role lies. Opportunities in print seem to be ever shrinking, magazines and newspapers are folding or downsizing, and the cult of the celebrity chef means that having an attachment to a TV programme is increasingly important to actually getting a commission. Opportunities do however exist, not necessarily in old school media but via the new media of the 21st century. I'd go so far as to say there is a new set of rules for keeping yourself in work.

As print pages shrink, for one reason or another, the world of food writing in the digital world expands. Many Guild members have already used blogs to promote their writing and ideas, and blogging is a brilliant way of doing two things. One, keeping your writing going whether you are in work or not; and two, proving to editors that you can write well. Blogs are unedited and, in my opinion, worth a thousand cuttings when it comes to commissioning someone who is untried. New media is also more democratic for the writer; you can say what you want how you want without needing someone to allow you 5 column inches first; once your opinion is out there, then you have a potential audience. In my current job (at the BBC's *olive* magazine) this is particularly important when we are looking for writers who live in the cities and areas we cover in our travel sections. We actively search out blogs about the cities we want to cover, so much better to have a resident write about their home town/city/area than send a writer on a whistle-stop tour and expect them to get to the bones of a place. And the beauty of a blog is that it reflects the writer's real voice and opinions making it easier to find a specialist on say budget restaurants, local markets or up-and-coming areas of a well-known city.

Being part of a food community is vital to food writing, and while you may not be able to jump on the next train to X food festival or afford to spend days searching out fabulous shops and markets in all corners of the country, online you can make friends and gather information very easily. Which brings me to twitter. Contrary to mis-representative reporting, twitter is not ALL about following celebrities and gossip. What twitter does is a lot of hard work on your behalf. If you follow the right sorts of people, then vast amounts of information will come to you. Twitter is about connecting to people and resources you don't know; if you follow restaurants you'll be among the first to know about special offers, publishers give away books and other tweeters post links to interesting pieces and blogs. On the other side of the fence, post a call out for information or a question yourself and if anyone out there can help you they will; and when you have a new post on your blog/book out/article published tweet it and instantly gain a new audience. Streamline who you follow and you won't be inundated with dross. Follow publishers, editors, agents, magazines and papers you would like to work for/with – if they need something you could be the first to know. If you get it wrong at the start then it isn't a problem; the beauty of twitter is that if someone is boring you, you can simply switch them off.

* * *

Many print formats are becoming multi-platform, so an ability to write for an online audience is a huge help. If you can format your own words and photographs then that's even better. There are many courses out there to help you build a web page or blog, learn to tag your online pieces so search engines find them, podcast or just file your photographs more efficiently. So get yourself online one way or another, it's great fun and more useful than you think.

Billington's Sugar

Billington's are celebrating 150 years of
perfecting their range of unrefined cane sugars.
Most of their sugars are produced on the tropical island of Mauritius.
Their Fairtrade range comes from Southern Africa and their organic sugars
from South America.

UNREFINED SUGARS

Not all brown sugars are the same. Many are only brown on the outside: underneath they are fully refined white sugar that has been coated with molasses syrup to add some flavour and colour.

Billington's sugars are all unrefined, which means they are simply produced by locking in, rather than refining out, the natural molasses of the sugar cane. It is this difference that gives unrefined sugars their superior flavour and natural colour.

There is an unrefined sugar for every application, whether it's for everyday use or your secret recipe. As all good cooks know, the best results are produced by using only the finest ingredients and, when it comes to sugar, that means Billington's unrefined cane sugar.

For 150 years we have been working closely with our growers to make sure that you have the best sugar there is - as nature intended it to be.

Unrefined Golden Sugars

Billington's golden sugars are light, free-flowing crystals with just the perfect amount of molasses locked in.

Unrefined Soft Sugars

Billington's soft sugars are unique. With their intense flavours and aroma, natural colours and appearance they are the perfect sugar for all culinary needs.

Unrefined Fairtrade Sugars

Fairtrade is all about better prices, improved working conditions and local sustainability for farmers and workers in the developing world. Billington's Fairtrade sugars are licensed by the UK's Fairtrade Foundation and the Premium on these sugars is paid directly to the Kasinthula Cane Growers Cooperative in Malawi.

FAIRTRADE DEMERARA CANE SUGAR

The ideal sweetener for Fairtrade coffee. Its rich flavour and crunchy texture also makes it a great topping for fruit and natural yogurt. It excels in cakes, biscuits and crumbles.

FAIRTRADE GOLDEN GRANULATED CANE SUGAR

The perfect Fairtrade sugar for everyday use, with a light golden colour and subtle flavour.

Unrefined Organic Sugars

In 1992 Billington's was the first company to bring organic unrefined sugar to the UK. Billington's work with local producers in South America, and their products have all been certified by the Soil Association.

ORGANIC UNREFINED DEMERARA SUGAR

This sugar is rich and deep in colour, with a coarser crystal. As the traditional sweetener for coffee it compliments the wide range of organic coffees now available. It is also perfect for topping fruit and natural yoghurt and is excellent in cakes, biscuits and crumbles.

ORGANIC UNREFINED CASTER SUGAR

A light, free flowing sugar with a subtle buttery taste. Its golden colour and superior flavour is perfect for adding a new dimension to all baking applications. It is the perfect baking sugar for all your organic recipes.

ORGANIC UNREFINED GRANULATED SUGAR

Light, dry and free-flowing with a subtle golden colour, it can be used wherever you would use white granulated sugar.

The Golden Sugar Range

GOLDEN GRANULATED SUGAR

Golden granulated is perfect for tea and coffee, for sprinkling on cereals and fresh fruit – wherever you would normally use white sugar.

GOLDEN CASTER SUGAR

This 'classic baking sugar' is light, fine grained with a subtle buttery taste. Perfect in shortbread, meringues and sponges.

DEMERARA SUGAR

With its rich aroma, crunchy texture and golden colour, unrefined demerara sugar is the ideal sweetener for coffee. Perfect also for topping cereals, biscuits, cakes and crumbles. Delicious too when sprinkled on porridge.

GOLDEN ICING SUGAR

With its mellow, rounded flavour and natural honey colour, unrefined golden icing sugar is perfect for icings, butter cream, dessert pastry, meringues and cake fillings.

SUGAR CRYSTALS FOR COFFEE

Unrefined sugar crystals dissolve slowly in coffee, providing a subtle sweetness and flavour. Their crunchy texture and flavour also make them a versatile topping for cookies, crumbles and ice cream.

The Soft Sugar Range

LIGHT MUSCOVADO SUGAR

Unrefined light muscovado is the world's finest light brown soft sugar, with a warm honey colour and creamy fudge flavour. Its richness and depth of flavour makes it perfect for cakes, biscuits, toffee sauce and savoury dishes.

DARK MUSCOVADO SUGAR

Unrefined dark muscovado is the world's finest dark brown soft sugar. It has a rich intense flavour and natural colour that works especially well in rich fruit and chocolate cakes, and adds extra depth to marinades, savoury sauces and chutneys.

MOLASSES SUGAR

Molasses is the ultimate soft brown sugar, packed full of natural cane molasses. It has the deepest colour and richest flavour of all sugars. Perfect for Christmas cakes, mincemeat and dark chocolate cakes. It is excellent in ethnic cooking, marinades and barbecue dishes.

The Unrefined Cane Sugar Specialists

Recipe index

Index

Guild of Food Writers' metric/imperial conversion tables

The recipes in this book come from many different sources and conversions vary. Use these tables as a guideline. Comparisons may confuse. Use either metric or imperial measures. Do not mix the two.

Metric/Imperial Weight Conversion

5 g	⅛ oz		375 g	13 oz
10 g	¼ oz		400 g	14 oz
15 g	½ oz		425 g	15 oz
25/30 g	1 oz		450 g	1 lb
35 g	1¼ oz		500 g	1 lb 2 oz
40 g	1½ oz		550 g	1 lb 4 oz
50 g	1¾ oz		600 g	1 lb 5 oz
55 g	2 oz		650 g	1 lb 7 oz
60 g	2¼ oz		700 g	1 lb 9 oz
70 g	2½ oz		750 g	1 lb 10 oz
85 g	3 oz		800 g	1 lb 12 oz
90 g	3¼ oz		850 g	1 lb 14 oz
100 g	3½ oz		900 g	2 lb
115 g	4 oz		950 g	2 lb 2 oz
125 g	4½ oz		1 kg	2 lb 4 oz
140 g	5 oz		1.25 kg	2 lb 12 oz
150 g	5½ oz		1.3 kg	3 lb
175 g	6 oz		1.5 kg	3 lb 5 oz
200 g	7 oz		1.6 kg	3 lb 8 oz
225 g	8 oz		1.8 kg	4 lb
250 g	9 oz		2 kg	4 lb 8 oz
275 g	9¾ oz		2.25 kg	5 lb
280 g	10 oz		2.5 kg	5 lb 8 oz
300 g	10½ oz		2.7 kg	6 lb
325 g	11½ oz		3 kg	6 lb 8 oz
350 g	12 oz			

Metric/Imperial Volume Conversion

15 ml	½ fl oz
30 ml	1 fl oz
50 ml	2 fl oz
75 ml	2½ fl oz
100 ml	3½ fl oz
125 ml	4 fl oz
150 ml	5 fl oz / ¼ pint
175 ml	6 fl oz
200 ml	7 fl oz / ⅓ pint
225 ml	8 fl oz
250 ml	9 fl oz
300 ml	10 fl oz / ½ pint
350 ml	12 fl oz
400 ml	14 fl oz
425 ml	15 fl oz / ¾ pint
450 ml	16 fl oz
500 ml	18 fl oz
568 ml	1 pint milk
600 ml	20 fl oz / 1 pint
700 ml	1¼ pint
850 ml	1½ pint
1 litre	1¾ pint
1.2 litres	2 pint
1.3 litres	2¼ pint
1.4 litres	2½ pint
1.7 litres	3 pint
2 litres	3½ pint
2.5 litres	4½ pint
2.8 litres	5 pint
3 litres	5¼ pint
1.25 ml	¼ tsp
2.5 ml	½ tsp
5 ml	1 tsp
10 ml	2 tsp
15 ml	1 tbsp / 3 tsp
30 ml	2 tbsp
45 ml	3 tbsp
60 ml	4 tbsp
75 ml	5 tbsp
90 ml	6 tbsp

Bibliography

Anthony, Patrick, *The Rye Royal Scallop Festival*, The Saturday Telegraph, 24 February 2007

Baljekar, Mridula, *Great Indian Feasts*, John Blake Publishing, 2005

Bareham, Lindsey, *The Big Red Book of Tomatoes*, Michael Joseph, 1999

Bateman, Michael, *The Sunday Times 1980;* & Maisner, Heather, *The Sunday Times Book of Real Bread*, Rodale Press, 1982

Berry, Mary, *Mary Berry's Complete Cookbook*, Dorling Kindersley, 1995

Blanc, Raymond, *Recipes from Le Manoir aux Quat' Saisons*, Macdonald Orbis, 1988

Boxer, Arabella, *A Visual Feast*, Ebury, 1991

Bradford, Richard Earl of, *Pie in the Sky*, Savour, April 2009

Campbell, Susan, *The Cook's Companion*, Macmillan, 1980

Capalbo, Carla, *The Food and Wine Lover's Companion to Tuscany*, Chronicle Books 1998; *Cook It Raw*, Savour, June 2009

Carluccio, Antonio, *Complete Italian Food*, Quadrille 1997

Cawley, Richard, *The Artful Cook, Secrets of A Shoestring Gourmet*, Macdonald Orbis, 1988

Glynn Christian, *Glynn Christian's Delicatessen Food Handbook*, Macdonald 1982

Clay, Xanthe, *It's Raining Plums*, Martin Books, 2001

Conran, Caroline, *Good Home Cooking*, Conran Octopus, 1985

Davidson, Alan, *North Atlantic Seafood*, Macmillan, 1979

del Conte, Anna, *Gastronomy of Italy*, Bantam Press, 1987

Dunlop, Fuchsia, *Observer Food Monthly*, 10 June 2001

Ehrlich, Richard, *Independent on Sunday*, January 1997

Esson, Lewis / Gill, A. A, *Breakfast at the Wolseley*, Quadrille 2008

Fearnley-Whittingstall, Hugh, *Hit the Sweet Spot*, The Guardian Weekend. March 09

Fletcher, Nichola, *Game for All*, Gollancz, 1987

Gordon, Peter, *The Sugar Club Cookbook*, Hodder & Stoughton, 1997

Gould, Kevin, *Dishy*, Hodder & Stoughton, 2000

Graimes, Nicola, *Brain Food for Kids*, Carroll & Brown, 2004

Green, Henrietta, *Food Lovers' Guide to Britain*, BBC Books, 1993

Grigson, Jane, *Jane Grigson's Vegetable Book*, Michael Joseph, 1978

Grimes, Lulu, *The Blog and Food Writing in the 21st Century*, 2009

Hanssen, Maurice (with Marsden, Jill), *E for Additives*, Thorsons Publishers, 1984

Hix, Mark, *British Regional Food*, Quadrille, 2006

Hsiung, Deh-Ta, *Decanter Magazine*, 1982

Humble, Nicola, *Culinary Pleasures*, Faber, 2005

Hyman, Clarissa, *Cucina Siciliana*, Conran Octopus, 2001

Jayne-Stanes, Sara, *Chocolate the Definitive Guide*, Grub Street, 1999

Lawrence, Sue, *Scots Cooking*, Hodder Headline, 2000

Linford, Jenny, *Food Lovers' London*, Macmillan 1991, Metro Publications 1995; *The London Cookbook*, Metro Publications, 2008

Luard, Elizabeth, *European Peasant Cookery*, Transworld 1986

Moine, Marie-Pierre, *Cuisine Grand'mère* Barrie & Jenkins, 1990

Muir, Jenni, *Time Out*, November 2007

Norman, Cecilia, *Microwave Cookery for the Housewife*, Pitman 1974

Norman, Jill, *Spices*, Dorling Kindersley, 1990

Owen, Sri, *The Rice Book*, Doubleday 1993/ Frances Lincoln, 1998

Patten, Marguerite, *We'll Eat Again*, Hamlyn, 1985

Roden, Claudia, *The Book of Jewish Food*, Alfred A Knopf, 1996, Penguin Books, 1999

Round, Jeremy, *The Independent Cook*, Barrie & Jenkins, 1988

Shaida, Margaret, *The Legendary Cuisine of Persia*, Lieuse Publications, 1992/Grub Street, 2000

So, Yan-Kit, *Classic Chinese Cookery*, Dorling Kindersley, 1984

Spencer, Colin, *Colin Spencer's Vegetable Cooking*, Conran Octopus, 1985

Stacey, Caroline, *Ethics of Eating Meat*, Food Matters BBC website, March 2009

Stein, Rick, *English Seafood Cookery*, Penguin 1988

Katie Stewart, *Times Calendar Cookbook*, Collins, 1972/Pan 1974

Sturgess, Emma, *The Restaurant Experience*, Frame Magazine, Spring 2009

Willan, Anne, *French Regional Cooking*, Hutchinson, 1981

Illustrations::

Page 45 *The Cook's Companion*, Macmillan 1980
Page 76 *Game for All*, Gollancz, 1987